"This book will help Christians learn how to apply their faith to watching movies, to think more deeply and discerningly about those movies, and to avoid the pitfalls of both cultural anorexia and cultural gluttony when it comes to the cinema. Grant Horner writes from the most helpful perspective: that of a biblically informed teacher *and* a plain and simple movie lover."

Brian Godawa, screenwriter, *To End All Wars*; author, *Hollywood Worldviews: Watching Films with Wisdom and Discernment*

"This book is a thinking person's guide to movie watching. Its most obvious virtue is its scope. The early chapters establish a biblical and theological foundation on which the rest of the book rests. Building on this foundation, the author covers a tempting menu of movie genres from comedy to romance to dark film. Illustrations are drawn from a seemingly inexhaustible reservoir of movies from over half a century of film history."

Leland Ryken, Professor of English, Wheaton College

"This is definitely one of the best times I have ever had while learning discernment! Dr. Horner is a brilliant storyteller. He captures human emotion in an economy of language—I found myself laughing as well as becoming choked up as I read his highlights from movie plots. The author's premise, that it is a sin for a Christian to *not* exercise discernment, is developed in a highly positive manner. By dividing the book into various movie genres, the author uses 'film culture' as a powerful tool to teach us how to discern the human condition from film. Dr. Horner's section on comedy and irony is sheer genius; by showing us why reality is filled with the comedic, we learn why the truths of Romans 1 are inescapable. In an age in which Christian discernment of popular culture is waning, this book renders a much-needed service; readers will come away with a new lens with which to view movies from the perspective of a biblical worldview."

Jay Wegter, Executive Director, Gospel for Life; Adjunct Professor of Theology, The Master's College; coauthor, *This Little Church Had None*

"If you're looking for just another 'everyone-says-that-about-Hollywood' kind of book—or interview—look elsewhere. Grant Horner is anything but predictable! He's a world-class mountain climber, a Classics professor who has students on waiting lists to get into his classes, and an all-around fascinating guy who weaves insights from Plato, Aquinas, Shakespeare, and C. S. Lewis into just about every discussion—whether we're talking about the big news story, the latest hit television show, or the blockbuster that just opened up over the weekend. You're sure to become a more discerning viewer after reading his *Meaning at the Movies*—I am."

Frank Pastore, host, *The Frank Pastore Show*

"Grant Horner has tackled a very appropriate subject for today's media saturated world. *Meaning at the Movies* develops a needed, insightful biblical perspective on how we, as believers, should process what is heard and seen in today's entertainment culture. It will encourage any reader, as it did me, to not just be a passive audience member, but to develop a desire to find what's at the heart of the films we watch. Mr. Horner explains how films mirror societal beliefs. By breaking down these varying secular worldviews, through a discerning Christian lens, we will be better equipped to respond to a culture in dire need of a Savior."

Rick Dempsey, Sr. Vice President, Creative, The Walt Disney Studios

"Grant Horner provides a straightforward, biblically sound answer to a complex contemporary question: Can a Christian love God while also loving movies? Rooted in a carefully constructed, creative application of the Scriptures and an encyclopedic fascination with the cinema, Horner affirms thoughtful, joyful engagement with popular culture. *Meaning at the Movies* will certainly empower, perhaps even transform, Christian education in the arts."

> **Charles T. Evans,** Executive Consultant, Paideia, Inc.;
> coauthor, *Wisdom and Eloquence: A Christian Paradigm for Classical Learning*

"This singular voice from the suburbs of Los Angeles reveals the unexpected theological vision of uprooted and fallen man in some of the great cinematic artifacts of the twentieth century."

> **Christof Koch,** Lois and Victor Troendle Professor of Cognitive
> and Behavioral Biology, California Institute of Technology;
> author, *Quest for Consciousness: A Neurobiological Approach*

"What is so refreshing about this book is that it does not fall into the usual 'Christian' trap of simple answers, shallow analysis, and judgmental portraits of the culture around us. On the contrary, Horner eloquently points out that the great Christian communicators of the New Testament were immersed within their cultures, and this 'worldly' interaction garnered them the tools to communicate the gospel. With a steady barrage of thoughtful analysis, vivid examples, and witty humor, Horner articulates how each genre of film, from horror to romance to comedy, has something truthful to say about human nature. He is pointed when necessary and whimsical wherever possible, resulting in a vibrant and imaginative expedition. This type of reading experience seems to be missing from the modern Christian cannon and helps illuminate an equally overlooked part of the Creator's nature. After all, to create was his first recorded act."

> **Jesse Negron,** story consultant, Hollywood;
> Creator and Director, *AFP: American Fighter Pilot*

"If the medium is the message, then Grant Horner shows us in his powerfully insightful book that film is the single most important message of our time. I absolutely love watching movies, but now that I've read *Meaning at the Movies,* I'll see them in a whole new light."

> **Dave Berg,** writer; former coproducer, Jay Leno

"The impact of movies is profound and impossible to ignore. For the faithful Christian, whether as a film*goer* or film*maker,* discernment of the underlying worldviews behind movies is critical. Yet many of us approach film viewing more or less thoughtlessly—as either a simplistic, black-and-white judgmental exercise, or without any critical evaluation at all, as if meanings did not matter. Grant Horner issues a thoughtful, powerful challenge to us as believers and lays out a clear road map, that we might bring an acute scriptural mind (the mind of Christ) along with the clear analytical skills to recognize truth from error with us into the theater."

> **Robin Armstrong,** filmmaker; Entrepreneurial Media and Real Estate Exec;
> Open Road Communications/The Gentry Group

MEANING AT THE MOVIES

BECOMING A DISCERNING VIEWER

GRANT HORNER

CROSSWAY

WHEATON, ILLINOIS

Meaning at the Movies: Becoming a Discerning Viewer
Copyright © 2010 by Grant Horner
Published by Crossway
1300 Crescent Street
Wheaton, Illinois 60187

Interior design and typesetting: Lakeside Design Plus
Cover design: Dual Identity Design
First printing 2010
Printed in the United States of America

Trade Paperback ISBN: 978-1-4335-1228-5
PDF ISBN: 978-1-4335-1229-2
Mobipocket ISBN: 978-1-4335-1230-8
ePub ISBN: 978-1-4335-2401-1

Library of Congress Cataloging-in-Publication Data
Horner, Grant, 1964–
    Meaning at the movies : becoming a discerning viewer / Grant Horner.
      p. cm.
    Includes bibliographical references.
    ISBN 978-1-4335-1228-5 (tpb)—ISBN 978-1-4335-1229-2 (hc)—ISBN 978-1-4335-1230-8 (mobipocket)—ISBN 978-1-4335-2401-1 (ebk) 1. Motion pictures—Moral and ethical aspects. 2. Motion pictures—Religious aspects—Christianity. I. Title.

PN1995.5.H67 2010
261.5'7—dc22   2009051490

Crossway is a publishing ministry of Good News Publishers.

CH		21	20	19	18	17	16	15	14	13	12	11	10
14	13	12	11	10	9	8	7	6	5	4	3	2	1

"This is . . . fascinating"
"Of course it is. . . . I wrote that with my heart!"
Joe Gillis and Norma Desmond in *Sunset Boulevard* (1950)

Contents

Preface

The Celluloid Mirror

"On both sides thus is simple truth suppressed."
William Shakespeare, *Sonnet 138*

"You think you can sacrifice someone else's life? You're an
animal!"
"No. Worse. Human."
Runaway Train (1985),
directed by Andrei Konchalovsky

THERE is an incredibly riveting moment late in *Runaway Train*—a
well-reviewed action movie based on a script by the great Japanese film-
maker Akira Kurosawa, directed by a Russian, and made in America.
Well into the story, we see three characters, two escaped convicts and
a female engineer, trapped on an out-of-control speeding train. They
cannot shut down the damaged engine nor can they jump off due to
the train's great velocity. They are hurtling across a frozen Alaskan
landscape to certain doom. It is only a matter of time. They form an
uneasy alliance, hoping to pool their meager resources in hope of finding a solution to their desperate quandary. Unbelievably, this brief and
fragile pact quickly devolves into a vicious, brutal conflict, with the
doomed trio in a fight to the death in a tiny locomotive compartment

that is rapidly becoming their mausoleum. "Manny" (Jon Voight in a phenomenal performance), the older convict and a hardened killer, comes up with an incredibly dangerous plan that just might work. He suggests all the risk be borne by "Buck," the none-too-bright younger criminal, who agrees. "Sara" sees this self-serving and manipulative plot for what it is, and in the ensuing argument and snarling fight, calls Manny an "animal."

But Manny knows better. Much better. He's worse than an animal. *He's human.*

Screaming violently while trying to kill each other with crude weapons, their faces contorted with wrath, the three finally stare deeply into each others' eyes; they slowly drop their weapons, begin to shake with grief, and then huddle together like long-lost friends. The wheels of the train pound out the rhythm of their inexorable journey to a grinding death as they cower together waiting for the end. They are like three friends attending their own funeral. The agony of the moment is unbearable. The camera pulls up above them and looks straight down upon their pitiful state: senselessly murderous humans, paragons of futility, moments before a death they will in no way escape.

It is hard to imagine a clearer picture of the human condition.

Perhaps the most important question we can ask of art is, "What does our art say to us *about ourselves?*"

Though this book is nominally about movies and theology, it is really, as all books are, about being human. As a believer committed to the God of the Bible and to the great flow of Christian thought from the ancient world to the present day—thought grounded specifically in the Old and New Testaments—I unapologetically base my view of human nature and human culture on two sources. These are the dual revelations of Scripture and the observable reality known as nature. This pair has long been called the Two Books of God (Scripture and nature). The former—while existing inside the latter—always takes precedence. Scripture guides interpretation of nature, while nature reinforces Scripture. Though the Bible is without doubt one of the core documents in human history, a vast number of even highly educated modern people are woefully ignorant about what it actually says. Wild speculation and utter misinformation abound in both mass media and private opinion. And of course movies themselves constantly present Christian faith as the province of lunatics, fools, and hypocrites. Which is part of what makes them so interesting to me.

How This Book Works

This book is not a series of movie reviews, or simply a set of theological interpretations of specific films, or a Christian critique of Hollywood as the source of all evil. If you're looking for a list of movies you should or should not watch to be a "good Christian," you'll have to look elsewhere. Those books have all been written before, and no doubt will be again. There will always be a market for them. This book is quite different. It is an extended meditation on why we have movies at all, why they are so powerful, and why Christians need to think deeply and theologically about film art—indeed, about all human cultural production. Furthermore, I do not take the position that believers should watch movies in order to "engage culture" or "be relevant": both of these ideas are wildly popular in Christian circles at the moment, but whenever I ask someone exactly what they mean by the terms, I inevitably meet with awkward silence. (We professors can be an annoying bunch.)

My primary concern here is how film works on our consciousness. My approach is biblical-theological. Because I believe man is a spiritual animal and that he is a hybrid of material flesh and immaterial spirit, and because the phenomenon of human consciousness seems to me to be the central crux of the issue of man's total being, it is natural for me to focus on how movies and consciousness interact. In fact, I think I may convince you that movies and consciousness have quite deeply interpenetrated one another—and that this is not without significance.

A New Theory of Culture

What follows, then, is a set of interconnected essays about how movies *work* and how they *work on us*. Because we humans are so dependent upon "methodologies" or patterns of thought that guide actions, I too

11

have developed a broad system for thinking about culture in general and movies in particular. I do not claim that this approach is either entirely innovative or is totalizing in its explanations, but rather that it is designed to open up and perhaps enrich conversation about culture, man, and God.

Built to some extent from aspects of systematic and biblical theology, particularly the ideas of Augustine, Calvin, and a number of the English and American Puritan authors with whom I spend so much of my study time, this theory will be explained in detail in the first chapter. It is most important however to note that the main source of the theory is my own close reading over a quarter of a century of the Old and New Testaments. I am not by nature a "systematic theologian," nor do I write here as an academic. The chapters that follow are written in a relaxed and familiar style that I hope you will find engaging and challenging, but very readable—almost like a good conversation after a movie. But what follows is undeniably a theological kind of conversation.

And while my own theological position is evangelical and conservative, I have also learned from sources as disparate as the early church writers and contemporary philosophers and cultural theorists. Here is the point: over many years of studying, thinking, and teaching through the tangled issues of Christianity and culture, I have come to the conclusion that the single most important passage of Scripture regarding human cultural production is the first chapter of Paul's letter to the Romans. This might seem an unlikely move; many great thinkers on the culture/Christianity problem stick closely to texts such as Acts 17 and similar passages. While I agree with many of their arguments, and while I have learned from many who have gone before me, I find myself compelled to focus my attention on the first great passage by Paul in the entire New Testament. Just as Moses' first words in the Old Testament are crucially important, so are Paul's in the New. My theory also considers the books of Ecclesiastes and the Song of Solomon, the Mars Hill sermon, and many other scriptural texts—but I find myself always returning to that opening chapter of Romans. Paul's brief words on the Athenian Areopagus (Acts 17:22–31) are grounded in the nature (and culture) of fallen man—on which we find Paul expounding most fully in the opening of Romans.

With all that said, I do earnestly hope that my explicitly theological viewpoint will not too quickly convince those who do not share my faith (or even my particular theological positions) to stop reading. This book is intended for believers, for almost-believers, for wish-I-could-believers, and for nonbelievers alike. It is a wide net, cast deep. A major part of my purpose is to demonstrate the persuasive power of a well-thought-out philosophy of man and his creation of culture—and one grounded in Scripture while observing nature. Moreover, I believe that these ancient biblical texts provide the best available explanatory model for why we create what we do—why we are driven to create *anything at all* that does not have immediate material value for us. Why, in the face of a natural world that seems bent on killing us as quickly and anonymously as possible, should we bother with anything as utterly wasteful as art? What serious purpose could it possibly serve? Furthermore, I am not only interested in the "end" or goal of art, what philosophers would call the *telos*; I am at least as interested in its *origins* as its end. The consummation of a revelation is always dependent upon its genesis.

Thus, I hope my readers will consider the arguments presented here as they are intended: the thoughts of a believer who has spent many years observing human cultural production and wondering, *where does all this come from?* Maybe you have wondered about that, too, believer or not.

A Map of the Book

I begin with an introduction that presents my theory of the suppression of truth and the origins of culture, particularly its relationship to the effect of film narrative on our consciousness. Part 1 features three brief chapters on the theological and practical elements of discernment, especially regarding film. Part 2 is built of five longer chapters featuring detailed film analyses; these essays deploy my theory of culture derived from Romans 1 as laid out in the first chapter, as well as the practical arguments in part 1. As such, the final five chapters model my approach to film critique in particular and cultural critique in general. In other words, it is necessary to read the introduction carefully and then chapters 1 through 3 in order to understand what I am doing in the analysis chapters.

The introduction, "Movies, Truth, and the Origins of Culture," delineates my theory of the origins of human cultural production. Here I discuss "screen culture" and its potent effects on consciousness; I attempt to provide a working definition of culture and the cultural objects we produce; and then I treat the question of human culture and its origins from the suppression of the truth of God as Paul describes it in Romans 1. Finally, a detailed analysis of the brilliant *Unforgiven* (1992) presents a concrete example of how my theory works practically in thinking through a popular and powerful film.

Chapter 1, "Thinking about Looking: The Lost Art of Discernment," is a theological study of the crucial process of biblical discernment—the recognition and proper valuation of ideas and their interrelationships in human culture. Chapter 2, "Welcome to the Real World: The Many Ways of Misunderstanding Basically Everything," functions as a kind of worldview catalog. This provides a general grid for grasping the philosophical underpinnings that all movies have. Chapter 3, "How to Interrogate a Movie," continues in this vein. Here we develop a series of helpful questions to ask and categories to explore when thinking about the films we watch. This brings part 1 to an end, and prepares us for the in-depth analysis chapters that follow.

Chapter 4 is titled "A Time to Laugh: A Theological Approach to Comedy." Everyone laughs, but we rarely think about laughter itself. Why is anything ever funny at all? Why is laughter pleasurable? I will show that in fact humor has a theological basis in perhaps the least expected place—the doctrine of the fall. Chapter 5 treats a much heavier subject: horror films. "Exorcising the Psycho: The Invention of Fear for Pleasure" is the application of my theory of the origins of culture from the suppression of truth to that popular genre of movies that has a single goal: to frighten its audience. Fear is a naturally unpleasant sensation. How in the world did it come about that we have a multibillion dollar industry that produces fear for pleasure? Chapter 6 turns to romance. "Hollywood Invents Romance: Of All the Gin Joints, in All the Towns, in All the World, She Walks into Mine" looks into the theological basis for love, both human and divine, and considers why this genre is so powerful in its attraction. Date movies may not be as entirely shallow as we thought.

Chapter 7 moves again into a realm of the more disturbing facets of human existence as shown in film art: the subgenre known as film noir. It is particularly interesting to think theologically about a large body of movies that pull back the curtain on human nature and show us in a clear mirror what we are really like. "Film Noir: The Dark Side, or Solomon Goes to Hollywood" does exactly that. Chapter 8 moves in a somewhat different direction. Instead of focusing on a genre I look closely at several films sharing the common theme of memory, consciousness, and technology. I believe these elements curve back into *the very nature of film itself*, which is a kind of technological representation of and replacement for memory—the foundational aspect of human consciousness. The films I deal with in this chapter, perhaps more than any others, show us what it means to be human. Thus, "The End of the Matter: Movies and Meaning, Memory and Man" is not only a summation of the previous chapters, but a final restatement of the theory of the suppression of truth and the origin of culture upon which the entire book has been built. I conclude with a brief coda on the city without memory—the city where movies come from, where sea, mountain, and desert all meet in an endless sprawl of stucco tract homes and strip malls and palm trees and affluent desperation—my own city, Los Angeles.

A Word about Spoilers and Content

I try not to spoil completely any plots at all. A significant part of the value of watching a narrative film is the linear discovery of what happens next. My wife often says to me about our favorite movies—the ones we rewatch periodically—that she wishes she could "forget" them in order to experience them again as brand new.

As a reader of this book you will be at something of a disadvantage if you have not seen a fair amount of movies and perhaps a greater disadvantage if you have not seen a particular film that you are reading about. I've tried to frame the discussions of particular plots in such a way as to make them valuable for the reader who has not seen the movie as well as the one who has, while not ruining the movie for either. I strongly urge that before you read a chapter with specific and detailed "spoilers" listed below, you watch those movies. You could also glance through whole chapters and try to watch the unfamiliar movies first, even if they are not on the spoiler list. This will help you to follow the chapter's flow much more easily.

Therefore I strongly suggest that you watch the following films before you read the chapters where I discuss them: *City Lights* and *Dr. Strangelove* (chap. 4); *Psycho* and *What Lies Beneath* (chap. 5); *Marty* (chap. 6); *Double Indemnity, Sunset Boulevard,* and *Scarlet Street* (chap. 7); *Citizen Kane, 2001: A Space Odyssey, Blade Runner,* and *Memento* (chap. 8). Of course, I discuss dozens of other movies throughout the book; these are just the ones that would likely be ruined by reading before watching.

Not unrelated to the issue of movie spoilers is the question of objectionable content. I am often asked if I can recommend any good, nonoffensive movies. The answer is simple: no. There are some who will be offended by every movie, and there are some who will be offended by none. This does not at all mean that there are no standards for a Christian when it comes to film. But I should say two things: first, if you are a believer, you should follow your own conscience as it is informed by Scripture about what constitutes an edifying use of your time and what does not. Second, just because I mention a film does not mean I necessarily approve of the content itself. The introduction explains what I mean by all of this, especially my contention that a "nonoffensive" movie can't be made. But be advised that my approach is not intended to produce for my readers a universal list of acceptable and unacceptable movies for any particular person. I will say, however, that your taste in movies should tell you a great deal about what kind of person you are. No doubt many of my readers will be irritated that I left a certain favorite film of theirs out of my consideration, while still others will agonize over some of the ones I *did* include! To either sentiment I will simply quote the Roman poet Horace: *ars longa, vita brevis*: art is long, while life is short. Thus editors are necessary—to force writers to end their books.

Movies are perhaps the most perfect mirror that we have so far constructed to show ourselves what we are. But like all mirrors, the mirror of movies is always in some sense a lie, in some sense, a distortion. How could it be otherwise after the fall of man?

Are you going to find God in the movies? No. Not a chance.

But he just might find *you* there.

Let's dim the lights, then, shall we? You can see so much better that way.

Acknowledgments

IN a movie they roll the full credits at the end; in a book it is customary to express your debts and gratitude at the beginning, and in ascending order, from professional to personal. Here I shall reverse both traditions.

In the purest sense, there is only one acknowledgment to make, and I'll make it in my beloved Latin:

Ad maiorem dei gloriam! Soli Dei Gloria!

To God alone. And yet he has blessed me with many images of himself, in those who surround me and encourage me. So I'll thank them as well, in and for him.

As Jesus says, the first shall be last, and the last first. One human only is both of these to me, the bookends of my bookish life on earth. How little I deserve her! So here I thank my wonderful, sweet, lovely, hilarious, and joy-giving wife Joanne, always tireless in efforts on behalf of her family and patient in her career of watching me read and think and write. She first taught me about art from an artist's perspective, and while we've seen many films together, I've yet to see such beauty on celluloid. Now we'll have more time for tea together. Maybe even . . . a movie. I am so thankful as well for my three wonderful kids, no longer children—Seth, Josiah, and Rachel, who have for many years put up with an admittedly odd father. Having you in my life is better than the best movie imaginable! All men should be so blessed.

I have been gifted with many other family members who have encouraged me in special ways over the years. First and most of all are my parents Wiz and Liz Horner, who sent me to school on weekdays—but took me to the movies on weekends, often accompanied by the pesky little brothers, Brian and Russell. All four wonderful. Special thanks, too, to Jennifer Bradshaw, who first suggested to me that I might be a teacher. She may just have been right with that.

I have been blessed also with the great intellectual and spiritual companionship of many friends: Gordie Waldock and Bick Moore who taught me much, and C. W. Smith who strongly encouraged me to write this book—Doctor Smith, who is even better now than he ever was, a modern patriarch presently enjoying his reward. My Morning March companions at The Master's College are always provocative in caffeine-fired verbal jousting about all things political, theological, and filmic: John Stead, Will Varner, Paul Thorsell, R.W. Mackey, Taylor Jones, Greg Behle, Tom Halstead, Dennis Hutchison, Sab Matsumoto, and Gregg Frazer—who is wrong about *Citizen Kane* and right about everything else. My English department colleagues Esther Chua and Jo Suzuki provide unbroken delight to me as we waltz through the world of ideas, while we are all privileged to follow the lead of our marvelous chair—a father, really, a *paterfamilias* in the richest sense—the inimitable John Hotchkiss. True thanks also to my dean, John Hughes, and to Allan Pue, who offered me my first academic position after a ninety-minute "interview" featuring a single question. I have been privileged to serve under these men, as well as my provost, Mark Tatlock, President John MacArthur, and the board of directors of The Master's College. Their leadership is what enables teachers and scholars to do their work.

I'd like to thank Brian Morley, who early on encouraged this project, and Steve Miller, who helped me immensely at the earliest stages. I owe a rich debt to Stanley Fish who sharpened my thinking more than I could have imagined while I studied under him at Duke University. I am always encouraged and challenged by the energy, verve, and dedication of Liz Caddow, and treasure her friendship and investment in me as we develop the humanities core for Trinity Classical Academy. And like any teacher, I owe more than they now realize to my many, many dear students. A teacher's years of solitary study plant deep the roots of thought; students are the hoped-for almond blossoms, fresh and bursting.

Of course, a writer would be lost without editors, so I thank Justin Taylor, editorial director at Crossway, for supporting this project, and for the marvelous and sensitive work of Tara Davis on the manuscript.

A great debt is owed to Anthony J. Tigner, Rob Ikegami, Liz Froemming, and Christy Rodarte who carefully read many early drafts of chapters and provided wonderful insights, suggestions, and editorial helps. *Animis opibusque parati!*

Frodo: I can't do this, Sam.

Sam: I know. It's all wrong. By rights we shouldn't even be here. But we are. It's like in the great stories, Mr. Frodo. The ones that really mattered. Full of darkness and danger, they were. And sometimes you didn't want to know the end. Because how could the end be happy? How could the world go back to the way it was when so much bad had happened? But in the end, it's only a passing thing, this shadow. Even darkness must pass. A new day will come. And when the sun shines it will shine out the clearer. Those were the stories that stayed with you. That meant something, even if you were too small to understand why. But I think, Mr. Frodo, I do understand. I know now. Folk in those stories had lots of chances of turning back, only they didn't. They kept going. Because they were holding on to something.

Frodo: What are we holding onto, Sam?

Sam: That there's some good in this world, Mr. Frodo . . . and it's worth fighting for.
The Lord of the Rings: The Two Towers (2002)

Introduction

Movies, Truth, and the Origins of Culture

"The effect of the unbroken flow of images . . . is uncanny.
If cinema is sometimes dreamlike, then every edit is an
awakening. *Russian Ark* spins a daydream made of
centuries."

Roger Ebert

"You know what your problem is? You don't watch enough
movies. All of life's mysteries are answered in the movies."
"Davis" (Steve Martin) in *Grand Canyon* (1991)

ALL the world's a screen.

The original phrase is *totus mundus agit histrionem*—"all the
world's a stage"—a famous saying of Petronius. Another formulation, by Shakespeare, adds that we are but players:

All the world's a stage,
And all the men and women merely players;
They have their exits and their entrances;
And one man in his time plays many parts.[1]

In a way, this statement has always been quite accurate, so much
so that sixteenth-century Protestant theologian John Calvin repeat-

23

edly used the same metaphor in his monumental work *Institutes of the Christian Religion*, calling the universe God's theater for displaying his glory and nature. I believe that by our point in history, film has become a significant theater displaying *man's* nature—in both its glory and its shame. The question then raised is, what kind of spectators are we? And what kind of actors? For we are in fact both. As Steve Martin's movie director character says in *Grand Canyon*, there may indeed be many mysteries that are opened up by gazing into the magical screen.

Alas, the stage metaphor alone is no longer sufficient. Our technology and our love for storytelling has transplanted and transformed the historically small, temporary, localized physical stage with its actors, backdrops, and props and replaced it with the incredibly complex art of filmmaking, where many thousands of elements (and many millions of dollars) all combine to produce the final cultural location of the moving screen image—infinitely repeatable, geographically distributed, not bound by time, and at least as apt if not more so to be loaded with rich cultural weight. *All the world's a screen.*

Think of how much of our lives we now spend looking at a screen. Film screens, television screens, and computer screens dominate our visual and even tactile experience; we are taught, we are entertained, and we purchase by screen interfaces; we get our news, make our decisions, and manage our money and possessions with two-dimensional screens. The electronic page has not yet replaced paper, but it has made serious inroads. I can still touch a screen to get a "hard copy" made of the image of the document in front of me. Screen-experience can be communal (a movie theater on Saturday night) or solitary (playing solitaire on your computer). Twenty-first century communication is almost overwhelmingly screen-based, with e-mail, social networking Web sites, and even our tiny cell phones having widely varied GUIs (graphical user interfaces). We have electronic "friends" all over the world that we have never met in all three dimensions. The simplest purchases in a grocery store are shown to us by a screen, nicely angled toward us so we are as visually involved in the transaction as the harried clerk (price, member discount, coupons, *total savings!*), and also somehow providing a pleasant screen-verification that we in fact now own the broccoli, milk, and nasal spray bagged in front of us. If it is on the screen, it must be so. The screen has in many ways become the world. And, as I will try to demonstrate in this book, most of the people in the technological West have built most of their ideas about the universe in which they live from looking at screens—and movie screens in particular. *All the world.*

My first question is, is this good, or is it bad, or does it matter at all? And what do we do with this reality as we now find it?

The purpose of this book is to help us think through these kinds of questions in regard to movies. Why do we think the way we do about the world? Is filmmaking an art, in the classical sense? Is it philosophy in some technologically advanced form? How influential are movies, really? Can they have a bad effect on us? Can they promote virtue in any way? How do we think in a biblical and theologically rich way about film in general and specific movies in particular? And why is film so incredibly powerful? If we had a truly biblical way to think about the culture of film, what would that look like?

As is well known, there has been a long and tortured relationship between Christianity and the arts and philosophy—and culture in general. If mankind is indeed fallen from God as the Bible alleges, and we are now depraved, blinded, and in a state of rebellion against God and all that he is and all that he requires of us, then it is to be expected that human cultural production would reflect these elements of man's nature. The question the Christian faces is, now that I have been saved *out* of the world, how do I live *in* it? Some will say, "Separate yourself entirely from culture," and this is often meant in a literal, physical way. You can indeed live in an isolated area, cut yourself off from exterior cultural influences such as television, music, movies, the Internet, books, art, magazines, fashion, and so forth, and raise your family as if the last one hundred (or one thousand) years of cultural change had not occurred. On the other hand, you could live in Manhattan or the tony West Side of Los Angeles, read widely, watch all kinds of movies and television shows, spend a lot of time on the Web, and participate broadly in cultural events. The digital age is of course breaking down most of these physical barriers; you can access almost anything anywhere with the Internet, just as you can lock yourself in a Manhattan apartment and try to seclude yourself away from the world in a concrete cloister.

Most Christians in America tend to be somewhere in the middle of these extremes. They read *some* things, but not everything; they watch *some* TV and movies, but draw certain lines when it comes to content; and in general, they adopt a moderately conservative approach to interaction with culture in general. The usual reasoning behind this stems from the recognition that fallen man produces fallen cultural objects (artifacts and ideas) that are often very attractive to our own fallen natures and that can cause us to sin. Yet longstanding arguments made from Scripture suggest that total or near-total separation from the culture we live in is not Scripture's standard, any more than indiscriminate acceptance of paganism is.

I take the position in this book that there are valid and valuable reasons for Christians to enjoy and thoughtfully study culture in general and film in particular. The believer should approach this enjoyment and study like all the rest of life: you must learn to seek God's wisdom and will in the choices you make, great and small. The key to a wise and godly life is to fill the heart and mind with Scripture and then make your decisions based upon the broad principles and the direct precepts found in the Word. I contend that Scripture does not call us to evacuate ourselves entirely from the pagan culture that surrounds us, but to use our wise and prudent interaction with that culture to help us grow in our appreciation of God's grace toward us, to see that what God says about fallen mankind is in fact absolutely accurate (even as found in pagan works), and to better equip us for interaction with the many human beings who do not yet know him. So why should Christians study film?

Simply put, film is the ultimate form of cultural expression in the modern world. Film is where culture is at. Film is the most powerful image of itself that humanity has ever produced. No one would deny that books, art, music, politics, social consciousness, and so forth are significant, but film is the one "cultural location" where all of these other categories may meet and have a discussion. In film, all the varied and disparate elements of the human experience come together and talk with each other. Have you ever seen a politically driven movie? Or watched a film that took your breath away because it was art, pure and simple? How many movies in the last twenty years have been based on classic literary texts? Film is a rich combination of storytelling, painting, philosophy, history, and politics all wrapped in technology. This supremacy of film may of course change in the future as film technology advances and is inevitably supplanted by newer technological/artistic methods. In some ways, film has helped create modernity itself, as it is a highly technological, mass-culture medium of art and philosophy, appealing to several senses, and embodying the spirit of its own age—an age that it helped to usher in. *All the world's a screen.*

Certainly Christians should not watch everything that is produced. At the very least, that would be poor stewardship of time, money, and attention. Disengaging from all film is an equal and opposite error, the other extreme from watching anything and everything indiscriminately. There are two distinct reasons for participating in a moderated and thoughtful experience of film viewing.

First of all, for most of us, movie going is a social event. We watch with others and react with others, and then share our responses, opinions, and critiques. We often end up in vigorous debates because many of us are highly opinionated about film. So film watching helps us engage *individuals*. It can be a very fruitful form of human interaction. I think it is an error to try to "engage" or "redeem" culture. It sounds nice, and it sounds theologically deep, but God does not call us to redeem culture *per se* and somehow create a "Christian" culture. True belief is always an exile, not a kingdom on earth. Furthermore, culture is not separated from God— individual people are. Culture is the product of both individuals and the masses. While individuals may be positively influenced by a Christianized culture, this does not guarantee that they will be so influenced, or that the spiritual results will be in any way significant to the individual. Millions of people have watched movies about Jesus—even theologically accurate ones—but this does not make them followers of Jesus anymore than watching *ET* makes me want to "phone home" or "be good." Nor would watching perfectly wholesome and inoffensive movies make you wholesome and inoffensive. But having a conversant familiarity with your culture is a critical point of intersection with the living, breathing individuals who also inhabit your cultural system. This is an observation made by many effective missionaries who enter alien cultures, then use features of those cultures—pagan though they may be—to establish rich, genuine contact with the people who know nothing outside those cultures.

Second, film watching helps us engage *culture*. I am not at all reversing what I just said, but actually following the logic through in a thorough manner. Cultural involvement is one aspect of living as a believer in a fallen world. How do we "engage culture" then? I believe there is only one biblically valid model, and that is to critique culture theologically, bringing Scripture to bear as an object of critical inquiry that dismantles error while also pointing out truth in human cultural production. This is what we see in the lives of Moses, Joseph, Daniel, and Paul as they live their lives in pagan cultures. And if you have any familiarity with Greek philosophy, you can clearly see that the author of the New Testament book of Hebrews knew platonic philosophy intimately and was making powerfully subtle arguments to dismantle it so it would not skewer a proper understanding of the old and new covenants. Similarly, Paul could argue brilliantly against the Stoics, Epicureans, and Platonists on the Areopagus in Athens, within sight of the great temples of the Acropolis, while Moses was learned in all the religion and superstition of the Egyptians. Daniel and his companions, the cream of the crop of Israel, mastered the learning of their Chaldean masters and used that learning wisely in the service of the one true God. On top of all this, it is a mistake, and unbiblical, to assume that Christians have the corner on truth. Bible-believing Christians have a corner on the gospel and on the person of Christ. Scripture is the revelation of God, and it is absolutely complete, without error, perfect, and the only true way to learn of God. But we should note that Scripture does not deal with every conceivable topic directly, and at the same time we should remember that Christians—even very mature ones—are not infallible. Wise and mature Christians should have a wild boldness when it comes to proclaiming the truth of God in Christ, and godly humility when talking about everything else. Furthermore, it is a bedrock principle of Scripture that man, despite his fallen state and utter depravity, still bears in himself the image of God and can discover certain things that are true even if he never knows truth itself in the person of Jesus—who said he was "the way, the truth, and the life." In fact, the most basic truths about God, man, and the universe are hardwired into all humans (Romans 1), a topic I deal with later in this chapter and extensively throughout this book.

Thus we may say that there is biblical warrant for studying the culture around us, in order to learn and to recognize the following things:

(1) All humans have certain basic *knowledge* of God, man, and the universe built into us.

(2) This results in certain *expectations* that are more or less universal among all people.

(3) These important *elements of humanness permeate our cultural production*. We all know, deep down, certain things, and we all, deep down, have certain expectations about the world and the ways we think things ought to be. While these are not perfectly universal, certain kinds of patterns of values, ideas, and questions do recur across widely divergent cultures and expanses of time.

(4) While Scripture is the ultimate source of authority and truth for believers, there are elements, *partial truths, present in all human cultural production*, including film. As I like to put it to students making intensive study of literature, art, film, philosophy, and theology: if it agrees with Scripture, it is true. If it disagrees with Scripture, it is still true, even in its falsity—because it is the nature of fallen man to argue against God. Or, to put it another way: *everything is biblical*. To agree with God is biblical. That's what God says we should do. To disagree with God is also "biblical," in the sense that this is what God says we actually do in our sinfulness. As the saying goes, the fool is convicted with the words of his own mouth.

(5) For the believer, these extrascriptural truths do not compete with Scripture, nor do they supplement it in the strictest sense; their value lies in their demonstration that *what Scripture says about man is true and valid*.

(6) The sum of all this is that for individual believers, cultural interaction forms an important opportunity (though not the only

one) to learn that Scripture is meant to be used—*to be an active agent of critique*—in the believer's life. The Bible exists to break you down and remake you, and to teach you how to recognize the true nature of the world around you. The Bible doesn't do you much good if it just sits on your shelf or rests in your mind as a series of carefully memorized religious precepts. Scripture itself claims "the word of God is living and active, sharper than any two-edged sword, piercing to the division of soul and of spirit, of joints and of marrow, and discerning the thoughts and intentions of the heart" (Heb. 4:12). This implies strongly that it is most effective as a sword, an object of penetrating, cutting, and opening (what we might call criticism) of man and man's condition. Furthermore, those believers who know the Word intimately are called "the mature," and they are those "who have their powers of discernment trained by constant practice to distinguish good from evil" (Heb. 5:14). Clearly, this "practice" involves saturating the mind with the Word—and then comparing it with the world. Discernment is judgment. Scripture in the hands of the wise Christian should open up an effective, sophisticated, and edifying mode of interpretation of the culture surrounding us, and ultimately, enable us to reach individuals with God's truth while minimizing the negative impact of fallen culture on us.

What are we to do, then?

Many Christians tend to view film as "mere entertainment." But really there is no such thing for the believer. Everything has meaning and relevance, because God rightly claims sovereignty over all aspects of our lives, no matter how minor they may appear. Every decision we make about everything we experience has real value to God. Film is not just mass media art or pop culture either. Film is the modern-day equivalent of philosophy. It is an artistic representation of what we believe, what we dream of, what we hope for—indeed, of what we are in the core of our being. Instead of arguing about fate in the marketplace in first-century Athens, we now watch Clint Eastwood shoot people in *Unforgiven* or Emma Thompson forgive Anthony Hopkins in *The Remains of the Day* (1993). Film is the celluloid frame of our waking dreams. And I'm not just talking here about artsy black-and-white movies made in Sweden or highbrow films from France based on obscure nineteenth-century novels. At its core, philosophy is a way of looking at the world, a way of explaining the world to ourselves, of orienting ourselves in the strange experience of being here and being conscious of ourselves being here. Film is intensely visual—just like humans are. The vast majority of our conscious experience is visual experience, and so film is the perfect medium for capturing what it means to be human. In fact, now that we have amassed over a century's worth of motion picture image production, and most of us have spent significant time in front of these screens, our memories of our visual experience is saturated with film imagery. So whatever else film is, it is not of no importance. It is an extraordinarily human endeavor and a richly human experience. Several generations before Christ, the Roman playwright Terence said *Homo sum: humani nil a me alienum puto*: "I am human, and nothing human is alien to me." Or, in a more sinister fashion, Dr. Tyrell says to Deckard in Ridley Scott's incomparably brilliant *Blade Runner* (1982) about his corporation that produces perfectly human robots: " 'More human than human' is our motto." And God said, "Let us make man in our image." God made us in his image; we make movies in ours.

Framing Reality

Our world is a framed world. Our eyesight has its limits every waking moment; we cannot see beyond the borders of our eyelids. Our other senses of course have their own limits, but vision is an especially framed sense. All that we see is as a picture in a frame, a film frame, a screen frame. Whether we consciously think about it or not, we experience a continual limitation and curtailing of perception. Only God sees all. We are ourselves framed in every way. We can only see what we are able to see. As some are colorblind, we are all spiritually blind to certain things in varying ways.

At first, a new pair of glasses is highly annoying to wear. You see the frame. Inside the frame: nice, focused images. Outside the frame: a blur. And always, sometimes for days or weeks, the maddening presence of a border—be it plastic or metal, thick or thin—that separates the visible world from the blurred world. But an interesting process of erasure takes place before long, and generally without

31

our notice. The frame slowly vanishes away. For one thing, it is
virtually impossible to focus on your eyeglass frame itself without
giving yourself a severe headache. It simply stays out of focus. And
before long it more or less disappears from our conscious perception. Oh, you can see it when you choose to, but the actual effect
of wearing eyeglasses is that our field of vision simply adjusts to
the smaller area of clarity provided by our lenses. My frames happen to be antiques from the eighteenth century with modern lenses
specially made to fit. The "frame" I look through to see my world
is quite small, and I often wonder what wonders of the past world
others have seen through my frames. But I do not notice in my conscious mind that 40 percent of my vision is essentially blind, blurred
outside the frame. I can see light, color, and movement outside the
frames, but if I want to actually see something with clarity, I must
see it through my framed lenses. And the frames have effectively
vanished from my sight. That which helps me see becomes invisible
in my world.

Film works in very much the same way. It works because it erases
your impression of it as a carefully produced product for visual con-
sumption. Rarely do we stop and think, *Aha, I am looking at a series
of carefully crafted images rapidly flashing before me at twenty-four
frames per second and constrained by a particular aspect ratio of
1.85:1.* I may notice black strips above and below the film space while
watching letterboxed movies on a home television, but how often do I
think of the curtains hanging to the sides of the screen in a megaplex
theater? The curtains are superfluous decoration these days in most
theaters; I recall a peculiar pleasure of my youth in watching the
first few seconds of film being projected upon the wavy and slowly
drawn-back curtains of theaters in the 60s and 70s. It was always a
wonderful moment when the perfect clarity of brightly illuminated
celluloid flashed out at my eyes when the curtains were fully drawn!
My point is that the power of cinema is that while you are watching
a well-made movie, you forget that this is what you are doing. Pay
no attention to the man behind the curtain, as the Wizard of Oz says.
In fact, forget the curtain, the border that separates the world of the
movie from the world of reality. The action in a movie takes place

inside a framed area—and yet we do not think about this frame consciously while we watch.

Now this is a very interesting phenomenon. As a general rule, if you are in the Louvre looking at a sculpture, you don't forget that this is what you're doing. The same could be said of a painting, or even listening to a great symphony. Reading an engrossing novel (whether by Gustave Flaubert or Stephen King) can "carry you away from yourself" in an extraordinarily powerful way, but the kind of "carrying away" we experience with audiovisual film art is of an altogether different order. Extended written narrative can be amazingly powerful. Film, of course, combines the visual with sound (after the late 1920s) to present a narrative arc lasting just one to three hours, and the effect is nothing short of astonishing. We forget how amazing movies really are because we have grown used to them, but for the vast majority of human history such a technological narrative art would have been unimaginable. All the world wasn't always a screen.

This idea of being "carried away" while watching a movie is nothing new. In fact, the ancient Roman writer Longinus wrote an entire book about the subject of being "carried away" by aesthetic experience nearly two thousand years ago. *On the Sublime* is still considered one of the great masterpieces of thought on aesthetics, consciousness, and art. Film scholars have developed the concept of "diegesis," meaning the telling of a story and the creation of the world of that story. If a movie is effective, the viewer enters the diegetic world of the film. In a sense, disbelief is suspended willingly, and the viewer surrenders to the world of the film, which replaces, to a large extent, the world of reality in which a viewer is simply staring at images on a screen. The viewer experiences various stimuli— visual and aural—and this affects the emotions, the rational mind, and even the body. (Stand at the back of a packed theater during an intense action sequence such as a violent fistfight or thrilling car chase and you will see hundreds of bodies unconsciously swaying and ducking.) Movies are so effective in part because they present their action by replacing our normal sensate experiences. The screen (in a theater at least) is surrounded by blackness, and the typical film aspect ratio (height to width) mirrors the broadly elliptical viewing range our eyes have with their "binocular vision." In other words, the screen becomes our eye, and the screen simply displays what has been recorded with another eye—the camera. But the camera-eye does not transfer directly to our eyes. The images, hundreds of thousands of them, are heavily processed and manipulated before we ever see them projected. These heavily processed images are paired with an extraordinarily complex soundtrack that reproduces with phenomenal precision what we would expect to hear alongside the images flowing before us. The illusion is nearly perfect. Yet it is delicate. An editing error, even a tiny one, can ruin the hypnotic effect. So can a badly delivered line by a miscast actor, an incongruous act or prop that seems out of place, or a glitch in the soundtrack. But when the work is polished, the screen is king, and it creates a world that seems as real—or realer—than the real world. The screen becomes the world, and as much as we may try to convince ourselves that we make the world, it in fact, more often than not, makes us.

Screening Consciousness

What is consciousness? Surely it involves present sensation, memory, imagination, and the processing and evaluating of information. It may be the "greatest unsolved problem" of both philosophy and science. If we are only material, then we have to wonder, *how can stuff know that it is?* Conversely, how can thought have a material form? Are emotions chemicals? How are memories made, stored, retrieved, and often lost? More than a few films deal with these fascinating questions.

Whatever consciousness is, it is all we have, apparently. This is not at all an unbiblical idea. We can see the topic broached from Genesis to Ecclesiastes, from Job to Revelation. God reveals himself first and foremost by saying "I AM."[2] Not to be conscious is not to be. Even poor Hamlet could make that distinction. When he says, "to sleep, perchance to dream," he shows us that he knows that even when we are "unconscious," that is, asleep (or dead), there is still a certain kind of consciousness, albeit different. God made man in his image, and like God, we are immortal—we never cease to be. Our consciousness goes on. Artists of all kinds are fascinated with consciousness, perhaps because it is so frustrating to represent. If you sculpt a thinking man from a rock, what is it about the rock that makes us think "thinking man" instead of "unthinking rock"? Think of the famous sculpture by Rodin, *Le Penseur,* "The Thinker" (1902), hunched over in thought. Of what is he thinking? His mind is a mystery to us. And what of those many paintings of people reading, thinking, meditating, or experiencing a life of thought? They are all inevitably ambiguous and vague. What is the Thinker thinking?

Film, it appears to me, may be the very best cultural representation, re-creation, or reproduction of human consciousness. Film is of course not exactly and precisely like our mind's experience, but it surely mimics it in very effective ways. And, as I will try to show in what follows, it also in some measure *creates* our conscious experience of the world. This is not without grave importance, especially for Christians. The study of film is important for Christians because it is the modern-day equivalent of philosophy. Philosophy is something everyone has; it is the set of beliefs we hold about our world. Am I saying that potty-mouth, gross-out comedy movies are *philosophical works?* Yes, they are. (I'm not saying you should watch them, of course.) They're not Plato or Kant or Aquinas, but they are a way of looking at the world, and they are also the result of looking at the world in a certain way. Philosophy does not have to be complex, abstract, or written in Greek or German. Philosophy is what you believe about things; it is your way of explaining the world. There is as much philosophy in the butcher shop as the university. This is why the Reformers, all of them educated in classical philosophy, often referred to biblical Christianity as *philosophia christi*—the philosophy of Christ.

Why is film so effective at recreating human consciousness? At least part of this is because it is both visual and linear, just like our own experience. Yet, like our own minds, film often moves back and forth to the past and even the future. It is a kind of material memory—a strip of celluloid (or now quite often a complex grouping of digital bits) that stores information and replays it on demand. This information is visual and audial and *linear.* Film represents a simulated consciousness; that is, as viewers we enter another world, another mind or minds, for a specified period of time. Some movies exploit this in a highly explicit way, such as *High Noon* (1952, a classic good-guy/bad guy western with a complicating moral dilemma about pacifism and justice), where screen time equals real time. The camera repeatedly cuts away from the action to show us a clockface that tells what time of day it is. Screen time matches viewing time; twenty minutes into the viewing, exactly twenty minutes have elapsed in the world of the film. An hour for Gary Cooper is an hour for us. Thus, we experience in a very realistic way the tension of the plot, even as the characters do. This one-to-one mapping of the film world onto the real world (and vice versa) can be a very effective tactic. In fact, classical Greek tragedy was built around this principle, which Aristotle called the "unity of time." The ancient Greeks thought that if you told a story by presenting a live audiovisual representation such as a play, the audience would be confused if you skipped around in time—you couldn't show a character's youth in scene one and his adulthood in scene three and his old age in scene four. No one ages that fast in real life. You couldn't even show (in the strictest interpretations of the rule) action over two or three days. No, what you saw in ninety minutes had to be ninety minutes worth of action. Later playwrights of course bent and broke this rule, and eventually filmmakers could show you ten, fifty, or a million years in less than two hours. Time can also be expanded: you can show a fifteen-minute event stretched over ninety minutes by cutting together different perspectives of the event as experienced by different characters.

A very popular device in film narrative is this idea of playing with timelessness, eternity, time travel, and time loops. We are fascinated with the idea of escaping the limitations of time. We think of movies like *Groundhog Day* (1993), where Bill Murray finds himself waking up on the same day over and over and over; *Somewhere in Time* (1980), where Christopher Reeve wills himself back in time to meet a beautiful girl whose picture has caused him to fall in love with someone from the past; *Peggy Sue Got Married* (1986), where an unhappy middle-aged woman passes out at her high school reunion and wakes up back in high school; and of course the bizarre and disorienting final sequence in Stanley Kubrick's *2001: A Space Odyssey* (1968), where (after collapsing man's entire evolutionary history into a few minutes of screen time) an astronaut apparently goes through some mystical time/space warp and sees himself aging, dying, and then being reborn. Christopher Nolan's brilliant *Memento* (2000) shows the fascinating link between memory and time as linear experience. Few films have ever been as demanding on the viewer's attention, and fewer still have created such an ingenious device for creating viewer identification with a major character. *Russian Ark* (2002) is, despite its apparent simplicity, even more demanding on the viewer, though not by confusing us with a disjointed narrative. It features a single shot of extraordinary complexity: over two thousand actors in period costume in Russia's State Hermitage Museum (the Tsar's Winter Palace) in an unbroken shot—no cuts whatsoever. The effect is nothing short of mind-numbing.

Because of the way narrative film style has developed over the last one hundred years, we have come to think of it as the only way to tell a story: hundreds of cuts back and forth between characters, scenes, and across time. But that is not how we experience life, with the exception of sleep. Our experience is one unbroken chain of visual and other sensory input. Not so with film, where we expect constant breaks and interruptions to the stream of visual data. Yet the art of editing has become so sophisticated, and our minds are so used to the convention of edited shots succeeding one another in a more or less logical fashion, that when we come across a film like *Russian Ark*—our minds go into overdrive trying to deal with the "uncut fiction," even though it is actually closer to real experience than movies are! The viewer keeps waiting for the cut, waiting for the edit or the cutaway to something else—but it never comes. It is like life, where, other than sleep or neurological anomalies, our conscious experience is not "edited," as film critic Roger Ebert noted in his review. Our conscious life is more like a movie than we realize, for when we see a movie that works more like life than a movie, we find ourselves longing for the movie that is more like a movie, edits and all. We don't want a movie that is like life—we want a life that is like a movie. *All the world's a screen.*

In one of the greatest ironies of film history, most film scholars consider the early Russian filmmakers to be the creators of what we now think of as "movies" in their standard form as the ultimate art in modern culture. In particular, Sergei Eisenstein showed the power of *editing*—putting together a sequence of different camera shots to tell a linear narrative—to make the art of film into the pervasive cultural power that it now is. But *Russian Ark* doesn't feel like a movie; it has all the vertigo qualities of life itself, even though it is deliberately dreamlike in its narrative. *There are no edits.* It is unbroken, and it overwhelms the viewer with its unbrokenness. The cameraman walks nearly a mile through the massive Hermitage museum in an hour and a half—shooting the whole time—climbing up staircases, overhearing conversations, seeing the Tsar and his doomed family, moving effortlessly through a massive and complex ballroom dancing sequence. The final moment, where a window in the museum opens up to perhaps the purest visual metaphor for eternity we possess, is staggering in its power.

What in the world does this tell us about ourselves?

I would say it tells us a great deal.

Interpreting Interpretation

Where does culture come from? Why have culture at all? It is a notoriously difficult idea to define. I would say the simplest formulation is that culture is the sum total of beliefs and practices distributed among various people groups throughout time. But it is more than just what we believe and what we do; it is also our whole framework for comprehending the world, for making sense, or trying to make sense, out of life.

Perhaps thirty centuries ago, Solomon decided to try to think his way through the meaning of life:

> And I applied my heart to seek and to search out by wisdom all that is done under heaven. It is an unhappy business that God has given to the children of man to be busy with. I have seen everything that is done under the sun, and behold, all is vanity and a striving after wind. (Eccles. 1:13–14)

Solomon decides to apply his heart, to earnestly seek out a true, deep understanding of "all that is done." He claims that this search for meaning, for an ultimate stance from which to make sense of everything in human experience, is a difficult task and "unhappy business" that God has given to mankind. This business of searching for meaning is, I believe, a direct result of the fall—it is in fact one half of the curse. In this half of the curse, we all labor under the desire to understand the meaning of our lives. This search is inevitably futile and results in intense frustration, or, as Solomon calls it over and over in Ecclesiastes, "vanity." So we scramble around, trying to live happily and trying to find meaning. We are unhappily unsuccessful in this, and then stumble into the second part of the curse: death.

I believe culture is what we produce in our futile attempts to understand the world. It is what we believe and what we do to deal with the twin problems of meaninglessness and death. Humans were designed to have the total fulfillment and infinite pleasures of knowing an indescribably beautiful God while living in an unending state of intensely blissful perfection. Instead, we find ourselves frustrated and trapped in continual futility, while still retaining a sense that we are immortal and should be filled with peace and joy. This only furthers the frustration of our existence. Culture is the attempt to create a system that allows us to live in peace, in pleasure, and with a sense of meaning, a feeling of fulfillment. And this is why movies are so powerful and so popular. They are the absolute center of modern culture. They attempt to explain us to ourselves.

Culture is the web of ways we have of both looking at the world and living in the world. It is the collection of our conscious interactions with our world, our neighbors, and ourselves. We could say that culture is how we are programmed to interpret and understand the world and ourselves as part of that world. I believe that narrative film—which has been part of human culture for a little more than a century now—is perhaps the richest aspect of human culture, for it shows us, in a form that seems to be quite universally accessible, what we are like. It does this by reproducing human consciousness after a fashion. The human mind, fallen away from God, has always sought to replace God. I believe that human culture in all its forms is inextricably linked with man's fallen state. Thus I will build my basic arguments about film upon the New Testament's bedrock text regarding the state of man in the present world, Romans 1:16–23:

For I am not ashamed of the gospel, for it is the power of God for salvation to everyone who believes, to the Jew first and also to the Greek. For in it the righteousness of God is revealed from faith for faith, as it is written, "The righteous shall live by faith."

For the wrath of God is revealed from heaven against all ungodliness and unrighteousness of men, who by their unrighteousness suppress the truth. For what can be known about God is plain to them, because God has shown it to them. For his invisible attributes, namely, his eternal power and divine nature, have been clearly perceived, ever since the creation of the world, in the things that have been made. So they are without excuse. For although they knew God, they did not honor him as God or give thanks to him, but they became futile in their thinking, and their foolish hearts were darkened. Claiming to be wise, they became fools, and exchanged the glory of the immortal God for images resembling mortal man and birds and animals and creeping things.

Virtually everything I will say in this book is based upon this central passage.

Man was originally created by God in his image. That is to say, we were like him in kind but not degree. We are spiritual beings with a conscious mind, memory, will, emotions, and desire. We were created to be immortal and to have an eternal relationship with him, a relationship built around his provision for us as creator and our worship of him as creatures. Mankind has now fallen away from him into selfish self-regard, and God has been replaced by our own wills and desires. Yet we were made to worship him, to give our attention to him. It is in our nature to be attentive to him in our consciousness. Now that the relationship is severed, there is a gap, a void in our conscious selves, and we are driven to fill that gap. Part of that attempt—an always futile one, of course—to fill the gap is what we call culture.

Our English word "culture" is derived from the Latin word *cultus*, which refers to agriculture, planting, and growing things up out of the fertile earth. (Interestingly enough, it also can be used to refer to worship or respect.) Culture is what grows out of the soil of humanity; it is the sum of a people-group's practices, beliefs, traditions, and ways of looking at and understanding the world. As I see it, the most important element of any culture is this last factor—how the people of a culture attempt to understand their world. If man's life is, in the words of philosopher Thomas Hobbes, "solitary, poor, nasty, brutish, and short," then only a sense of some meaning beyond those elements of life can provide comfort and pleasure. I believe that all humans are primarily driven by a desire for meaning, in the broadest sense; we want our lives to have some value beyond our mere moment-by-moment experiences. The most basic human attempt to gain meaning beyond the present is to hope that the present will continue indefinitely and will be filled with pleasure as opposed to pain. Obviously, this is the human desire for eternal life. But since most people come to the conclusion that eternal life is probably not real, they then revert to cramming as much pleasure into each fleeting moment as possible. So, for most of us, meaning becomes equated with pleasure, and yet we are always confronted with the fear of the end of our lives.

This is why we create and propagate and cling to religious and philosophical systems, and why many search for ultimate value and meaning in art, creativity, or some form of aesthetic or pleasure experience, including athletics, communing with nature, using drugs, or finding some kind of cause larger than the self to give meaning to life. There is little doubt that satisfied, happy people are those who are secure that their lives have real meaning and significance, in the deepest sense. This driving desire for meaning is as universal as anything in human experience, because it is shared by all cultures however different they may be in their answers to the question of meaning. As a Christian, I believe ultimate meaning is found in union with the one true God, and that that God is the God of the Bible, and that that union is based upon the gospel of grace. All other "meanings," pleasant and useful as they may be, are partial, temporary, and unsatisfying.

Over many years of studying cultural production, from high culture to pop culture, I have come to the conclusion that what Scripture says about human beings is startlingly accurate—amazingly so, in fact. I have come to the conclusion that there are in fact teachings in the Old and New Testaments that do not just shed great light on what humans produce in their cultural systems, but go a long way toward explaining why we have cultural systems at all. Let me lay this theory out briefly.

Suppressing the Origins of Culture

In the first chapter of Romans, the apostle Paul, who had been a Jewish religious zealot involved in the persecution and murder of Christians before his conversion to following Jesus, begins his long theological text by making a few simple but profound points about human nature. According to Paul, the first and most important thing about mankind is that it presently exists under the wrath of God. God is angry with man, both as a race and as individuals. God's anger is "being revealed" (v. 18, NIV), suggesting that it is not yet fully revealed, though some elements of it are already manifest. Scripture teaches that mankind has fallen into a state of total rebellion against God, who is holy, pure, and perfect. Man is now selfish, self-absorbed, and utterly evil. He cannot reform himself and cannot please God and cannot pay the debt he owes by religious acts or charitable deeds. In the human sense and on the human level he may look good, be kind, be selfless, be very religious, and even give his life to save another, but this is mere surface and never sufficient to cover each man's own sins. So God's wrath abides, it lingers, over man, and every man goes around crippled by guilt, stricken with fear (especially of death), and attempting to do some rather strange things. The strangest of these is the attempt to "suppress" the truth of God. Verse 18 says men "suppress" the truth in their "unrighteousness"; that is, we actively deny what our inner voice tell us—that there is something beyond and above us, that that some*thing* is a some*one*, that that someone has a claim over us and rightly so, and that that someone is offended by our rejection of his just claim.

I believe that this suppression of truth is in fact the origin of culture.

If God is in fact God—that is, a sovereign Creator and Ruler without bounds, unlimited by time and space, unchanging and unmoved, the ultimate source of everything, and infinitely good, wise, and holy (set apart from all else and utterly unique in his perfection)—then it seems to follow that his truth does not change. And while the ultimate revelation of his truth is Jesus Christ, he also reveals his truth in Scripture, which always everywhere points to Christ. Furthermore, the universe itself points to God and his glory:

The heavens declare the glory of God,
    and the sky above proclaims his handiwork.
Day to day pours out speech,
    and night to night reveals knowledge.
There is no speech, nor are there words,
    whose voice is not heard.
Their voice goes out through all the earth,
    and their words to the end of the world. (Ps. 19:1–4)

I believe *everything points to God*. This is the very purpose of God's entire creation. Even those conscious beings in his creation that reject him still ultimately point to him (this is part of the point of Phil. 2:10–11: "at the name of Jesus every knee should bow, in heaven and on earth and under the earth, and every tongue confess that Jesus Christ is Lord, to the glory of God the Father"). Properly understood, all aspects of creation—including human cultural creation—in the final analysis function under God's authority and reveal a basic knowledge of God that lies within us all.

But when man fell away from God, man lost all that gave real meaning to his existence, and he perverted that basic knowledge of God we all carry within. Man denies his own nature when he denies God—in a real sense, man negates his own existence by rejecting his creator. This causes the futility observed by Solomon and anyone else with a longstanding, carefully observed view of what life is really like. Man's basic activity, according to Romans 1, is the *suppression* of the truth of God. But what precisely is suppressed?

The first thing that is suppressed is that the truth itself is plain! Scripture tells us that what may be known of God is plainly revealed to man. This means that the inimitable glories of the visible universe that point to a glorious God present an outward witness to his existence and rule, and the inward witness of God is no less powerful. All humans have an inbuilt sense of his "eternal power and divine nature," and this inbuilt knowledge comes from God himself. No activity occupies more energy in the fallen human than the attempt to reject, cover up, deny, reduce, and suppress this knowledge. However, this is like trying to tell yourself that you do not exist or denying that you had biological parents. The statement negates itself, and if pursued, may drive you mad. Man is surrounded by a constant stream of evidence to which he is blinded by his own decision to suppress what the evidence points to. In addition to these basic truths about God, I believe we have wired into us the recognition, degraded as it may be, of certain qualities that characterize God. These qualities include truth, beauty, perfection, justice, creativity, and happiness—and that he is a being to be loved and feared. Anywhere we find these (even in movies), we are attracted to them. Whether a man believes in God or not, he tends to respond positively to these qualities for reasons he may not be able to articulate or understand. The futility comes when, in the face of all the evidence, man knows he must interpret all of this evidence *somehow*. The ultimate end of this futile process is either an intellectually incoherent atheism or agnosticism or an attempt to create a religious system that fits the desires of the imagination. Neither brings peace and satisfaction.

God creates a world and rules over it. The world he creates is in accord with his will, that is, it truly is what it is and what he has made it to be. Some of his creatures in his world, the ones created in his image and thus free in their wills as originally created, fall away from him and become his enemies. They have a knowledge of him and of his power and attributes built into them, and everything in his universe points to him—yet these rebellious creatures actively suppress this truth. They suppress it in two stages of equal importance: first they suppress the actual knowledge of God, and then they suppress the fact of the first suppression. Remembering something you have suppressed would negate the suppression. If you try to forget something, you defeat yourself by remembering each day to forget it. So the rebel creatures must live in a state of continual, active suppression, suppressing both the original object and the suppression itself. Man must follow every suppression with a further suppression. Mankind in his fallen state is thus primarily characterized by the act of suppression, knowledge of which is then suppressed. Interestingly, many thinkers have posited similar views of man, while (of course) suppressing the truth of God. Freud and Nietzsche come to mind.

But here's my real question: *what exactly happens to the truth that is suppressed?* This truth, or, more correctly, these truths—about the existence and nature of God, his rule and power, and our own nature as rebels originally created in his image and made for enjoyment of him yet still responsive to things like truth, beauty, and justice—do not, I believe, simply go away. If truth is true, then it does not change and it does not ever really go away. If it does not go away when it is suppressed, then what happens to it? Here is where we find fascinating intersections with the thoughts of men like Freud and Nietzsche, who, while themselves rejecting the revelation of God, both contend that humans are driven by the energy of things that are repressed and deeply buried in our minds. Freud identifies sex and Nietzsche the Will to Power, both of which are only partial explanations at best. Now, I am no Freudian psychoanalyst, nor am I a Nietzschean philosopher, but I think that in the broadest sense they are onto something. If there are true truths about the universe (and about our place in the universe) that we repress or suppress, and these repressed objects of knowledge are the engines that drive us, then they do not in fact go away. They return.

I believe that suppressed truth is never in fact totally eradicated. It never vanishes, it is never annihilated—it never goes away. At least one purpose of God's implanting truth in man is to leave man without excuse (Rom. 1:20). The nagging, gnawing, inbuilt revelation of God is by its nature irremovable. So, if the truth that is suppressed does not disappear, what happens to it? I believe it changes form and returns. It becomes truth altered, truth metamorphosed, truth perverted. After describing the suppression of truth, Paul tells us that man's foolish heart was darkened, and then the truth of God was "exchanged"—that is, "the glory of the immortal God" was perverted into "images resembling mortal man and birds and animals and creeping things" (Rom. 1:23). What replaces God is an image of some kind, whether a real object or an intangible idea, and since we are designed to worship, the produced image becomes the object of our rapt attention.

God must be replaced. The irony is that since God truly is God, any replacement is futile, because even the replacement inevitably points back to him. The replacement is in the image of something God made, directly or indirectly, and beyond that, the fact that a replacement is required and desired shows that something is being rejected and replaced. The truth of God inevitably reemerges in one form or another. As I see it, all human cultural production, from worshiping a golden calf to watching German opera, is a return of suppressed truth. I call this the "conservation of truth principle."[3] In the same way that matter cannot be vanquished but only change form, truth does not simply go away without a trace. The trace always reconstitutes itself as truth in some form, adulterated though it may be. Truth can be suppressed, but only temporarily, and will always bubble up to the surface again if you try to drown it. As Launcelot says in Shakespeare's *Merchant of Venice*:

> Nay, indeed, if you had your eyes, you might fail of
> the knowing me: it is a wise father that knows his
> own child. Well, old man, I will tell you news of
> your son: give me your blessing: truth will come
> to light; murder cannot be hid long; a man's son
> may, but at the length truth will out.[4]

Truth by its very nature will not remain suppressed forever. A murderer may escape conviction by men, but he will not escape God's judgment. The ultimate example of the final failure of suppressing the truth is of course found in the death of those who deny God and find themselves being judged by the One who made them and offered them only love and grace.

Suppressed truth inevitably reemerges in culturally variant forms, all with flavors of truth, and is therefore highly appealing to humans hungry for meaning but desiring to avoid the ultimate source of truth. The re-emergent truths have been perverted by human depravity and mixed with untruths and partial truths. They now *appeal to the flesh, accord with demonic forces*, and *oppose God*. James writes of the fallen human state and by extension all that fallen humans produce, and characterizes it thus: "This is not the wisdom that comes down from above, but is earthly, unspiritual, demonic"

(3:15). Man's suppression of God produces thinking and cultural production that is opposed to God, is like demonic rebellion against God, and completes the circle by justifying sinful flesh to itself by continuing the process of suppression. As the Puritan poet John Milton wrote in *Paradise Regained*, all philosophy is but "subtle shifts/conviction to evade." It is nothing more than gossamer arguments designed to suppress from our consciousness that we feel guilty before God.

We cling to utterly unrealistic views about human nature, and we struggle with a recognition that "something is not right" with the world. From this most people tend to go in either of two directions: they become idealists detached from reality or they become cynics detached from humanity. Hence the two great classical genres of Comedy and Tragedy. Everything will work out in the former; everyone will die miserably in the latter.

What will it be? *The Sound of Music* (1965) or *Unforgiven*? Do we escape to the Swiss Alps singing "Edelweiss," or do we die on the barroom floor, rolling in blood and broken glass, dreaming of a house we'll never live in?

Vengeance and the Unforgiven

Let me provide an example to clarify some of the admittedly abstract arguments above and to provide a picture of what the rest of this book will be doing. God is a god of justice. While he is patient in his justice, and for the time being many wrongs go unrighted, the time is coming when he will right all wrongs, reward all rights, and bring the entire universe back into a state of continual and complete justice. Man, made in God's image, also has a sense of justice. Being fallen, he is neither just himself nor able to understand the ultimate justice in God's plan for allowing temporary injustice in the now. Fallen man is thus (once again) frustrated with the vanity of justice in the world he sees and knows. We want to be assured of justice in the case of everyone around us, as this makes our life secure. But we would rather not have justice meted out against *us* when *we* misbehave, because we don't want to be punished. Justice is for the other guy.

God clearly states, "Vengeance is mine, and recompense . . ." (Deut. 32:35); it is not for us as individuals to right wrongs done to us. Followers of God are required to forgive, even forgive their enemies. Yet all humans have a burning urge to bring justice to those who wrong us and those dear to us. We want to bring justice to the oppressed and injured even if we have never met them and they live halfway around the world. Resisting the urge to right wrongs requires superhuman strength. It is utterly unnatural. Our passion for justice is both good and bad: good, because God loves justice and hates injustice; bad, because we often turn justice to our own ends, we often do not give justice that is just and right and rightly proportioned, and we do not have the patience to wait for God's timing of justice. Deferred justice is injustice. People should get what they deserve: honor for the honorable and punishment for the evil. But as we look around, we see that life is deeply unjust: the honorable are dishonored, the good are injured, and the helpless are trampled underfoot. We might say that, as far as actual experience goes, what you deserve has nothing to do with what you get.

In Clint Eastwood's rich and spectacular revisionist western *Unforgiven*, the venerable star of many westerns directs himself in the role of William Munny, an ex-assassin who got religion, then got a wife and family, then lost his wife, and is now in need of cash to provide for his children. He has a chance to do one more job, and his mission is more than just. He and his old partner contract with a group of beleaguered prostitutes in the town of Big Whiskey; the whores there want the assassins to kill two cowboys who were involved in a vicious mutilation of a young prostitute. Along the way, an act of violence is added to the original set of crimes that is so horrific that Eastwood's character—up to that point a model of cool self-control and disinterested detachment—loses his "new man" and reverts to the cold-blooded murderer he had been before. At the end of the film, after one of the most spectacular short gunfights ever filmed, William Munny stands over a very bad man—one who should be a "good guy" on the side of justice—and points his rifle right at his head. No escape is possible. The man on the ground does not plead for mercy; he knows he's a dead man. Yet he says, with serious indignation despite his own consistently horrendous brutality to several others in the movie, "I don't deserve to die like this. . . . *I'm building a house!*" The running joke in the film is that this character is building a rather shoddy home of which he is inordinately proud. He is now in disbelief that he is about to die on the floor of a sleazy bar; he had been planning on enjoying his house. Eastwood's William Munny stares down blankly, his soul gone, and says dryly, "Deserve's got *nothin'* to do with it." Then he chooses again to become a murderer and pulls the trigger as the camera remains fixed on his stony face.

It is difficult to imagine a truer picture of the human experience. Everyone has a built-in sense of what justice is, and a desire to see it done—at least, as we see fit. Our perceptions of justice and its application to others and ourselves is every bit as fallen and error-ridden as everything else in our consciousness. Munny will be wrong to murder this man. He should have a trial, due process, a jury of his peers. He should have a chance for the law to work, and the law takes time. If Munny shoots the unarmed man on the floor, he will absolutely be a lawless murderer. But in acting "unjustly" he will also be righting a wrong—the torture and murder of his best friend and co-assassin. Munny knows that in Big Whiskey the law would never bring the perpetrator of those deeds to justice. The problem is that the man William Munny wants to murder is the law—he is Little Bill, the town sheriff, played by Gene Hackman. This character is simultaneously the most genial and most brutal person in the film. He is worse than English Bob, the would-be assassin from Britain; he is worse than the brute that cut up the prostitute; he is worse than William Munny. Justice says he must die. But in the place of justice there is injustice: the cruelest man is the law personified.

> Moreover, I saw under the sun that in the place of justice, even there was wickedness, and in the place of righteousness, even there was wickedness. I said in my heart, God will judge the righteous and the wicked, for there is a time for every matter and for every work. I said in my heart with regard to the children of man that God is testing them that they may see that they themselves are but beasts. For what happens to the children of man and what happens to the beasts is the same; as one dies, so dies the other. They all have the same breath, and man

has no advantage over the beasts, for all is vanity. All go to one place.
. . . (Eccles. 3:16–20)

The intense desire for justice—which all people confess is a good thing—results as often as not in actual injustice. Justice comes from God, who is perfectly just in all his ways. We desire justice even though we suppress the truth of God as a whole. That suppressed truth remains and returns as a reconstituted element of culture (a sense of justice), which is undeniably perverted. Little Bill wants to keep dangerous bad guys out of his town, but his sense of justice can be rather self-serving; he is unjust in his own actions over and over. His own sense of justice involves him coolly equating the brutal mutilation of a young girl with the payment of a fine, and further assumes that if a man builds a house, he should get to live in it. *Even if he just brutally tortured another man to death.*

Furthermore, it isn't merely wrong for Munny to shoot Little Bill; it is wrong that he should be in a position *to have reason* to shoot him. Not just morally wrong—it is *a wrongness with the very state of the world*, which was created to be a theater for the display of God and his perfect mercy and justice. We live in this world, and we have both a sense of and a desire for justice. And we do not find it. And we are frustrated, and we cannot understand. And we make movies that show this frustration, and the best ones show the terrible complexity of our moral situation. In *Unforgiven* the initial victim is a woman who prostitutes her body; the initial perpetrator is "just a guy out for a good time"; English Bob is a stuck-up British killer followed by a fawning writer who believes in and helps create his mythic heroism for pulp magazines; the supposed "heroes" are assassins who know with no shred of doubt about their own natures that they are cold-blooded murderers. Yet they are going to bring justice to Big Whiskey. And the local sheriff is a monster and a sadist. And he's building a crooked house. Here is a western without a clear "good guy." Concerning man, the film is biblically accurate.

In the movie's most powerfully memorable scene, an inexperienced young would-be assassin who has joined up on the contract killing shoots his first human being (in an outhouse with his pants down), though he has been lying about being an experienced murderer. The Schofield Kid, whose goal in life was to be a good killer, tries to express to Munny, the previously hardened but now softened murderer, what is happening inside his soul after he just took a man's life for money. "It don't seem real . . . how he ain't gonna never breathe again, ever . . . how he's dead. And the other one too. All on account of pulling a trigger."

Munny replies with a deep sense of self-knowledge, "It's a hell of a thing, killing a man. Take away all he's got . . . and all he's ever gonna have."

"Yeah, well, I guess they had it coming."

"We all got it coming, kid."

Madness is in their hearts while they live, and after that they go to the dead.

Unforgiven is the western movie version of the book of Ecclesiastes. Solomon with a six-shooter.

So, what does the title mean? Who, then, is unforgiven?

Part 1

PRACTICAL CONSIDERATIONS

ONE

Thinking about Looking

The Lost Art of Discernment

"Those who have their powers of discernment trained by
constant practice to distinguish good from evil."
Hebrews 5:14

DISCERNMENT means thinking as God thinks.

Of course, we can never think at God's level of depth, perfection, or excellence, but for the Christian, discernment is the crucial gift and skill of learning to use the mind, which is informed by Scripture and focused on God's glory. It may be the thing most lacking among contemporary evangelicals.[1]

One of the most popular and influential movies in the last decade of the twentieth century is *The Matrix* (1999). It's an action-packed, visually stunning, and energetic film that dives directly into the most difficult philosophical questions. What if everything we think is real is in fact *not real at all?* What if we are just slaves of some malevolent force, unaware of our true condition? *The Matrix* is the kind of film that draws many repeat viewers; I've talked to many Christians who've seen it more than three times, and it has probably sparked more discussion among young Christians than any movie made in the last twenty years. I use it regularly in my college courses on film analysis. We look at the fascinating cinematography, the disorienting plot, and the way the film represents technology (as so many science fiction movies do) as a frighteningly malignant and rebellious force.

While teaching the movie over the last decade, I have noticed something odd. The vast majority of young Christians who watch the film for the first time say that what they like most of all are its *distinctly Christian* themes. According to them, there are Christ figures, symbolic representations of God the Father and the Holy Spirit, a very unusual birth/resurrection/ascension sequence for one character, references to the Old and New Testaments sprinkled throughout the film, and an overall plot structure that seems to work perfectly as an allegory of Christians trying to reach a dying, deluded world with the truth that will set them free. It generally takes about an hour of discussion and probing questions before most of the students come to realize that not only is the film *not* Christian, it is about as far from Christianity as it can be. Having affinities with Christian images and ideas means nothing more than just that: it has similarities and resonances with Christian symbols. But that's as far as it goes. In fact the producers, Larry and Andy Wachowski, have been quite open with their personal philosophical views that undergird the film—and they are the polar opposite of what the Bible teaches.

The point is this: discernment takes hard work. We easily confuse error and truth; it is the most basic consequence of living in a fallen world. Truth and error are often so entangled in this world that we can even despair of detecting them, much less separating them. But we must learn to discern. How many Christians have walked out of theaters entertained but unenlightened? It is my belief that movie going can be edifying to a certain, limited degree, but only when done with careful, deliberate discernment. How many times have *you* walked away from a film unaware that you have bought into subtle philosophies and worldview positions that could undermine your faith? We should walk away—we *can* walk away—stronger for having been exposed to error, *and exposing it as error*.

How many young girls have *not* formed their views of romance based upon movies such as *Titanic*? How many young men have *not* formed their views on masculinity primarily due to action movies? How many married men and women have chosen to commit adultery partly because they absorbed a series of film portrayals of affairs (even nonexplicit ones) that did not show the pain and misery that always accompanies adultery? Have any middle-aged adults bought into euthanasia because they enjoyed a good movie that showed how an aged person's quality of life is what gave meaning to that life— and only a "high quality of life" justified the continuance of that life? How many Americans bought into a pro-abortion position (or even a weakened anti-abortion view) because they watched a beautifully photographed and well-acted film like *The Cider House Rules* (1999)—never once recognizing that the film is actually little more than a poorly disguised commercial advertising the moral benefits of taking unborn life?

The answer to all difficulties, dilemmas, and questions in the Christian life has always been the same: *what does the Bible say?* Sadly, many churches that call themselves "Bible believing" are slowly sliding away from scriptural authority because they are willing to place other sources of "wisdom" on a par with God's Word, rather than exercising biblical discernment by using Scripture to judge the validity of other authority-claims. Once this slide begins, discernment decreases exponentially, because discernment is not the default position—it is always rooted in a mind saturated with Scripture.[2]

Discernment and Art

Discernment about the arts is particularly problematic. Believers have an "anti-art" extreme on one end and an "anything goes" attitude on the other. Very few Christians ever think about the exercise of discernment beyond a basic level (for example, they might say no R-rated movies; no movies with bad language, or violence, or sex/nudity; no movie that has any plot elements involving adultery—even if the film portrays it nongraphically and entirely negatively, etc.)

Christians are commanded to be obedient to God. We are to be in the world, not of it; we must not love the world, though we are certainly going to be surrounded by it. We are not called to separate physically from the world (we can't do that until we die), but I believe we must "separate" *while in the world.* We are to separate, to discern truth from error, right from wrong, and then make right choices leading to God-honoring responses. Our actions must be characterized more by internal separation of truth from error than by external separation from the elements of the world that are clearly sinful. Standing next to an immoral woman will not ruin your moral condition (Jesus did it), but lusting after her beauty in your heart will. Our task is to discern, divide, decide, and do. We need to *discern* the errors that surround us, thoroughly *divide* those errors from the truth so often entangled in it, *decide* how to respond practically, and then *do* what we have rightly decided to do.

Proximity to evil, real or represented, does not somehow taint the believer. Many situations, perhaps most, will not do this—but only if you are aware of your natural sinfulness, recognize your tendency toward evil thought and action, saturate your mind thoroughly with Scripture, and have a heart filled with a love for God's glory. This doesn't mean you should expose yourself to everything available—in fact, in a fallen world, you will already be surrounded by evil and worse yet, you are yourself burdened with a sinful nature. You are not some being who is as pure as the driven snow that needs to preserve your perfection. Your mission is to discern and decide. There are different grades of discernment and varying levels of exposure. You can get closer to some things than others, and there are other things that should be avoided entirely once their nature is clear, but each of these decisions is a form of discernment.

Christian discernment is thinking as God thinks. His mind is infinite, perfect, complete, and wondrously beautiful. He misses nothing, understands everything, and appreciates and enjoys all the marvelous works of his creation. God is much more than an artist, but he is not less than an artist. His work is lovely; he is the creator of beauty itself, and he takes pleasure in beauty. The beauty that gives him the greatest pleasure is of course his recognition of his own beauty, the beauty of holiness (Pss. 110:3; 96:9). Human standards of beauty change over time—glance at the history of fashion magazines or compare movie stars through the decades. But the greatest beauty is God's beauty, and it is eternal and unchanging.

The Lord God has created almost innumerable elements of this world for us to experience, and he has also given us minds sensitive to his fingerprints, which are everywhere visible throughout his creation (Rom. 1:19–20). Making man in his own image, as a being who is intelligent, emotional, creative, and capable of perception, memory, imagination, and anticipation shows a particular aspect of God's will for us: he wants us to *experience things*. He wants us to think, to feel, to create, to enjoy, to remember, imagine, and hope. He wants us to do all these things within the boundaries of his care, his holiness, and his will (1 Cor. 10:23–33). His goal is not simply for us to *have* experiences, but to *choose* experiences and to *respond* to experiences in such a way that we grow more and more obedient to him (Phil. 4:8). He desires for us to desire to live lives that please and glorify him, and thus to edify ourselves and each other—which will in turn bring us the pleasure of obedience. Obedience to God is the greatest pleasure there is. He wants us to make right choices by acknowledging his rule in our hearts and his will for our lives.

So what do Christians "do" with movies? Should we act the same about movies as those who do not know the God of the universe?

Like everything else in human life, a radically different approach to film is necessary for believers. Non-Christians will generally have as primary motivations for film-watching entertainment, pleasure, vicarious living, an event to share with friends or loved ones, and so forth. For the believer, every moment is an important decision; some of these decisions will please God, and others will please only ourselves. We need to increasingly choose the former over the latter. Our primary goal should be to please God; and if God is what he claims to be, then these same decisions will result in our pleasure as well as his. Every scrap of our experience needs to be rooted in a consciousness of the presence of God. We do not move through one existential moment to another, seeking meaning only in ourselves. Those who love God are eternal beings, and *every decision makes a mark on eternity*.

There is a general perception that most "artsy" people are often weird, flaky, or liberal as far as morality goes. Whether this generalization is true is essentially irrelevant. In God's eyes, all of us are equally sinful. Some may flaunt it more than others who care to look socially respectable, but ultimately none of us is worse (or better) than anyone else. Artists and people who love the arts without being themselves talented or creative find deep pleasure, meaning, and satisfaction in aesthetic experience. For many humans, this alone gives meaning to life. The Roman writer Horace said *ars longa, vita brevis*—art is eternal, life is short. This, of course, is exactly backwards. All human life is eternal, but our *response* to art is one of the many ways we can glorify God throughout eternity. The MGM logo surrounding the roaring lion is the Latin phrase for "art for art's sake"—but they *do* make money, don't they? Art, like everything else, should be "for God's sake," as a toolman uses tools to please and glorify him. Aesthetic pleasure, like all pleasures, is from God, but, like all pleasures, it must be used for God's glory, not merely our temporary enjoyment.

Some Christians fear all art and creativity, but without biblical warrant. We should avoid sin, not beauty and thoughtfulness, design and craft; we must resist *evil*, not every form of pleasure or enjoyment. Contrary to what some Christians think, there is not a bizarre kind of virtue in ugliness! How many churches have you been in that were tacky, ugly, or featured some lowbrow aesthetic? Or made every attempt to eliminate anything that might engage the senses, which God made? God does not expect or desire that you leave anything at the church door but your rebellion. He wants your mind, your body, your personality, your emotions, and yes—your aesthetic capability.

Some other conceptions of Christian worship are primarily or largely aesthetic, such as the "High Church," with its mystical aestheticism of candles, incense, cathedrals, statues and icons, jeweled reliquaries, rich classical music, and so forth. None of these things is inherently wrong, but since we are highly distractable humans, everything tends to draw our attention, eventually, away from God. Beautiful buildings are not convicting, and neither are statues or stained glass windows. True conviction comes from the Word and the presence of the Spirit. Many contemporary churches use certain kinds of musical performance, drama, visual arts, film clips, and poetry for didactic purposes. God can use these things, of course, but he doesn't need them. Their use requires great care and discernment because they can quickly become mere entertainment serving only to distract a passive audience from the central object of worship: the glorious majesty and beauty of God Almighty. It is considerably tougher to preach real hard for three minutes than pop in a video of the Simpsons to illustrate a point.

The Complexity of Worldview
A basic thesis of this book is that for effective interpretation and discernment, the viewer must be able to decode a film's worldview—its

controlling philosophical position. Film, like all art, is open to varying interpretation. It is an untenable argument to claim that any film or other work of art has only one single valid level and range of meaning. Experiencing art is clearly a subjective event, and the very process of interpretation, which for the Christian should involve worldview analysis and discernment, is an opportunity for the Christian to exercise God-honoring obedience.[3] This presents a real challenge for the discerning viewer. Any art that is merely absorbed without critical, biblical reflection is art that you are using merely for pleasure, not for purpose. God is not antipleasure, but he does not expect us to use pleasure for its own sake. We must always be asking ourselves, "What does God think about this?" We need to use any and all experiences with art and culture to practice biblical-critical discernment.[4] As the writer of Hebrews tells us:

> For though by this time you ought to be teachers, you need someone to teach you again the basic principles of the oracles of God. You need milk, not solid food, for everyone who lives on milk is unskilled in the word of righteousness, since he is a child. But solid food is for the mature, for those who have their powers of discernment trained by constant practice to distinguish good from evil.

Many Christians fall into the trap of oversimplifying worldview. Human beings (reflections of God!) are inconceivably complex beings, and our thoughts and beliefs and explanatory systems are richly varied and extraordinarily interconnected. Human thought is like a massive web, all of it linked together by common threads, but with many various strands, links, and sectors. The seventeenth-century poet Thomas Traherne said, "To think well is to serve God in the Inner Court." To think well, we must be wary of oversimplification, but we also have to be realistic about starting *somewhere*. I would thus like to offer a very basic definition of worldview, one designed specifically to aid the Christian in the area of discernment regarding film or any other essentially narrative form of art. I have couched it in the form of a question:

"Who believes what about what and why?"

The question consists of five elements: "who," "believes," "what #1," "what #2," and "why." When these questions are dealt with, then we will have a workable level of understanding a particular worldview.

For film and narrative literature, the "who" aspect is the place to start. We must first discern whose beliefs we are decoding, and in film art there are many "whos." The most evident belief-holders are usually the major characters, and many of them will exemplify different ways of looking at the world. Indeed, this is the central engine that drives plots—conflicts between characters' worldviews. Character "A" thinks he may kill character "B"; character "B" has a different view of the matter. Hence, a chase scene and shootout. But with movies and with literary texts, there are other layers to consider. For example, a novel or film may contain a group of very evil men, and although the novelist or director has "created" these characters, he or she may not necessarily agree with or approve of their view of how the world works and how to live in it. Film itself is especially complex, because in most cases it is a collaborative and commercial enterprise. The producers, the business executives providing the financial backing and management for the film, may have a strong worldview influence (including but not limited to a desire to profit from the movie) and may thus exercise powerful editorial and content control over the "art" produced by the filmmakers.[5] So trying to find a film's worldview simply by listening to what characters say is only one level of discernment.

The next element is the idea of "belief." All humans believe something about everything, and we live, like it or not, according to what we actually believe. Our beliefs are our actual assumptions, presumptions, and presuppositions about the world, some of which are derived from observation, some from intuition, and some from sources we may not be able to readily identify.

Next come the two "whats." This chapter is primarily a treatment of "what" kinds of things people believe about "what" kinds of things. In other words, we will be looking at the *content* of the beliefs as well as the *objects* of belief. For instance, a content issue might be "doubting our senses" in regard to the object issue of "what the physical universe is like"—one of the major premises of a film like *The Matrix*. This will become clearer in the sections that follow on worldview and on philosophical positions, but it is an important distinction to make.

The next issue is the "why." Things have causes, many of which can be traced back to their source. I believe it is clear from Scripture that the source of all human thinking is the tension found in the dichotomy between our basic, built-in understanding about the existence and nature of God (Rom. 1:19–20) and our inherent and total sinfulness that is a result of the fall of mankind in Adam (Rom. 5:12–14). This results in darkened hearts (Rom. 1:21) and the suppression of truth (as I discussed in the introduction). That is, we are unable to correctly perceive or represent to ourselves the true nature of the universe (including ourselves) in a way that is entirely accurate. This is a very important point. Mankind cannot represent himself either entirely accurately *or entirely inaccurately*. Thus, all storytelling-art functions as a representation of this tension inherent in man's attempts to convince himself that he *is* something that he *is not* (i.e., good), and that he is *not* something that he *is* (i.e., sinful). As we examine a number of movies in detail throughout this book, this will become increasingly evident, and it is the central issue for effective biblical discernment in film viewing.

To state a positive, general definition of worldview, then, we could say "a worldview is any collection of ideas and their attendant attitudes that attempt to explain and systematize, at some level, how the universe works." We need to be always asking the question, "who believes what about what and why?"

Remember how I mentioned the common opinion among Christian viewers that *The Matrix* is in many ways compatible with Christianity? Spend a few minutes carefully reading any of the dozens of amateur reviews of the film as published on any of the various Christian film Web sites. Some of these responses are almost frightening in their foolishness and lack of biblical knowledge and worldview understanding. This is a direct result of not asking "who believes what about what and why?" from an informed and biblically grounded position. Watching movies is not inherently wrong, as some Christians might say. But watching movies, even selectively, without exercising biblical-critical discernment is a mistake of a very serious nature.

How many times have you been entertained into a state of spiritual numbness and intellectual stupor? Is it possible to appreciate film art while simultaneously using the experience in a way that pleases God and edifies ourselves? I believe it *is* possible—and necessary. Christians should be the very best film viewers—the very best cultural critics, in fact—because we have the potential capability to discern truth from error and also to understand the real purpose of enjoyment of human creativity, which is to glorify God by practicing discernment.[6]

Welcome to the Real World

The Many Ways of Misunderstanding Basically Everything

"Claiming to be wise. . . ."
Romans 1:22

THOUGHT does not occur in a vacuum.

Ideas are related to other ideas. Ideas come from ideas. These ideas lead to new ideas. Truly original ideas are so rare, they are almost nonexistent. Most ideas that claim to be new are merely rehashed versions of old ideas (see Eccles. 1:9–10). In order to understand the ideas present in the world, we have adopted the habit of categorizing them according to relationships with other ideas. Film is no different; the vast majority of plots are variations on just a few basic themes and character types. As a result, people who think carefully about the movies they watch tend to categorize them into certain divisions— genres, for instance.

But categorized lists can be dangerous and deceptive. Such lists will necessarily be collections of generalizations and oversimplifications. Nevertheless, if used thoughtfully, the list below will prove helpful for establishing the groundwork to use when attempting to discern patterns of worldview beliefs. Too many Christians are unaware of the worldview systems of those who do not accept Christianity; we find security in maintaining vague ideas about people who are "just wrong," rather than working hard to understand their worldviews as *yet more evidence for the truth of what God says in Scripture.*[1] It is no exaggeration to claim that all the worldviews men have held throughout history are variants of a few basic themes and can be found described to some extent in Scripture.

Each worldview below is described briefly but thoroughly enough to explain its stance on all the major aspects worldviews tend to exhibit. This is neither an exhaustive list nor a comprehensive description, but all worldviews stem from these basic categories. As we analyze individual films in later chapters, these basic categories will become apparent in the specific worldviews of the individual movies.

Christian Theism

According to classical biblical orthodoxy, there is a God who is himself invisible to us. He reveals himself primarily through the work of the Holy Spirit in our hearts, using the Old and New Testaments, and secondarily through nature. He is perfect, eternal, unchanging, just, loving, and, above all, *holy*—that is, utterly separate from and different than us. There is no evil of any kind in him or his thoughts or actions. He is perfectly good. His holiness transcends our most perfect conception of what we think holiness is—he is absolutely, entirely of a different order of being.

This God created the universe and everything in it, including man, who was made to be like God in kind though not degree. Man was created good and perfect, and, like God, he was originally created as a free agent with intellect and will—the ability to reason and to choose. God gave man a single command, which he disobeyed, resulting in his alienation from a perfect God who cannot bear the presence of sin. The whole human race is descended from the first man and has inherited his state of alienation from God, and each individual also now exhibits enslavement to disobedience. We are both born sinners due to our lineage and willingly continue in our sin as expressed in our own thoughts and actions. God is perfect and is therefore right to judge the race, corporately and individually, which has rebelled against him.

God's love for us, however, is revealed in his substitution of himself, in the person of his son Jesus Christ, to pay our debt. In essence, he paid to himself the debt we owed but could not pay. Thus both his mercy and his justice are revealed at the cross: his mercy in that he paid the penalty of death required of rebellious mankind and his justice in that he insisted the penalty be paid—though in this case by a substitute who was perfect and innocent. This mercy is received through individual faith. It is not enough that the penalty was paid for sinners; each individual must come to a point of personal faith in the redemptive work of the cross. We must see the death of the perfectly obedient and holy Son of God as direct payment for *our own transgressions*. Our individual sins—lies, lustful attitudes, sexual immorality, drunkenness, hatred, stealing, pride, and so on—were what nailed Jesus to the cross. His resurrection demonstrates his power even over death and that God the Father accepted the sacrificial payment. The penalty of death has been paid, and all who will acknowledge their sin and their need of a Savior can receive his utterly free forgiveness. This is not mere mental assent to either myth or history. Christians are those individuals who have thrown themselves on God's mercy, trusting nothing else to make them right with God, and who are now indwelt by the Holy Spirit of God by faith in him.

We now live as forgiven but still sinning humans, striving against the sin nature that still lives within us. The world we live in is characterized by enmity toward God. Christians still sin, though they must struggle against it, and those who are not believers are entirely enslaved to sin, unable to gain victory over it in any permanent or absolute sense. God has provided an inspired text to teach us about the nature of spiritual realities and to teach us how to live as saints in the world. Our primary goal is to obey God in our lives by teaching others about him with love and humility, and to obey him further by working our way through the experience of living in a fallen world—discernment being the crucial skill. The world is a place of deception, both human and demonic, and we must be on our guard to separate truth from error, always recognizing our own tendency, even as believers, to make errors and mistakes and to be sinfully arrogant, self-satisfied, and independent.

Deism

Many theologians and historians view deism as a relic from a bygone era. It is said to have sprung up and vanished, more or less, during the Enlightenment, the period from the mid-seventeenth to the early nineteenth centuries, when science as we know it began to take all areas of thinking under its umbrella. I'm not so sure about this. Deism in the classical sense may have vanished at the end of the Enlightenment, but ideas never occur in a vacuum and rarely vanish entirely without a trace.

Deism is *not* a monolithic system—it was never systematized into a coherent body of doctrines or philosophies. Many deists were people who held widely divergent views on how the universe actually worked, or the nature of God, or the nature of man. Deism is a conception of the universe as a thing invented by a powerful God, often conceived as the Judeo-Christian deity. But in this worldview, God is a distant, even disinterested Creator who treats the universe almost like a clock: it is manufactured, wound up, and then left to tick. As such, this position tends to strongly de-emphasize the personal nature of God as well as his immanence (presence), and instead views God as primarily transcendent (distant or otherworldly).

God is therefore not a providential being in the biblical sense, running and ordering the details of the universe according to his plan. The universe, jump-started by God, has been left to itself. It runs itself, we might say. In this religious conception, God is not someone we can pray to in the biblical sense; we are here on the spinning globe, left to ourselves, and we must do the best we can. God does not hear our prayers in any kind of personal, concerned way. As a result, many deists emphasize a kind of ethical and scientific pragmatism. We must figure out how the world as a more or less closed natural and mechanical system actually works, and then figure out how best to live in it. Deists often develop a system of scientific inquiry and explanation that is paralleled by a system of practical ethics.

But if God is transcendent and disinterested, then ethics and morality are problematic. Where do they come from? Is morality relative, situational, or merely rational? Do we trust ourselves to produce ethical/moral systems, and if so, can they be absolute? And if not, then how can we exist socially in any rational way?

The deist's ethical system is generally close to Judeo-Christian thinking, emphasizing love, kindness, hard work, service, generosity, justice, and so forth. Since God made the world and left it as he made it, the universe is not generally thought to be in a degraded or fallen state. The idea of the fall of man, or man as a sinner in need of forgiveness and change, is foreign to most deists. Man is what God made him to be, and he can figure out the world and how to live in it. If man is in some kind of "fallen" state, then his reason should enable him to get back up again. Man's reason is supreme, and it is intact, not depraved.

Naturalistic Materialism

James Sire made a marvelous observation: "Deism is the isthmus between two great continents—theism and naturalism."[2] He couldn't be more right. Naturalism flows out very, well, *naturally* from deism. As God is distanced from his creation, we tend to see more of the creation and less of the Creator (cf. Rom 1:19–23). The progression goes something like this: At first man receives and accepts the revelation of God. Then man comes to rely more and more on the reason God gave to man, and finally man views his "reason" as an end unto itself, sufficient to interpret and understand everything—including God, who is reasoned right out of existence.

I call this worldview "naturalistic materialism" because naturalism alone is not sufficiently clear. It can mean a study of or appreciation of nature, which is both good and biblical. The worldview in question is important because it is "materialistic." The central truth of the universe is not God, but matter. Everything that is, is matter. Matter can change forms and even become energy, but in the end, it is all there is. This worldview is most clearly recognizable in the system of thought known as naturalistic evolution. In fact, the two are inextricably linked. If matter is all there is, how did it reach such a state of bewildering variety—including matter that is *consciously aware of itself?* It must have gone from one form of matter to another, slowly changing and growing more complex over time. It certainly could not have begun in its present complex states—or *more* complex states, from which we have degraded (a thought too degrading to be entertained).

Naturalistic materialism generally denies the existence of any kind of deity or any invisible spiritual realities at all. This leads to several difficulties. Where does man get his emotional capacities? Or desires? Or religious sense or philosophical thought? What are memories and dreams and imagination? The answers of naturalistic materialists vary, but their basic tactic is to insist that these things are also more or less "material," that they are really only electrochemical events in brain tissue. Even these "nonmaterial" things are the products of evolution; they developed to help us survive.

As with deism, ethics and morality become a problem for the naturalistic materialist. Right and wrong become issues of pragmatism or personal preference. There can be no absolutes, since we ourselves are the product of random, material recombination of molecules. Right and wrong are *whatever we agree to call right and wrong*. This may vary from place to place, era to era, even person to person. This is the only realistic position that the naturalistic materialist can hold with any intellectual honesty and consistency. But the dangers should be obvious. If we follow the logic to its conclusion, then how can you argue against me killing you and taking your money if it will help me survive and reproduce to pass on my genetic material? Naturalism as we know it (evolution) is driven by competition, not cooperation. No coherent reasons for holding *any* moral or ethical position, other than protecting yourself and perhaps your children, can be derived from such a system. Most people who hold these views try to sidestep the issue by appealing to pragmatism of some sort, or they simply follow out the implications and claim to be moral relativists, although I will show later that this is a logical and practical impossibility.

Following from all this, human life is meaningless except in one area. If we are the products of random materiality, then the state we enter at death is identical to the state we were in before we were born: we do not exist. There is nothing but this life, and there never will be. Life is going nowhere but toward death, at the precise and unalterable rate of sixty seconds per minute. We cannot even anticipate, as a general rule, how much life we'll get to have. Life, then, must be made as good as possible while it lasts. And the one thing most humans will agree on is that the one thing everybody thinks of as good, the one thing everyone is pursuing, is *pleasure*. As a result, we see the combination of two things. First, there is no absolute morality or ethic. We really should only watch out for ourselves. Second, the pursuit of pleasure is all we have. Life is short, so fill it up. The sum of the equation seems to be a perfect image of human life as most actually live it: the pursuit of personal pleasure no matter who gets hurt. But *is* everyone so reckless all the time? Of course not. So there must be something causing some level of restraint. Part of it may be the knowledge that total, outright, reckless hedonism is destructive physically and socially (you'll kill yourself, and if you don't, no one will be able to stand being around you), both of which are nonpleasurable situations. So we restrain ourselves—in order to prolong certain other pleasures.

Nihilism

Nihilism is perhaps one of the most misunderstood worldviews. It isn't exactly a philosophical "system," because it is "antisystemic." Neither is it "coherent," because it is "anticoherence." It does not have a list of doctrines, teachings, or anything else that could be called "truths," because it questions or denies the very idea of "truth." Some try to trace nihilism to certain founding teachers, such as Nietzsche, but that demonstrates a glaring oversimplification of Nietszche's writings. Describing nihilism is like trying to catch a greased pig while wearing a blindfold. In fact, such a metaphor in many ways is a nihilist's view of every other worldview's attempt to explain and understand the way things are.

Nihilism is in some ways a logical outgrowth of certain forms of naturalism. James Sire writes:

> Naturalism places us as human beings in a box. But for us to have any confidence that our knowledge that we are in a box is true, we need to stand outside the box or to have some other being outside the box provide us with information (theologians call this "revelation"). But there is *nothing* or *no one* outside the box to give us revelation, and we cannot ourselves transcend the box.[3]

71

As a result, we can't really know *anything at all*. Any attempt to claim actual knowledge, actual certainty, actual truth, is absurdly arrogant and ignorant. In fact, the very conception of "truth" itself is a lie, about which we have forgotten that that is what it is (to paraphrase Nietzsche). But nihilism is less an argument about the nature of reality than about the nature of what and how we can know about reality; it's really a questioning of the branch of philosophy known as "epistemology"—the study of the nature and extent of "knowing." A nihilist is a radical skeptic, but *not* a moral relativist, again, a category which does not and cannot really exist.

If nihilism leads to a worldview where nothing means anything and everything means nothing (including, one might ask, the very worldview that leads to such a conclusion, thus apparently negating it), where everything that is, is beyond knowledge (or at least reassuring certainty), and where everything is going nowhere, then what must it be like to live with such a worldview? It seems that the only possible result would be utter despair. And despair is a hard thing to sell to potential converts! Although Nietzsche claimed that his worldview was actually a kind of "joyful wisdom" that brings happiness because it frees us from the tyranny of mere morality and other absolutes, it has proven throughout the generations after Nietzsche to be anything but joyful.

The influence of nihilism is pervasive (which ironically was a fear of Nietzsche's, rather than an aim of his philosophy)—more than most people realize. Anyone who tries to live as if there is no ultimate absolute meaning to anything is functioning as a nihilist to some degree, though a perfect adherence to nihilism is never actually possible. To believe in nihilism, one would have to believe nihilism itself were "true," that nihilism "means" "x," which misses the whole point of nihilism. (We'll see this problem crop up in several movies later on.) If you say that you don't believe in anything, you have still affirmed belief in nonbelief. Of course, the nihilist's response to this is that the nonnihilist is still trapped within the lie of believing that there is "meaning," and that it is accessible. The nihilist will simply shrug in such a case and feel sorry for the poor, ignorant person who believes nihilism is contradictory, because contradiction is something you have to believe in as a meaningful category in order to attack nihilism—which claims there is no such thing as meaning.[4]

Existentialism

Existentialism is largely a response, a defense mechanism even, to nihilism. Sire rightly points out that the goal of existentialism is "to transcend nihilism."[5] Nihilism promises pleasure in the form of release from the tyrannical illusion of the absolute, but delivers insecurity by calling every conception of the absolute an illusion. Existentialism reacts by emphasizing the subjective nature of existence. If naturalistic materialism leads to nihilism by emphasis on objective, random materiality, then we must somehow account for human self-consciousness, and then decide if it has value beyond the merely material. Are our thoughts, memories, emotions, dreams, and hopes *really* no more than electrochemical reactions? And can they even be trusted? (This is an essential question we tackle in the last chapter, especially in films such as *Blade Runner*, *Memento*, and *Citizen Kane*.) Is there an alternative to seeing this as a morass of meaninglessness? Yes, says the existentialist. We can use our consciousness and our self-consciousness to *make ourselves what we want to become.* Our existence, as an existentialist would say, precedes our essence. We "are" (existence) comes before "what" we are (essence). We exist; we are conscious; we are conscious of ourselves; we have the ability to experience many things and to change as a result. We "make ourselves."

This is where we find meaning in the random materiality of our existence: we can experience, and we can experience change. Existentialism almost always results in the same basic view of ethics: whatever I choose to do is "good." There is no outside, objective "good," but what I choose to do is good, at least for me. This sounds like moral relativism, but again, such a position is not actually possible. *Everyone* has *some* kind of standard, some kind of line that they will not cross (and many more lines they want others not to cross). Many of these "lines" are accepted by almost everyone and by virtually every social group. For instance, you would be hard pressed to find people groups anywhere that would approve of openly practiced immediate-family incest, or eating your own children, or regularly executing members of the group (say, two per week) for no apparent reason. Thus, there is really no such thing as actual, *pure* moral relativism—different people have different views, but there is always some kind of ultimate standard—and therefore there is no moral relativism.[6] This again shows the attempted suppression of God's moral absolutes. We deny the existence of moral absolutes, yet we always keep at least one such absolute for ourselves, even if it is only to say "there are no moral absolutes . . . absolutely."

Eastern Pantheistic Monism

Eastern philosophy and religion is complex and richly varied. In some ways the two main threads of Eastern thought, Buddhism and Hinduism, are similar, but in other ways they are vastly different. Furthermore, each of these threads has numerous strands of variation, so it is nearly impossible to make any kind of accurate, brief, general statements about Eastern thought. Nonetheless, for the sake of practicality, I will attempt to provide a general overview of the kinds of thinking most prevalent in Eastern culture, particularly as portrayed in movies.[7] Keep in mind then that what follows is *not* a description of either Buddhism or Hinduism *per se*, but rather an amalgam of some elements of the thinking that may be found in strains of either or both religious/philosophical systems.

Film art has produced many works that have been strongly influenced by Eastern philosophy, and for a good reason: it is intellectually appealing to many westerners and has great entertainment value. This is primarily because of the Eastern view of reality, which is quite different from the Western view. Exoticism is always in vogue; *Casablanca* (1942), one of the most popular movies of all time, built an entire cultural myth around the romanticism of this visual look and feel. As we look at specific films in later chapters, this point will become evident, but first let's examine a few core worldview issues foundational to understanding Eastern thought, generally known as *monism.*

Monism asserts that all reality, the entire universe, is one; it is united and has one essence, which is usually understood as *consciousness*. There is no duality, no separation, no division among what really is. Everything is united, linked together in the deepest sense. In general, the monistic unity ("oneness") of the universe is understood to be God, but not in any way that resembles the personal, transcendent Judeo-Christian deity, who is by nature *not* us, just as we are *not* him. In the West, any person who claims to be God is branded a lunatic or a heretic (hence the Jews' response to Jesus' claims to be one with his Father). But the Eastern conception of God, this *consciousness*, is universal and includes everything that is real. Anything that is not this universal consciousness is not really real. That is why a follower of Eastern thought can say "everything is God" and "I am God" with a straight face. The universe—every rock, each splash of water, human being, star, thought, snail, emotion, tree, and memory—is all one.

Humans do, however, conceive of many things we think are real, but that are not. These things are "illusions," or *maya*, and the only way to escape them is to recognize that they do not exist. This is not mere knowing; it is an existential realization (e.g., we don't "know" we are actually God, we simply "come into" that realization). Therefore knowledge, study, doctrine, and rationality—the hallmarks of Western philosophical and theological thinking—have essentially no place in Eastern thought. This is why Eastern thinkers will not argue with Western thinkers on worldview issues. They don't "think" we are "wrong" in the ways we might think they are. Right and wrong are categories dependent upon distinction and rationality, but in monism everything is one, there are no distinctions, and rationality is an illusion because it is based on making distinctions when there are none. All that matters is consciousness of the oneness of everything; such consciousness will remove from us the illusions of distinction. Thus, in the same way that we are one with God and the trees and the stars and all thoughts, we can make no real distinctions in what we call "morality." In other words, there are no real categories of good and evil. The very idea of "category" is itself an illusion, because there is only one category: the one. Nevertheless, pantheistic monism (God is all, all is God) holds that the universe, though undifferentiated by categories of good and evil, is always already perfect. It lacks nothing and cannot be improved. All we can do is reject illusion more and more.[8]

This is where Eastern thinking gets a little troubling, because almost every westerner has heard of one certain aspect of this worldview that just doesn't seem to fit: karma. Karma is an essentially fatalistic idea that your past actions control your present condition, and your present actions will determine your future condition. Evil deeds must be paid for, while good is rewarded. This is based on the concept of multiple lives, with each life reaping the benefits or punishments of the previous incarnation. We are consciousnesses that are slowly evolving (and in some cases devolving) through a series of lives, learning more and more to reject illusion and accept the true oneness of the universe. But our actions are themselves really only illusory, so eventually even karma as a system of rewards and punishments for good and evil will dissipate—recognized for the illusion that it is.

The Discerning Eye

If you watch a film with the powerhouse combination of a mind saturated with Scripture *and* a working understanding of the major worldview systems, you will in many cases be able, even with a single viewing, to analyze a film with a high degree of discernment. This is just as important with classic, older films as it is with the most cutting-edge movies, and it works equally well across all genres, from Clint Eastwood westerns to Ridley Scott science fiction, from historical romance like *Sense and Sensibility* to gangster movies like *GoodFellas*, from lighthearted comedic entertainment directed by Ron Howard to heavy, philosophical "art films" made by Ingmar Bergman.

Suppose you are watching Chris Nolan's innovative and bewildering film *Memento*. The story unfolds in an extremely bizarre and highly disorienting way (a worldview issue in itself) but since I don't want to ruin the film for those who haven't seen it yet, I'll refrain from discussing the film's structure in detail here.[9] But there are plenty of other things we can consider. For example, what exactly is memory? Do we use memory to stay anchored in reality, or are memories deceptions, lies we tell ourselves to make ourselves happy? Leonard Shelby, the main character, says that memories are almost totally unreliable; that they can change the shape of a room or the color of car; that they can be distorted; that they are *only an interpretation*; and that remembrances of things past are ultimately irrelevant if we don't have "the facts." What does a thoughtful viewer do with this kind of content? I contend throughout this book that film is the most ironic of all art forms. And this movie is no different: how can we deny the sweet irony that we hear these words from the lips of an actor who has *memorized* his lines—lines about the inherent falsity of memory? As I write this, I am remembering the film, which I just watched with my eldest son, my father, and my brothers yesterday in North Carolina (for about the seventh time—if memory serves). I also remember my wife and two other children, who right now are on the other side of the continent, and I remember which highways to drive west on for three thousand miles to get home. I remember how to go over the Appalachians, how to get to the Mississippi River, the plains of Kansas, the majestic Rockies of Colorado, and the deserts of Arizona. I've driven it before. I remember where my house is, just north of Los Angeles, and so on and so on. But memory, of course, is not perfect—something we would expect as a result of the fall.

So I bring my map.

But how faulty is memory, exactly? The final few moments of *Memento* eventually call everything we've seen into question, but the film refuses to clean up the mess. The life of Leonard Shelby (who cannot form memories and lives in a fog of the short-term present) and most of his relationship with his wife and with Sammy Jankis are seen only through Leonard's flashbacks, but there are some strange things going on in how these flashbacks are edited near the end of the movie. Nolan's film brilliantly uses extremely unconventional narrative technique to create audience identification with the protagonist. While watching, we empathize with him, because we are as disoriented as he is—perhaps more so. Leonard has suffered a head injury and is unable to form new memories. His whole life is a series of sudden, disorienting "moments" where he feels like he is just waking up. He has no idea where he is, what he has just done or said, or who might be manipulating his weakness. Every few moments, he has to ask himself, "what's going on here?" and he slowly learns that, other than the notes he writes to himself (and especially *on* himself), there is little in the world he can trust. The viewer feels the same way: *What is going on?* I need a map!

So what does a thoughtful, theologically informed viewer do with a film like this? What do we buy into, and what do we reject—and to what degree? How do we decide on the film's level of accuracy about memory, life, and humanity? Is human nature portrayed accurately, from an orthodox, biblical standpoint? What, precisely, constitutes our life? Are we the sum of our memories (which are faulty), plus our present consciousness, plus our curiosity and hopes for the future? Or are we more—or less—than these things? Where do they sell *that* map?

The thoughtful, hardworking Christian viewer has the potential to cultivate a sophisticated ability to think carefully, critically, and biblically about everything he or she sees. This is not merely a pragmatic, useful skill—it is something required of every believer who desires to obey God. We are not to absorb the world mindlessly, which is what many unbelievers do. What will happen the next time you watch a movie? Will you think your way through it biblically and with an informed understanding of its worldview issues? Or will you passively absorb whatever the director wants you to absorb?

If you've seen *The Matrix* you probably recall the powerful scene where Morpheus is standing over the recently rescued and utterly disoriented Neo. He says to the newly awakened character, "Welcome . . . to the real world." But did you ever stop to think that, based upon the philosophical questions the movie quite relentlessly raises, that such a welcome is actually impossible to make? If you can be entirely deceived about what you think is real, then how could you ever know that your "rescue" actually brought you to the "real world" instead of depositing you in yet another simulacrum, another false reality, a "world that has been pulled over your eyes?" In human history, the absolute reality of God, his rule, and his world may be suppressed in various ways. But in all human cultural production we see over and over again a final, ultimate insistence on a real world that is just that—real and absolute.

78

We must evaluate, critique, and discern our way through all the elements of this fallen world. To do anything less than this is to dishonor God by ignoring the blessings of his wisdom, to waste the opportunities for learning and discernment he has given us, and finally to lose part of the opportunity we have to be salty in this bland and dying age.

THREE

How to Interrogate a Movie

"And I applied my heart to seek and to search out by wisdom
all that is done under heaven. It is an unhappy business
that God has given to the children of man to be busy
with."

Ecclesiastes 1:13

HAVE you ever watched a movie and then thought, *Hey, that was pretty
existentialistic,* or, *Wow, that sure was Derridean deconstructionist,
with more than a touch of late Nietzsche. No idealistic structuralism there at all, no sirree Bob!* Or maybe you recognized that the
film pushed the view that the universe is a place of randomness or
of mechanistic determinism or of progressivistic optimism. Oh, sure,
that's the usual postmovie discussion in the lobby or in the car or at
the coffee shop, right? Well . . . maybe it's a little more like, "Those
were cool explosions" or "Wow, she was gorgeous" or "Man, that
had more twists and turns than a roller coaster. But it's only entertainment, and *it doesn't mean anything.*"

But it *does* mean something. Nothing is indifferent or meaningless. But we must realize that ideas that are presented in movies
are not always clear, fully developed worldviews. Every worldview
is the aggregate, composite result of a collection of philosophical
positions—individual beliefs, presuppositions, and accepted proposi-
tions. Worldviews are made up of one or more philosophical positions
working together and providing a framework for understanding the

Practical Considerations

world and living in it. A worldview is like a salad; the ingredients are the various individual philosophical elements that make up the whole final flavor. All worldviews are philosophical positions, but not all individual philosophical positions are full-fledged worldviews.

In order to understand a worldview, it is very helpful to be able to grasp and take apart the various elements that make up the system.[1] It is often easy to detect philosophical elements in a film: an individual character may be clearly existentialist, or nihilistic, or romantic. But does that mean the *film* is promoting that position? Not necessarily. What if the character is destroyed or suffers greatly as a result of his philosophical position? Perhaps the film presents a negative view of certain ideas—but then again, perhaps not. Maybe the movie presents destruction due to existentialism or nihilism as a good thing—or an inevitable thing, or a thing to revel in. A film can show adultery to be horrible, destructive, and foolish (and several movies have done just that), but if the film is graphic in its representation of the affair, does it tend to talk its audience out of adultery—or into it?

Our thinking about movies needs to be more sophisticated than "it's got cussing, so I won't watch it" or "there's an affair going on, so it must be persuasively immoral." Therefore it will be helpful to consider some root philosophical issues as individual conceptions that work with and among worldviews, but are often independent of them—and may even work simultaneously across differing worldview frameworks.

Human Nature

Perhaps the single most important philosophical question to ask when watching a film is, "What is the nature of humanity according to this movie?" If one's view of the nature of man (in theological terms, "anthropology") is skewed, *then everything else will be off*. I cannot possibly emphasize this enough: anthropology is the key. Error at this point inevitably leads to greater error in many other places. Every film contains presuppositions—and most contain overt statements—about the nature of mankind.[2] The spectrum is deceptively simple: man is good, man is bad, man is both, man can change categories, or man is morally neutral (i.e., categories of good and bad are fictional or somehow irrelevant). This has always been a major theological issue—

82

maybe *the* major issue after the existence of God. It sparked many of the central debates in the early church, including the famous arguments between Augustine (who held that man was totally, inherently sinful after the fall) and Pelagius (who taught that man was injured by the fall but still had some capacity for good and for reaching out to God).

Beyond this basic question are a series of more complicated issues. Is this the view of the director, the screenwriter, the actor, or some combination? What about the producer? Or producers? (This is the "who" question from chap. 1.) Since film is such an incredibly complex collaborative art, this issue is probably not resolvable. The real issue is, what is the overall view of the nature of man presented by the film as seen by a reasonably perceptive viewer? This can largely be determined by considering plot, characterization, and the tone or mood of the film.

Plot

The vast majority of film art follows classical narrative continuity editing practice. That is, the footage is shot over a period of weeks or months in a complicated process of organizing sets, locations, weather, actor availability, and so on, and then these short strips of raw film are slowly and painstakingly assembled by the editor into a final linear form that portrays a story or stories that flow from beginning to end—just like real life does. In other words, the filmmaking process itself is strangely jumbled: later scenes may be filmed earlier, shots from the middle of the movie may be photographed on the first day, and actors might have to play a death scene on Tuesday morning and a scene from earlier in their character's life on Wednesday afternoon. Out of this nonlinearity comes a more or less coherent story told from beginning to end. Film theorists also distinguish between "story" and "plot." "Story" is everything that "happens" to the characters, but "plot" is the part you see. A movie that features three generations of an immigrant family adapting to America may last only two and a half hours, so by necessity most of the supposed action, the whole "story" (which covers perhaps seventy-five years), must be compressed into a shorter version referred to as the "plot," which omits many actual events that may or may not be referred to in the film itself. We see a couple meet; in the next scene they are holding hands. Six minutes later (in theater time that is) they are getting married—a rather rapid courtship by anyone's standards! The intervening "story" elements are eliminated (an editing technique called ellipsis) for the sake of narrative practicality. We are so used to narrative continuity editing that we hardly ever think about it consciously, but as we have seen and will continue to see, our mental "processing" of editing is very important indeed.[3]

But however compressed the plot may be, it will invariably be based on some kind of conflict. It may be a simple, raw battle between good and evil (*Star Wars* [1977], *Stagecoach* [1939]), or it may be a subtly nuanced exploration of a character's inner struggles with conscience or some other intangible (*A Simple Plan*, [1998]). Many films that seem promising at the start because they feature a careful treatment of such inner struggles eventually succumb in the final moments to an externalized version of the battle of good and evil. We go from a thoughtful study of human psychological stress to a shootout in an abandoned warehouse. This is the only real weak spot in *A Simple Plan*. Instead of keeping the audience riveted on the brilliant study of human destructiveness rooted in greed and distrust, we end up with a shootout with a stock villain we have never met before. The film finally recovers with a more subtle coda, but the gunpowder really only functions as an anticlimax.

Nonetheless, this shows that plot is based on conflict of some kind. There has to be some kind of struggle, some risk of things not turning out well, some danger or fight or attempt to overcome something. Without it, movies would be intolerably boring. How many movies have you seen that spend two hours showing a happy marriage? Friends who get along swimmingly? A work environment with no tension, just lots of happy productivity and kindness? Pure boredom! In a real-life marriage, nastiness and suffering are miserable, though common. But it sure makes for good movie plots! We see the pain and the struggle, and we want the protagonist to win out over whatever thing is evil or destructive. It may be the resolution of a troubled relationship or a shootout in a warehouse, but we want the good guys to win. But after that, we want the credits to roll. No one wants to actually *watch* someone living happily ever after—we just want to know that they do.

Characterization

This desire for a happy ending may reveal more about the audience than the characters themselves. Throughout cinematic history, audiences have been trained to root for the good guys. We are shown in a number of ways who they are and who the bad guys are, and we are manipulated emotionally to identify with and care for the protagonists, not the antagonists. This audience/character identification tends to make us feel that we ourselves are "good people" struggling against the evils out there in the world. Who can watch the end of *Braveheart* (1995) and not feel an almost irresistible urge to go out and fight for good? (While visiting the Highlands of Scotland recently with my father and brothers, I kept feeling an urge to knock down any Englishman I could find—not just because my family is Scottish, but because I have seen Mel Gibson's movie more than once.) We want to believe we are good, and brave, and stalwart, and able to resist evil, and that we are victims not primarily of our own misdeeds and selfish attitudes, but of the inexplicable evil of others. Some films, however, play with these conventions of good guy/bad guy. They may be thoughtful enough to show major character flaws in the protagonist and also intrigue the viewers with some positive elements in the antagonists. We will consider this effect on the viewer in later chapters when we discuss specific films, but let me say that the viewer-identification factor is much more effective than most of us realize, and it has deep and genuine power, both for good and for bad.

Tone or Mood

Many films function at very complex levels of meaning. No movies have a single, simple underlying theme or way of looking at reality. Many films are deeply ironic—they may look like comedy or tragedy, but the film itself often subtly questions its own visible message.

Raising Arizona (1987) is sometimes considered a shallow, madcap screwball comedy with improbable characters and events, but that is only what appears on the surface of a superficial viewing. Underneath are more serious—and darker—undercurrents about parenting,

85

personal accountability, marital commitment, social responsibility, and American materialism and shallowness. Some viewers will see the film as an attack on the very institution of marriage and family, but a thoughtful consideration may lead to a very different conclusion. The final sequence features a tremendous shift in mood: as H. I. McDunnough dreams of the possible future of the infant he has kidnapped and now returned, he understands for the first time what it really means to be a parent—deep personal sacrifice for the good of the child, which leads to a true sense of family in the traditional meaning. The wild, cartoon-like adventure in the rest of the movie (where the kidnapped child is nothing more than a commodity for a series of selfish though generally sentimental idiots) fades away only to be replaced with a dreamy reverie about adult hopes for a small child's life. Silliness is replaced with earnestness. But then, in the final moments, H. I. wakes up and makes a bizarre statement, wondering about where his "perfect family" dream took place. He thinks "maybe it was Utah," undoubtedly a reference to the unrealistic image of a "perfect" Mormon family! Does this mean the serious dream reverie was only a joke? Or should we just "chill out" and view parenting as an out-of-control roller coaster ride (the clear message of *Parenthood* with Steve Martin [1989])? Or should parents strike a balance between seriousness and a sense of humor? A film's mood or tone is a key to unlocking its worldview.

The Nature of Reality

There are probably as many theories about art (what it is, what it does, how it does what it does) as there are examples of art. The core question about art has always been, "Does art imitate life, or does life imitate art?" The answer is probably both, particularly for film art. Most movies, at least in classical narrative cinema, are about actual or possible realities that we could imagine as part of real life. Even the wildest fantasy films work because most of what they show is recognizable to the audience.

Additionally, it is clear that film art has an impact on real life. For example, there has been a noticeable increase in interest in Scottish history and culture among Americans since the success of *Braveheart* and *Rob Roy* (1995). People buy books, surf Web sites, look up their genealogy, and even travel overseas as a direct result of watching these movies. Attitudes about bravery, heroism, death, romance, and politics have been altered in many viewers. During WWII, American public opinion was molded in many ways by films featuring "American" heroism in the face of Continental evils, whether in the form of aggression or appeasement. Humphrey Bogart's "Rick Blane" in *Casablanca* comes to mind—stepping out of his personal isolationist philosophy as he does and recognizing that his little problems "don't amount to a hill of beans" in a world threatened by aggressive fascism and genocide.

But beyond these simple observations, a survey of film history shows a particular fascination with the nature of reality, from the early trick photography of George Méliès all the way to *The Matrix* a century later. It is deeply ironic, though it should be expected, that the art form most capable of imitating reality and immersing the participant in a reality that isn't really real should feature so many individual works that play with conceptions of reality. Many, many films revolve around the reality that humans can be easily fooled or deceived about reality. Suspense movies depend on this heavily by manipulating the emotional states of ticket buyers who are never in any real danger. There is a whole subgenre, the "con" movie, that deals with characters who trick and deceive each other while keeping the viewers at various levels of understanding about what's really going on; and there are of course films that "con" the audience to some degree or another. The best example of this is probably *The Sting* (1973), where the biggest con is played, not on Doyle Lonergan but on the hapless viewer who is shocked by the unexpected twist in the violent ending. I remember my father taking me to see the movie when I was about twelve and going from a state of emotional devastation to utter euphoria moments later. Now there's a movie that lived up to its re-release tagline: "Remember how good it made you feel?"

Recent examples of movies with audience-cons include *The Sixth Sense* (1999), which is a clever film but fairly easy to predict due to both lack of originality combined with the unfortunate practice of some reviewers revealing too much about the plot. (*Jacob's Ladder* [1990] features an almost identical story told in a far more effective way.) *The Usual Suspects* (1995) is considerably more effective because of its subtle and ingenious use of the "unreliable narrator" technique. Such films are fun the first time, but a repeat viewing is often even better, because now that we know the secret, we can enjoy looking for and finding all the clues we missed the first time around. The first time, we get the pleasure of discovering the plot, but the second time we get the pleasure of discovering how the plot really works and how it fools us and shows us how poor our perception abilities really are. I believe these are especially interesting films in that they work because our fallen natures have left us with weakened abilities to perceive things correctly.

Many movies play with conceptions and perceptions of reality. Let's face it, there's a lot of entertainment value in these imaginative games. But more important is the worldview issue—and it's also much more evasive. What is the nature of reality, according to the film? *Sixth Sense* features a fairly stable reality, despite its supernaturalism. Reality itself is settled; it's the untrustworthy self-perception of one character that drives the plot. A film like *The Matrix* is considerably more subtle and thoughtful. The plot is driven by the idea that reality as we think we know it *does not exist*—it is a carefully designed non-reality. The film plays with the audience's expectations and assumptions all the way through. For instance, we get neat explanations for the little glitches in the "reality" we all experience, such as déjà vu or why so many foods "taste like chicken." A basic human instinct that the movie plays with very effectively is the hunch most of us seem to have that there is something else out there: something invisible, powerful, and incomprehensible that somehow controls that thing we call "reality." In some ways, the film is both an example and a symptom of our fallen state as detailed in Romans 1.

Nonetheless, *The Matrix* is more of a breakthrough in special effects than of playing with the reality question. Nearly six decades earlier, *Citizen Kane* (1941) posed similar questions even more subtly. The story of one man's life is told through the eyes of several people who knew him. We get the events of Kane's existence from many perspectives, all of which do not quite add up. The whole film is structured like a mystery story, where a faceless reporter attempts to learn the meaning of Kane's final word. Audience expectation is built all through the movie as we proceed from one interview and flashback to another, leading us closer and closer to the meaning of "Rosebud." When the mystery is finally "solved," the thoughtful viewer is left somewhat hamstrung, because the explanation seems to explain everything and nothing, just like all the interviews and flashbacks. We get a story, but we don't really know *what it means*. The reporter says he has been playing with a jigsaw puzzle, but does not claim to have solved anything. The question arises, "Can we really know anything about anything?" Is reality objective and tangible, reachable and "real," or is it subjective and mutable, unreachable because it's so subjected to interpretation, opinion, and mistaken human perception?

For the discerning viewer, these are fascinating questions that go back to the root issues of philosophy and that are also extremely important in developing a Christian worldview. Is reality objective or subjective? Or both? Or do we need some other category to explain it? What can we know, and how can we know it? To what degree is our fallen perception clouded and prone to error? Can it be repaired? And, importantly, to what degree do we allow our views of reality to be formed by movies—which are essentially nonreal representations of someone else's views of reality?

Determinism/Randomness

Is the universe a place of randomness or determinism? Is there someone or something in control of the universe, guiding it according to some will or plan? And to what degree? Or is the universe a place of random, meaningless chance, with no rhyme or reason, no plan, no goal or end, no reality beyond the material, which sloshes around in this place called space? Or—and here's a real twist—could the universe be *random but meaningful* or *determined but meaningless*? Is the universe coherent at all?

This is not a theology book *per se* or a rigorous philosophical treatment of the difficult issue of randomness versus determinism. These concepts are among the most complex and divisive among theists of all kinds, having separated Erasmus and Luther and also encapsulating the basic differences between Calvin and Arminius. Christianity is still battling over these issues, with renewed arguments between those who believe in the sovereignty of God in the tradition of orthodoxy and those who claim that God is "open," that he changes and grows, and that he is surprised and is not much more in control of the universe than we are.

Movies are always philosophical; they may not sound Platonic, or Cartesian, or Hegelian, but they always represent one school of thought or another.[4] The best philosophers have already articulated the various patterns of thought that the rest of us develop or fall into. Movies are one expression of those patterns—they always contain some kind of philosophical worldview. Some films seem very deterministic, presenting a twentieth-century counterpart to Sophocles' ultimate tragedy *Oedipus Rex*, where the main character manages to fulfill a terrifying prophecy by the very process of trying to evade it. One of the most popular American movies ever made is *It's a Wonderful Life* (1946), a deceptively complex film driven by what is actually a very simple plot. George Bailey, a man who has spent his life serving others and waiting for his own life to "get going," finds himself in a desperate situation and comes to the brink of suicide. God sends a rather inept angel (a theologically unimaginable entity) named Clarence down to earth to show George the value of his unique contributions. Clarence shows him what the world would have been like if George had never been born. George is so terrified by the vision of an "alternate reality" that he begs to have his life back, with all its problems. This brings up the question of the deep interconnectedness of all reality, much like the movie *Back to the Future* (1985), and thus begins to sound more like Eastern monism than the Western theism that seems assumed by the film! If something in the past can be changed, what would be the effect on present reality as we know it? Would it be partially different? Totally different? The idea of alternate realities seems to go against any possibility of either philosophical determinism or theological sovereignty—despite the presence of Clarence and the heavenly host.

Flesh and Bone (1993) is even more subtle. In this brilliant film, the main characters find themselves on what seems an inexorable, fated path of destruction. Over and over again, a series of apparent coincidences bring several humans together into a swirling maelstrom of horrible, senseless violence. At the end of the film, it is clear that the evil protagonist's son is fated to become exactly like his father, a brutal monster of a man. They are "flesh and bone"—like father like son. But then the son makes a startling decision to break away from his fated path, and so the movie takes a decidedly "freewill" approach. But then you could also say that the son was *fated*—just like Oedipus!—to kill his father, and the bizarre coincidences that drive the film and bring everyone together in one place are not coincidences at all, but some form of deterministic poetic justice. So the discerning viewer will ask, "What *is* the worldview of this film—fatalist or randomist?"

That films often tap into these very human curiosities is fascinating. Many of the most popular and influential movies ever made deal directly with these themes. Are we free? Are we hapless victims of some kind of overarching fate? Can we change fate, or are we actually trapped in a kind of helpless, hopeless "freedom"? The answer to these questions says a great deal about your view of the meaning of life.

Optimistic Progressivism/Pessimistic Decay

In the seventeenth century certain English theologians vehemently debated the status of the universe. They all agreed that the world was a fallen place. The question was, was it *fallen* (and perhaps improving as Christ redeemed humans to himself) or was it *falling* even more? Some argued that the world was actually decaying, spiritually and physically, while others claimed that the world was improving overall.

Humans have always tended to categorize themselves into pessimists and optimists. These two positions are usually oversimplifications, but they are useful terms. Films can also be divided into such categories, but the discerning viewer must again beware of oversimplification. Characters themselves may be very optimistic in a pessimistic movie. Such a film will function primarily as irony, and, if done well (i.e., subtly instead of overly-preachy), can be very effective. More importantly, though, is the film's conception of what *drives* the characters' optimism or pessimism. And we must also ask, what drives the film's worldview regarding these categories? Optimism is more than a sunny disposition, and pessimism is not merely a bad mood.

Schindler's List (1993) is considered unbearably depressing by many people. Nazi genocide is certainly reason enough for making a film feel very pessimistic. But then again, the characters of Oskar Schindler and Itzhak Stern seem to infuse the movie with a deep opti-

91

mism. So, is the movie optimistic, pessimistic, or both? Here is an example of why we can't look at a film with narrow vision, focused only on a single issue. The film also contains profound insights into human nature. Schindler is clearly written to play over against Amon Goeth, the Nazi monster. Yet this is no mere case of good-guy/bad-guy conflict. Goeth is played at times sympathetically, though Steven Spielberg is certainly no fan of Nazis. And Liam Neeson's nuanced portrayal of Schindler is one of his best ever. He uses the Jews even as the Nazis do, and of course he manipulates the Nazis themselves; he is a womanizer and a liar; he is greedy. He is in many ways just like Goeth, with one difference: he begins to respond to his conscience and follows through, while Goeth never does.

This is a key issue in film discernment. Is the movie optimistic or pessimistic, or is the answer somewhere in between? Without considering this carefully, most worldview analyses will be futile.

Moral Absolutism/Relativism/Pragmatism

Another issue is morality and ethics. Each person, each worldview position, and each example of film art will exemplify some view of what is good and evil, right and wrong, preferable or to be avoided. At opposite ends of a chart would be moral absolutism and amoral nihilism/existentialism. Absolutists believe that there are ultimate, unchanging categories of right and wrong, good and evil. This leads to a belief in the necessity of justice, because without some sense of the absolute in morals and ethics, justice becomes irrelevant. There are of course different opinions of what these absolutes might be, but the absolutist position stands squarely opposed to supposed moral relativism or (more realistically) individualistic moral anarchy, where everyone does "what is right in his own eyes."

A different position, perhaps a middle position in some respects, is moral/ethical pragmatism. In this case, there is in fact a moral absolute: the absolute of pragmatism, individuals doing what seems best in each situation. For example, lying might be wrong in some instances (dealing with business acquaintances) but perfectly acceptable in others (your date shows up in a dreadfully ugly outfit, which you compliment profusely.) Most moral absolutists find themselves functioning, at least occasionally, as pragmatists. Is it really a lie to hide a new pet dog for your neighbors so their kids won't know what they're getting for Christmas? Should you dissimulate when the Gestapo shows up at your door to ask if there are Jews in your attic? Can you tell your four-year-old about Santa Claus?

Film art is loaded with these kinds of issues. In fact fiction itself has often been attacked as a lie, and therefore destructive, as far back as Plato's *The Republic*. We will further explore the issue of how morality and ethics are presented in film in the following chapters.

Modernism

As I will be using the term, modernism is somewhere between a worldview and a philosophical position, depending on how it is held. Essentially, modernism is a belief that we can reach answers and understand most of the basic realities of our world. It is not essentially or merely "scientific," but rather "scientistic." It holds that observation and rational induction should lead us to actual objective and final truths (truths that will help us live better), and this "scientism" is strongly opposed to theism. Science itself, in its purest form, continues to emphasize doubt, which can slowly be whittled down, down, down by the careful practice of the scientific method of observation, hypothesis, experiment, and revision of hypothesis. Scientific thinking is therefore always changing. Scientistic modernism claims to get to the root of things, to "explain" things. There are so many kinds of modernism, and they are often so dissimilar and even contradictory, that I would prefer to call it a position or positions, rather than a full-fledged, more-or-less coherent worldview.

Examples of strong modernist positions are psychoanalytic theories, evolutionary theories, "objective" historical study, structuralism, and deconstruction. Each of these intellectual position claims to study and explain how things really work. The psychoanalyst subsumes all things in human consciousness under some system (Freudian psychosexual development, for example), and explains everything in terms of that paradigm. Evolutionists have their own paradigm for explaining how things got where they are—and where everything might be going. Some historians claim disinterested objectivity, a desire to study carefully and explain history "as it really happened," supposedly free from subjective interpretation. Structuralists attempt to look for underlying patterns of meaning that they then decode to explain the world to us, and then the deconstructionist comes along and explains why you can't do that at all. You could throw in the Marxist who views everything as materially-driven class struggle, or the analytic philosopher who claims that everything eventually succumbs to careful descriptive analysis, or the punk rocker who believes that by questioning and reversing societal norms, he or she will become independent, free, and happy. The hallmark of modernist thought is that there is some totalizing system of explaining everything. The ultimate modernist position would be to try to combine as many of these systems as possible into an overarching, coherent, totalizing system to explain the universe. This is much easier said than done, since so many elements of these systems are contradictory or mutually exclusive. Therefore, these systems compete for our acceptance by engaging in a war of persuasive rhetoric.

Postmodernism

Postmodernism is perhaps the most misunderstood and misrepresented philosophical position in the world right now, among both Christians and other worldview groups. Christians generally use it as a catch-all boogeyman (anything we don't like we label "postmodern"), and while it is most definitely *not* equivalent to biblical Christianity, there are some striking parallels. Most people think that postmodernism is a single, unified, monolithic system of thought. It is not. Most people think that postmodernism is moral relativism. It is not. Most people think postmodernism is some degraded form of thinking that has replaced "modernism," which at least believed in truth. Ironically, nothing could be further from the truth. Christianity was the *primary target of the modernists.*

Postmodernism is "incredulity toward metanarratives." That is, a postmodernist thinker looks at modernism's claims of achieving totalizing systems that can explain how everything really works, and says, "Bunk!" The postmodern position is not one of pure skepticism, however; it is skeptical about the arrogant truth-claims of all the kinds of systems mentioned above, while not denying truth as a category. However, let me offer this as a statement about postmodern filmmaking: it is generally quite different from classical "modernist" moviemaking.

It questions received notions about reality, perception, memory, and thought. It makes the viewer very aware, in many instances, that *they are watching a movie*—and this goes against classical narrative cinema, which operates by making the viewer forget they are *only watching a movie*. A key idea in some postmodern thought is that humans seem to prefer a simulated reality over the "real" reality—and then to lose the distinction between the two. Again, later consideration of specific films will make this clearer.

It is easy to fall into thinking that film art is mere entertainment. Even most people who enjoy actually thinking about movies and critiquing them intelligently don't usually think in terms of worldview or philosophical position. And those who think in terms of philosophical worldview often don't make their final judgment about a movie by comparing this to scriptural revelation. For the Christian viewer, this is an imperative: we must think about what we see and hear, look for philosophical positions, analyze worldview issues, and finally make a sound judgment based on careful, critical comparison to what God says about the central issues of human experience.

You don't need a master's degree in analytical philosophy to watch a movie. But it helps tremendously to be aware, at least in general terms, of the various philosophical positions that are circulating in the world. And this is not valuable only for thoughtful movie going; it helps us decode books, magazine articles, talk radio debates, political arguments, and even the trends we see in education—both public and private, elementary and high school, as well as college and graduate level studies. We needn't be experts, but we had better not be ignorant.

What we do need to be experts in is God's Word. This final source of authority is perfect and infallible in its ability to help discern the philosophical worldviews that surround us and drive the movies we often so unthinkingly watch. Some readers will no doubt balk at placing Scripture next to celluloid. Some will think film is "above" biblical critique. Others may say that the Bible is too "holy" to be sullied with comparison to worldly movies. Both positions betray foolish and idealistic ignorance about the nature of art and the nature of what God says to us.

The Word is designed to help us make right decisions. Art is one of the things we have to make decisions *about*. Everyone is constantly making decisions about art (even those who try to avoid it entirely are making decisions about it—their decision is to avoid it entirely!). How can we make right decisions without having our minds saturated with Scripture? We can't.

The next time you watch a movie and don't think biblically, you'll be disobeying God. But there is another option. The rest of this book—several longer chapters dealing extensively in exactly the kind of theological analyses I have been arguing for—will show you what that option is.

Part 2

ANALYSIS

A Time to Laugh

A Theological Approach to Comedy

"Gentlemen, you can't fight in here—this is the War Room!"
President Merkin Muffley (Peter Sellers)
in Dr. Strangelove, or: How I Learned to Stop Worrying
and Love the Bomb (1964)

"A joyful heart is good medicine, but a crushed spirit dries up
the bones."
Proverbs 17:22

WHY is anything ever funny at all?

Humor is one of the strangest parts of human experience. It is everywhere and virtually constant. It can bring great joy and great pain. Can you imagine spending an hour with your friends without a single joke or ironic remark? Humor is irrepressibly human. We almost seem made for laughter. Even in the darkest times laughter often makes a surprising appearance (Jewish humor was famously rampant in the ghettos of World War II). Life without humor would be very dark and drab indeed. Climbers like me are well known for their black humor while in the mountains and on the cliffs—it is a coping tactic for high-stress situations. Like everything else in human life, there is a strong theological truth at work here. Because comedy itself as an abstract subject is such a rich and fascinating subject, this chapter will be less an analysis of several specific movies than an essay on what humor is and why it is so central to human experience. Of course, along the way we'll be looking at movie examples. I teach an entire course on comedy, and I can assure you there is no lack for material! My goal here is to provide some framework to help understand comedy in the broadest sense, because while we all laugh often, we rarely think about humor in a theological way. And that's not funny.

Man was originally designed for pleasurable, intimate fellowship with God. This relationship entailed an unending life of joy, pleasure, peace, and a sense of being exactly what we were meant to be. In the beginning there was no lack of fulfillment, no insecurity, no fears about the future or regrets about the past, and there was a wonderful moment-by-moment sense of total satisfaction. No desires would be unmet, no selfishness would be present to ruin those pleasures, and any sense of lack or loss would be unimaginable. Man was designed perfectly, and he was designed to experience that perfection perfectly.

Part of that design was freedom. And because the freedom was real and genuine, it included the freedom to walk away from freedom itself, to walk away from joy, perfection, and satisfaction. Having abandoned the real freedom of knowing God for the "false freedom," the slavery, really, of freeing ourselves from his loving rule, we now find ourselves in a peculiar position. We retain our natural desire for the joy we know we are made for, but we are unable to obtain it any sustainable form. Joy, which should be constant, is temporary. Peace is fleeting, if we find it at all. All the satisfactions we find in life— love, financial security, fulfillment in work or leisure—eventually disappoint. We are slaves who were designed to be free. If you live with any level of self-reflection at all, the inevitable result will be a certain level of dissatisfaction and at least some sense of irony. This sense of irony results from the recognition of an undeniable discrepancy: *things are not as they ought to be.* This in turn leads to desire for improvement as well as explanation: we want to understand why things do not meet our desires and expectations, and we want to make things better. This is again a factor in the origin of culture. For example, politics and philosophy, as well as art, derive from this recognition that something is wrong and it needs to be made better. Rights need to be wronged, the world needs to be explained, and the ugliness around us needs to be made beautiful. But as I will show in what follows, the truth of this ironic situation is largely suppressed, as is the suppression itself.

What does all this have to do with Charlie Chaplin, Peter Sellers, and Steve Martin?

They are, like all comedians, first and foremost *ironists*.

Irony, Movies, and Man's Situation

> I have seen everything that is done under the sun, and behold, all is vanity and a striving after wind. (Eccles. 1:14)

Irony is central to human experience.

Let me begin by defining what I mean by "irony." The English word is derived from the ancient Greek word for a "lie" or "deception"—words that present ideas that do not accord with reality. In other words, there is a discrepancy between what is said and the real world. Consider the following sentence: "This is not a sentence." In a fashion that is far more complex than may at first appear, the words and the reality do not agree; there is an essential difference between what is said and what is meant, between surface and depth, between message and medium. This produces a strange experience, a kind of disconnect that is both pleasurable and also slightly disorienting. This is why the best jokes usually require just a moment of thought before they strike us as funny.

The modern conception of irony is much the same, because irony always involves a discrepancy of some kind, whether or not it involves language. In literary theory there are several different forms of irony, such as verbal, dramatic, and situational irony. Verbal irony is like the Greek idea of a discrepancy between words and reality. If I see a man and a woman that I know hate each other, and then say with a smirk and a roll of the eyes what a great couple they'd make, I'm being verbally ironic. Let's say I'm watching a movie that starts off with a joyous wedding, followed by a long series of flashback scenes that show how much the couple originally hated each other. In that case the succession of "hate scenes" will be followed, we know, by a series of increasingly amorous "love scenes" culminating in the wedding. The reversal is "dramatic" because we (the audience) know something during the hate scenes that the haters do not know. We have an ironic foreknowledge; their hate is humorous because we know it will change to love over time. We could deepen the plot by having the two future lovers as lonely hearts that happen to both be employed as interviewers in a matchmaking service and who first meet over the phone when they interview each other to set up their dating profiles. When they finally meet in person and realize who the other is, they are embarrassed and angry. This is situational irony. And it is of course the classic Romantic Comedy setup formula. Despite hundreds of incarnations it often works well, not in spite of its predictability but because of it. Which is wonderfully ironic!

Irony is absolutely central to comedy, humor, and laughter. Laughter is in fact the psychological, spiritual, and physiological response to recognition of irony. It is the recognition of a discrepancy—where expectations are met with their opposite. America's great nineteenth-century humorist Mark Twain quipped, "Suppose you were an idiot, and suppose you were a member of congress; but I repeat myself." Irony almost always displays multiple levels of meaning when examined carefully, and Twain's joke is no exception. The surface joke is obvious. Congressmen are idiots. The second level is the recognition, which follows after the first laugh, that we should have known a member of congress was by default an idiot, and by thinking the two categories were separate we were functioning like all the other voters. We see these linked chains of irony everywhere. We expect the man on the screen to walk down the street in control of his body, but he steps on the carelessly tossed banana peel and slips—the classic comedic pratfall. We laugh at this unexpected turn of events, at least up until it becomes so clichéd that it is no longer "unexpected." For example, if we see someone eating a banana in a movie and then they toss the peel, we expect the gag to come to completion. In other words, *the unexpected becomes expected*, and the whole situation then becomes newly ironic at another level. Irony is like a deep well, and once you peer inside, you can never look away. When you begin to look, you see irony everywhere, and your vision of the world begins to change, which is itself ironic. The most ironic thing about the world is that it is ironic. This is the irony of irony.

There is yet another kind of irony called "cosmic irony." This idea again goes back to the Greeks as well as other ancient cultures. It is the sense that the universe itself is primarily characterized by irony—that things are not as they first seem, that expectations are not met, that situations reverse over time.[1] Everything is thus characterized by irony; nothing escapes the status of the ironic. The unexpected is to be expected, which is not what we would expect. Oddly enough, this cosmic irony is linked to fate—the universe is fixed, even though it functions through a series of reversals of patterns that seem random and unpredictable. In other words, the universe is a place of *predictable change and unpredictable fixity*. And how can you possibly live with satisfaction in such a doubly ironic world? If this sounds to you like Solomon's musings in the book of Ecclesiastes, then you already understand what I'm talking about. The great wise man of the Old Testament has many echoes of Ecclesiastes in the Proverbs as well: "Even in laughter the heart may ache, and the end of joy may be grief" (Prov. 14:13).

One of the finest film examples of cosmic irony, comedic or otherwise, is Harold Ramis's popular 1993 movie *Groundhog Day*. This movie is a great case in point for how "mere" popular entertainment can be philosophically rich: it was successful financially and is also very thoughtful. Irritable television weatherman Phil Connors is covering the Groundhog Day festivities in Punxsutawney, Pennsylvania, and finds himself waking up day after day in a time loop. Every day is February 2, and only Phil recognizes the repetition. Everything is exactly the same as it was the "previous" day, unless Phil interacts to change things. Bewildered at first, he eventually figures out that he is trapped over and over again in the same day. He begins using his growing knowledge of his repetitive world to manipulate people selfishly, doing things without regard for consequences that he knows will never come. But eventually Phil changes and starts to use his vast experience to help people, even saving lives and changing the world for good. The time loop plot device sets up numerous hilarious situations, of course: Phil is repeatedly accosted by an amazingly obnoxious insurance salesman, but then turns the tables on him again and again in a particularly satisfying sequence; he impresses everyone with his foreknowledge of what will happen next; and he uses his inside information for romantic gains, being permitted numerous dating errors since he can learn from his mistakes and avoid them the "next day."

But then something happens. While all of this is at first enjoyable for Phil, he eventually suffers from terrible boredom. "I was in the Virgin Islands once. I met a girl. We ate lobster, drank piña coladas. At sunset, we made love like sea otters. That was a pretty good day. Why couldn't I get that day over, and over, and over . . . ?" Variety and its necessary correlate, uncertainty, seems a requirement for human happiness. Phil asks a minor character, Ralph, what he would do in his situation: "What would you do if you were stuck in one place and every day was exactly the same, and nothing that you did mattered?" Ralph's dry, resigned reply says it all: "That about sums it up for me." If ever there was a movie line that captured how most people view their lives, this might well be the one. Because it isn't just pure variety that we desire—it is variety combined with freedom from boredom combined with endless guilt-free pleasure. Phil wants his Virgin Islands day over and over, because it was pleasurable. Ironically, endless repeated pleasure would satisfy his longing for variety—by ending variety in a different way. "Well, what if there is no tomorrow? There wasn't one today." Phil's tense-twisting comment goes to the heart of the modern existentialist situation: I can tell myself that life is meaningless, and therefore I can live only for personal moment-by-moment pleasures, but then I become painfully bored. The French existentialists feared this inescapable trap they called *ennui*—a stultifying dullness worse than death.[2] If there is no tomorrow, there will be no accounting for today, no judgment. Therefore we are free to do as we please. But the price is terrible boredom, which is just another way of saying meaninglessness. Like all self-fulfilling prophecies, this one is rich in irony. Phil's cyclical "Groundhog Day" life is a fairly accurate portrait of linear human experience: we start out in life bewildered and disoriented; later we learn to have a good time; then we become bored and disillusioned. But life does not have to be this way.

We were designed to experience the one experience of the universe that is unchanging in its endless variety: seeing and knowing and being in fellowship with God. Scripture teaches that God does not change, but his infinite being provides an infinite variety of endlessly unfolding experience for those who love him. We think we will be bored if we have the same thing over and over again; variety and pleasure, and pleasure as variety is what we desire. This is why people think being a Christian will be boring. But that is because while we are still separated from God, we cannot properly conceive of him as he really is, and because we still think we can replace experience of him with experiences of his creation. But there is no boredom, no meaninglessness with God. It is the other way around: boredom is nothing other than the result of replacing God with everything that is less than God.

In *Steamboat Bill Jr.* (1928) Buster Keaton, the only silent star that could even begin to challenge Chaplin, pulls off a spectacular comic stunt that still wows people today. Keaton famously performed his own dangerous gags, many of which could have killed him, but his greatest is one of the best-known short clips from the silent era.[3] It is barely a dozen seconds long, and there is absolutely no margin for error: Keaton is standing in front of a two-story house during a powerful windstorm, which is demolishing the town around him. Suddenly—with Keaton's character facing the camera and unaware of what is happening—the entire front wall of the building behind him falls forward in one gigantic section as if hinged at the base. This is an actual wooden wall weighing several tons—and it falls right on Keaton. But he is standing just where the small open attic window hits the ground, and after the building slams onto the earth in a cloud of dust, he walks away. The scene is done in a single take with no cuts and no trick photography. The visual effect is astonishing.

Like all humor—indeed all narrative—this brief shot is loaded with irony. We have dramatic irony: the audience knows something that Keaton does not. There is dense situational irony: Keaton's character is trying to survive a hurricane, and a building that should provide shelter nearly kills him. In fact, most people have seen only the clip of the falling building and thus miss the irony of the whole setup. Keaton is blown quite hilariously through town *on his bed* by fierce hurricane winds. He slides up and down the streets, as if in some surrealistic dream bed/taxi, in and out of a barn full of animals, past shops, making turns, touring the whole village on his windblown bed, and finally coming to rest in front of a house. All the while Keaton maintains his slightly confused, deadpan "why me?" face for which he is so famous. He takes refuge from the obviously tottering house under the bed, as if that will save him. Then we see an old man leap from the second story window onto the bed, thankful that it has slid into place just in time to provide a rescue for *him*. He then runs off, and Keaton comes out from under the bed, wondering what just landed on it and vanished; the bed then blows away, leaving Keaton standing in front of the house, which tips forward, nearly crushing him. As the old man leaps from the window and is saved, the window provides a reversed "rescue" for Keaton—it is the only part of the house that can fall on him and *not* kill him. As we watch in horror while the house falls forward onto our hero, we are certain he will die—but he lives.

The situational irony in this sequence of shots slips over into cosmic irony, the irony that observes the topsy-turvy nature of the universe. It's a universe of expectations that are reversed, a natural world that kills people with storms and other disasters, a world where people ride beds through town and where one minute a window frame is used actively as a means of escape by one man who knows he is in peril, and the next minute the same frame passively creates safety for a man who does not even recognize the danger of his situation. The window frame is like the film frame: it vanishes even while it creates. The window (a classic metaphor) provides a view and an escape and is a constant reminder that the world is upside-down and topsy-turvy. It is a world where a piece of eighty-year-old plastic run through a machine can bring laughter to a viewer whose grandparents weren't even born when Keaton's window stunt was filmed. Even fictional narrative film is a window on the past—we have captured actual things done by actual people, some of whom are now gone from this world. I can watch Keaton and gain an intimate understanding of his comic genius and rich sense of irony. But he is gone, and I cannot meet him in the real world. He is always only celluloid and light to me. What am I to him?

The book of Ecclesiastes tells us, "There is no remembrance of former things, nor will there be any remembrance of later things yet to be among those who come after" (Eccles.1:11). This is a universe where things that have not yet happened have already been forgotten. This is the universe of Solomon, the universe of Ecclesiastes. The only thing we can expect is the unexpected:

> Again I saw that under the sun the race is not to the swift, nor the battle to the strong, nor bread to the wise, nor riches to the intelligent, nor favor to those with knowledge, but time and chance happen to them all. For man does not know his time. Like fish that are taken in an evil net, and like birds that are caught in a snare, so the children of man are snared at an evil time, when it suddenly falls upon them. (Eccles. 9:11–12)

Chaplin, Blindness, and the Irony of Grace

So far we've done some basic thinking-through of comedy and how it is thoroughly rooted in irony. The basic ironic discrepancy for man is that while he is made for perfection and joy, he finds himself in an imperfect situation and one utterly devoid of anything like consistent joy. Our expectation is for exactly what we do not get. For some, the recognition of this irony leads to using humor to cope with life and provide some kind of meaning—a kind of irony about the irony of life. If this orientation is optimistic, it functions as comedy in the classic sense. It is like the comedy of Shakespeare, where a dangerously topsy-turvy world ends happily and results in the resolution of problems (which are never very serious) and ulti- mately, in a marriage. The greatest Shakespearean example is from *Much Ado about Nothing* (ca. 1600), where Benedick the reformed bachelor says to his single friend at the end of the play, "Prince, thou art sad; get thee a wife, get thee a *wife!*" The solution to sadness? Fall in love and get married!

However, if the orientation of one's irony tends toward pessi- mism, we end up not with comedy but tragedy. Classical tragedy always concludes in a manner quite the opposite of classical comedy: everyone dies. Think of Shakespeare's greatest tragedy, *Hamlet* (ca. 1600). By the last scene, every major character ends up dead. And while modern film is a long way from the classical comedies and tragedies of Shakespeare or the Greeks before him, there is a lesson to be learned here. For human beings, there really are only two endings to the play in which we are now actors, the play Petronius showed us on the first page of this book. Those endings are joy and grief, a funeral or a wedding. The ultimate death is separation from God, which results from rejecting the open invitation to his wedding. Perhaps only Christians can really laugh in the deepest sense, and without pain. We have real hope grounded in and resulting from an understanding of our present ironic state and the sure knowledge that *the discrepancy will come to an end*. And hope is a powerful driving force in the best film narratives. It is so powerful that it often goes far beyond words.

It amazes me how many people who really love movies simply have no interest in silent films. They seem to think that having no sound is equivalent to having no sight. Nothing could be further from the truth. In many ways silent movies were (and are) far more subtle than many later sound films. As is often the case with art, restrictions are not necessarily limits—and they often enhance. We could wonder how much more visually subtle film art might be now if the silent era had extended into the 1940s or even 1950s.

But everyone knows about Charlie Chaplin, even if all they have seen are brief clips or still images. During the height of his career he was probably the most recognized person in the world. In many ways, Chaplin invented Hollywood—he was the first movie superstar. And he was not just some slapstick comedian. His career, spanning over six decades, included writing, directing, choreographing, and even scoring his films, many of which he also produced. When he arrived back in Hollywood in 1972 to receive an honorary Oscar, he was greeted as he hobbled slowly onstage with thunderous applause that lasted several minutes. Hollywood's elite knew that he was in a real sense their Adam, the one from whom they sprang.

Chaplin, whom I consider one of the greatest artists of the twentieth century, chose as his medium film, and his mode, comedy. His work had mass appeal the likes of which we rarely see in contemporary film. Why is this so?

The comedic spirit is richly universal—everyone can engage with it. Even the most humorless person can be made to laugh with the right scenario. A person without a sense of humor is a sad case indeed. Personally I love to laugh and to make others laugh. My best classroom lessons are punctuated with laughter, whether slight tittering or hearty, head-back guffaws; the worst moments in front of students are when my hilarious comments sink like a lead balloon.

Why does humor help us learn? Why is it pleasurable? Can it edify? Why is it so universally experienced? Let's turn to the film Chaplin considered his masterpiece and try to find out. It is silent, and it is all about seeing.

City Lights (1931) has a very simple parallel plot. Chaplin is his usual character, the Tramp, a kind of lovable bum who affects a quiet dignity and tries unsuccessfully to stay out of trouble. He meets a lovely girl (Virginia Cherrill) selling flowers, and realizes she is blind. She assumes he is a wealthy young man, and he does not correct her misunderstanding because he is thrilled to be with her. He is able to satisfy his desire to gaze at her constantly because she cannot see him doing it, and she does not know what he actually is—poor. The Tramp also meets a drunken millionaire (Harry Myers) and saves him from a suicide attempt; the drunk takes Charlie as his new best friend and invites him home. Living with the rich man allows Charlie to perpetuate the illusion of his own wealth to the blind flower girl— he can borrow the millionaire's car and has access to lots of cash. But when the millionaire wakes up sober each morning, he does not recognize the Tramp and throws him out of his house, a cycle that is repeated several times. As time passes the Tramp falls hopelessly in love with the girl who cannot see him, even as the millionaire loves the Tramp when he is "blind drunk." Charlie embarks on a series of escapades to raise money to pay for an operation to restore the girl's sight. He even has a prizefighting match, and the ensuing boxing scene is one of the funniest sequences ever committed to film, and surely the greatest comic fight ever. He finally ends up in trouble with the law (innocently) by trying to help the flower girl and, right after he gives her the money for the operation and all her other debts, he is dragged off to prison. Months later the Tramp is released and has a chance encounter with the girl—who of course has never seen him and does not recognize him. He can see her, and his face lights up simultaneously with love and fear—love and delight because his sacrifice has given her sight, and fear that once she sees that he is a tramp and not a wealthy man, she will not love him. His fear is that she will be like the rich drunk and reject him when she sees him for what he really is.

The humor is continuous and shifts from simple slapstick to sophisticated situational comedy, ranging from social class jokes to very low-key sexual humor to a very funny visual gag regarding a street cleaner and an elephant parade. The opening shot even makes fun of the squawky soundtracks of the "talkie movies," which were the new rage and which Chaplin despised. Chaplin was famous for demanding multiple takes—sometimes dozens and dozens of them—to get the scene just right. And it pays off. Even viewers who have never seen a single silent feature are surprised to find how well the eighty-seven-minute film plays, without a single line of spoken dialogue.

Many modern viewers, raised on movie explosions and racy scenes, simply fail to grasp the extraordinary subtlety of the film's final moment—a very brief shot laden with incredibly powerful emotion. This only demonstrates our visual poverty. We don't know what to do with a "mere" close-up of the human face. We must learn to truly *look* in order to truly *see*. The movie is about sight and blindness; it is a nearly perfect metaphor for the two possible human conditions. The movie will teach you new things about how to see and may be the best cinematic representation of sacrificial love ever produced.

City Lights is a rich and powerful example of the suppression of truth and the origin of a specific cultural object. The desire to be loved unconditionally is basic to the human condition. We all have a conception of unconditional grace and love, but we are unable to make it a reality. Human love is never perfect, and it never satisfies perfectly and permanently. Only God's love can do this. Yet we project this kind of perfect unconditional love—which is characterized primarily by grace—onto human relations in both real life and fiction. In real life, most people end up disappointed due to unrealistic romantic idealism, which inevitably drowns in a world of selfish people. But in fiction we can create and enjoy the hoped for, desired for, longed for dream of unconditional, gracious love. This is exactly what makes *City Lights* such a thunderingly powerful film, subtle and silent as it is.

Chaplin spends over eighty minutes gaining deep audience sympathy, even empathy for his Tramp. We see him as gentle, sacrificial, genuine, and sensitive. His manipulation of truth is initially accidental, and should he clarify his actual impoverished state he would lose his girl *and* his ability to help her when no one else will. In the final scene, the girl—never once named—sees the Tramp but does not know who he is.[4] He of course recognizes her instantly, and he sees that she sees. His face is beaming love for her; she interprets this as a "love at first sight" crush and begins to laugh at him. "I've made a conquest!" she says, delighted. He is terrified that she may recognize him, and scurries away from the front of her new flower shop. (Ironically, her shop is on a street corner we have seen many times in the story already, a corner where the Tramp is always taunted by bratty newspaper boys.) She offers him first a boutonniere for his tattered jacket, then a coin in an act of charity no doubt prompted by her own experience as a recipient of kindness from a stranger. (This ironically duplicates and overturns their original meeting scene where he buys a flower from her.) As she presses the coin into Charlie's hand, her highly developed sense of touch—the result of years of blindness—tells her that the hands she now holds are the hands of her benefactor. Charlie recognizes this recognition and is terrified. He knows what comes *when he is seen clearly*—rejection. He is ugly. He is poor. He is unlovable.

What happens next is nothing short of magical. She asks him (with an intertitle—remember, the film is silent), "You?" The camera cuts from her face to a close-up of Charlie's face. He nods and points to his own eyes, while smiling tentatively. "You can see now?" he asks in return. The camera cuts back to her face; her expression is subtle yet unmistakable. She smiles ever so briefly and says, "Yes, I can see now." But in her face we see her heart. She is disappointed. She had pictured a tall, handsome, wealthy benefactor. But this man before her who was merely a tramp at one time is now utterly stricken, a broken man in every sense, a convict who hardly belongs in the bright outer world. The girl nods, torn by the revelation, affirming that she can see, but does not like what she sees. The camera cuts back to

Charlie. The look on his face is also subtle but clear: it is the look of hope. Will she love him? Again, the camera cuts back to a close-up of her face, as she grasps his hand tightly and begins to smile at him with gratitude and satisfaction—and love and acceptance. She is now willing to trade her dream for reality, because she knows his poverty is intimately tied to her newfound riches of vision. The dream departs when the eyes open after sleep. Finally the camera cuts back to a very tight close-up of Charlie Chaplin's face, holding the shot for just a moment before fading out.

At this point, Charlie's expression, which has been called the greatest moment in film acting, has to been seen to be believed. It is an expression of pure joy. I'm not quite sure how he manages it, actually, and it would be oddly unbearable if the shot lasted for more than its three brief seconds. But there is no mistaking the meaning of his face—it is the face of one who is loved utterly, and knows it. He is accepted by one who is entirely satisfied with him, yet should not be. It is as if *he* has been made wealthy by *her* voluntary poverty, instead of the other way around. It is the soul of joy on the face of man. His face is the face of a recipient of grace. I wonder what it would be like if Christians, who should have such faces all the time, did. As Solomon wrote:

> Behold, you are beautiful, my love,
>   behold, you are beautiful!
> Your eyes are doves
>   behind your veil. . . . (Song 4:1)

Comedy, Cynicism, and Joy without Regret

Chaplin's film is a masterpiece of comedy, both "funny" comedy (in the modern sense) and "happy ending" comedy (in the classical sense.) Both senses depend upon ironic reversal. And both are intimately bound up with laughter.

Solomon, author of Ecclesiastes and much of Proverbs, mentions laughter more often than probably any biblical writer. He asks the ultimate question on the subject: "I said of laughter, 'It is mad,' and of pleasure, 'What use is it?' " (Eccl. 2:2). In other words, what does it do for you, other than provide enjoyment that doesn't last?

The clearest command about humor in the Bible is in the New Testament. "Let there be no filthiness nor foolish talk nor crude joking, which are out of place, but instead let there be thanksgiving" (Eph. 5:4). Believers are not to joke crudely. Now, we can probably haggle over definitions and talk about the individual conscience, but I think the safest guideline for our tongues is to avoid anything that we would hesitate to say in a public situation with a broad Christian audience, or anything that our own conscience reacts against, or anything that does not edify ourselves and others. There is certainly a difference between hearing inappropriate humor and repeating it; I can hear it inadvertently in a public setting and not be defiled by it if I do not approve of it (even though I may recognize it as funny). Laughter is often tacit approval and must be taken seriously. How's that for irony?

Ecclesiastes 7:3 says, "Sorrow is better than laughter, for by sadness of face the heart is made glad." This does not mean that laughter is wrong or humor is of no value. It does tell us that laughter, like everything else, must be understood with discernment. It has to be placed properly on a continuum of value, and on that continuum, sorrow has more actual eternal value. Laughter is not value*less*, but its value becomes truly functional only for those who have experienced sorrow. I think there are two ways this works: first is that those who have experienced great suffering will respond more strongly to the joy of laughter. Second—and this is crucial to understand—those who have sorrowed to repentance and turned to God are the only ones who can truly experience fully joyful laughter: "For godly grief produces a repentance that leads to salvation without regret, whereas worldly grief produces death" (2 Cor. 7:10). As James says, "Be wretched and mourn and weep. Let your laughter be turned to mourning and your joy to gloom" (4:9). But we must recall that he is speaking to those who need repentance and are reveling in sin. When they have repented of their worldly laughter, then they can finally experience true laughter that is not punctuated by guilt, laughter "without regret." Only believers can fully grasp the ironic situation of the present world, because if they are wise in Scripture, they know why the world is as it is, and they have real hope in the final righting of all things. Laughter is like honey: "If you have found honey, eat only enough for you, lest you have your fill of it and vomit it" (Prov. 25:16). Honey is wonderful, delicious, pleasurable, and useful, like everything God made. And too much of it—like too much of anything God made—begins to cause negative consequences. Laughter is no different; if you approach everything with nothing but laughter, if humor is the center of your approach to the world, then your natural tendency of sinful self-righteousness will quickly degrade your sense of humor into a sense of cynicism, which is the malignant twin of benign and edifying comedy.

"A joyful heart is good medicine, but a crushed spirit dries up the bones" (Prov. 17:22). Cynicism is a bone-crusher, a spirit-crusher—it destroys the object of cynicism and eventually the cynic himself. A young cynic is a sad thing; an old one is a tragic thing. Almost any human relationship can be healed, except the one infected with deep cynicism.[5] And the border between rich comedy and caustic cynicism is wispy and permeable indeed.

Which brings us to black comedy and to *Dr. Strangelove*. There is, as Solomon wrote in observation of our sadly fallen world, "a time for war, and a time for peace" (Eccles. 3:8).

RAF officer Lionel Mandrake is slightly worried: his superior officer has without warning or reason unilaterally ordered a flight of B52 bombers to nuke Russia at the height of the Cold War. No one else seems to know anything about this, and the painfully polite Englishman is vaguely suspicious that something might be "dreadfully wrong."

> **Group Capt. Lionel Mandrake:** Erm, what about the planes, sir? Surely we must issue the recall code immediately.
>
> **General Jack D. Ripper (firmly):** Group Captain, the planes are not gonna be recalled. My attack orders have been issued, and the orders stand.
>
> **Group Capt. Lionel Mandrake (confused):** Well, if you'll excuse me saying so, sir, that would be, to my way of thinking, rather—well, rather an odd way of looking at it. You see, if a Russian attack was in progress, we would certainly not be hearing civilian broadcast.
>
> **General Jack D. Ripper:** Are you certain of that, Mandrake?
>
> **Group Capt. Lionel Mandrake:** Oh, I'm absolutely positive about it.
>
> **General Jack D. Ripper:** And what if it is true?

Group Capt. Lionel Mandrake (very disconcerted now): Well, I'm afraid I'm still not with you, sir, because, I mean, if a Russian attack was *not* in progress, then your use of Plan R—in fact, your order to the entire Wing . . . oh. I would say, sir, that there were *something dreadfully wrong somewhere.*

General Jack D. Ripper (firmly): Now why don't you just take it easy, Group Captain, and please make me a drink of grain alcohol and rainwater, and help yourself to whatever you'd like. . . .

Every semester when I teach one of my basic film courses, we watch Stanley Kubrick's dark comedy masterpiece *Dr. Strangelove, or: How I Stopped Worrying and Learned to Love the Bomb.* This film is always a kind of cultural test for the students and almost a personality indicator. Half of them sit stolidly through the movie, wondering what is supposed to be so funny, and the other half are on the floor in tears of laughter. (I'm with the latter group.) Humor is an aesthetic category, and hilarity is in the eye of the beholder. I have been asked many times, "So what is so funny about accidental nuclear war?" Not everyone quite grasps black comedy, or wants to, and admittedly British humor and even the brilliant Peter Sellers (who plays three roles in the film) can be an acquired taste. I love his *Pink Panther* films; my wife, who I fear is a finer judge of movies than I am (and has a considerably better laugh), can't stand them. Then again, I love the utter silliness of *Monty Python and the Holy Grail* (1975), so I'm probably a hopeless case! But that's okay—it's only a flesh wound.

I happen to find Kubrick's film outrageously hilarious not in spite of its lurid premise, but because of it: a nutty Air Force general named Jack D. Ripper (Sterling Hayden) singlehandedly decides to lob a few nukes at Soviet Russia forcing a nuclear war he is sure the United States will win. While the plot is horrific, the eminently quotable script provides a brilliant glimpse into the depravity of the human heart and our rather ridiculous view of ourselves. Perhaps the clearest line is uttered by another hawkish general, played by George C. Scott: "Gee, I wish *we* had one of them Doomsday Machines!" The device in question is a superbomb capable of destroying all life on earth. While it is fictional and merely a plot device in the movie, it has its radioactive counterpart in the real world during the era of US/Soviet nuclear proliferation and Cold War tensions. There's nothing funny about it. Which is precisely why it is so funny. Our world is inescapably ironic—and the less you recognize this state the less humor you will find in movies like *Dr. Strangelove*. In fact, I have noticed that people with a very underdeveloped sense of irony are made distinctly uncomfortable by darkly comedic films like *Dr. Strangelove*, *Network* (1976), and *Fargo* (1996). Certainly these films are not for everyone, and like all movies they contain material that is offensive in them. Nonetheless, they are fascinating to consider in light of what Scripture says about the nature of man. Just look at the sardonic subtitle to Kubrick's movie and think about what American fears were really like in 1964.

At one point in *Strangelove*, the president (played by Sellers) makes a radical decision. He knows he will not be able to recall the squadron of B52s ordered by the rogue general Ripper; they will only respond to a coded message and no one knows the code. Russia is going to be nuked and will respond with a deadly retaliatory strike. The president decides to tell the Russian premier what has happened in hopes that he can defuse the retaliation and perhaps give them enough information needed to shoot the planes down—better to lose a few planes and men than start an accidental thermonuclear conflict! He invites the Russian ambassador into the "War Room" where all the Joint Chiefs of Staff meet with the president. Towering over them is the "Big Board," an electronic map of the world showing military threats and movements. General Buck Turgidson (played by Scott) is horrified that a "dirty commie atheist" is being ushered into the inner sanctum of the American defense system, and within moments the general and the ambassador are engaged in a childish scuffle on the floor. The president rushes over and scolds them like the children they are: "Gentlemen! You can't fight in here! *This is the War Room!*"

But what else *would* they do there? The irony—verbal, dramatic, situational, and of course, always cosmic—is as thick as quickdry cement on a blazing summer day. You don't know whether to laugh or cry (I generally do both). The reason they have to fight in the War Room is not just because they are in a room dedicated to fighting, but because the room is what classical rhetoric calls a *synecdoche* or *pars pro toto* (part for the whole)—it is a part that represents the whole. As the room is, so is the world—and the world itself is nothing more or less than a War Room.

From the first human death (a brother murdering a brother, itself a *pars pro toto* picture of the rest of human history) to the last, we are characterized by horrific violence. And, as Jesus reminded us in the Sermon on the Mount, violence is not only physical enactment; it always begins in the mind, and to God the hateful thought is equivalent to murder. The final sequence of *Strangelove* features the now iconic image of B52 pilot Major "King" Kong (Slim Pickens in his most famous role) astride a bomb in order to repair the jammed bomb-bay doors, waving his cowboy hat, screaming "Yee-ha! Waahoo!" like a hysterical rodeo champion, and riding a nuclear bomb like a bronco down to its target—and his own doom.

So where do dark comedy and its corollaries come from? Why is "inappropriate" humor (sex, bodily functions, gory violence) so popular? *Because it is funny.* Fallen humanity loves to revel in ironic reversal. So sex (which is sacred) and bodily functions (which are private) and violence (which is grievous) are all flipped upside down: sex becomes profane, the body and its processes become publicized, and violence becomes a source of laughter. The only thing funnier than riding an angry bull is riding an armed warhead. Reversal is where it's at. I'm not just talking about R-rated movies, either—the *Tom and Jerry* cartoons I loved as a kid are a festival of violence played for lighthearted fun. So where is the proper balance for Christians? Can we laugh at a funny sexual or bodily situation or a scene of violence played for fun, or do we offend God when we laugh mindlessly at something along these lines just because it strikes us as hilarious? And this question may be only one part of the equation.

Let's be honest. We have a natural tendency to laugh at these things because they strike us as funny. Laughter is generally an involuntary reaction. Aristotle described comedy as poking fun at the ignoble—the ugly, stupid, grotesque, and ridiculous people in the world. Okay, fair enough, but do we know *why* we have such beings in the world? And why do we laugh at them, and ourselves, and our ironic absurdity? Maybe laughter is *serious*. Maybe it is—pardon my irony—no laughing matter.

The reason jokes like the War Room scene in *Dr. Strangelove* are so funny is because they are, despite being wildly over-the-top, terrifyingly accurate. The world is in fact run by fools and idiots, and we are quite capable of destroying ourselves, one at a time or *en masse*. And the individual is paralyzed in this situation. Worse yet, the individual can come to recognize the absurdity and irony of this situation and the irony of his impotence. The cultural response of this film to the absurdity of the Cold War (indeed, all wars and all human violence) is perfectly understandable. Recognition of a hopeless situation, where we are powerless before a merciless blade of destruction, leads to despair. And the only two possible cures for despair are suicide and laughter. The two might not even be so different.

The great irony of film comedy (and all humor) seems clear to me. The "controlling suppression" of film comedy is that the central truth which is suppressed and returns is the very reason behind our present state of irony. That reason is of course the fall of man. The only valid explanation for who, what, and why we are is the one explanation most universally denied by human cultural production. That explanation is the one found in the biblical text—the narrative of the fall of man into sinful rebellion, resulting in misery, dissatisfaction, and hatred. The fall is why we are bored with our day-after-day-always-the-same life and long for eternal pleasure; it is why we cling desperately to the shimmering hope of perhaps being loved unconditionally though undeservedly, seeing and knowing even as we are seen and known (1 Cor. 13:12); and it is why, after devising the means to destroy ourselves utterly, we are compelled to make a funny movie about it. No wonder so many comedians struggle with depressive personalities. In an incalculably rich final irony, the most classic "bit" in film humor (the slapstick banana pratfall) is a miniature reenaction of the theological doctrine of the fall, an ultimate *pars pro toto*—this time played for laughs against ourselves. We have been falling because of a piece of fruit for a very long time. And we still are.

For what happens to the children of man and what happens to the beasts is the same; as one dies, so dies the other. They all have the same breath, and man has no advantage over the beasts, for all is vanity. All go to one place. All are from the dust, and to dust all return. Who knows whether the spirit of man goes upward and the spirit of the beast goes down into the earth? So I saw that there is nothing better than that a man should rejoice in his work, for that is his lot. Who can bring him to see what will be after him? (Eccles. 3:19–22)

A time to weep, and a time to laugh; a time to mourn, and a time to dance. (Eccles. 3:4)

FIVE

Exorcising the Psycho

The Invention of Fear for Pleasure

"She just goes a little mad sometimes. We all go a little mad
   sometimes. Haven't you?"

> Norman Bates in *Psycho* (1960)

"I'm not Regan."
"Well then, let's introduce ourselves. I'm Damien Karras."
"And I'm the Devil."

> Regan MacNeil and Fr. Damien Karras
> in *The Exorcist* (1973)

ON Saturdays my parents would usually let me stay up a little bit later
than other nights. My younger brothers would be sent off to bed at
9:30 or 10:00, but I could toddle around the house until the stagger-
ingly risky hour of 11 p.m. When the time finally came to go to bed,
I would comply humbly, but only because I knew that my parents
would be in bed at 11:30 and surely asleep before midnight. And
midnight was when the weekly "Creature Feature" came on television. I willingly curled my skinny eleven-year-old frame up for two
hours of contraband televised terror. This was the apogee of living
dangerously if you were in the fifth grade in 1974.

   I would first glide silently to the kitchen to concoct some trillion-
calorie milkshake-with-cookies-and-Snickers monstrosity and then

glide into the basement television room. I would hold my breath as the TV warmed up (back when they still did that), then turn to WDCA channel 20 and watch the late-night fright-fest hosted by Count Gore De Vol. The Count, a campy vampire host, would introduce and screen cheesy old black-and-white horror movies, interspersed with gruesome jokes, political commentary about Watergate (which I barely understood), and a moderate amount of sexual innuendo (which I understood not at all, fortunately). Yes, Mom and Dad, it's true: I spent the grave-dark Saturday nights of my youth shuddering in the basement while the family slept above. The hardest part was when I had to turn off the television and all the lights and make my way back to my bedroom, two flights up—in the "wine dark" house, as Homer would have called it. Some nights, if the movie had been particularly scary, my shadowy trip back upstairs would last for ten shuddering minutes, as every creak and trick of moonlight sent my heart into my throat. And I'm not going to elaborate on the obligatory yet gripping "check under the bed before going to sleep" ritual. Movies.

The worst one was a trilogy made by the Italian director Mario Bava in 1963. It was called *Black Sabbath,* and the movie later inspired the moniker of the heavy metal band of the same name. It is "hosted" and narrated by a jovial Boris Karloff, who also appears in a chilling vampire tale in the second segment. I saw this movie a number of times in my youth. Each time I was so frightened by the third sequence called "A Drop of Water" that I was jumpy for days and really did lose sleep. There is a dead old woman in the story who is so frightening (despite being patently fake and quite over-the-top) that I still have her visage burned into my memory. She rises from the dead in revenge over a ring stolen by the lady who laid her out for burial. Her bulging eyes won't stay shut after being closed by the undertaker, which I found horrible beyond expression. I finally had to plead with my parents to remove a certain antique rocking chair from my room. I dared not tell them why: there is one just like it in the movie. And the old lady shows up in the thief's apartment, rocking in it, eyeballs a-popping. Dead. And smiling. And angry. I absolutely couldn't stand it.[1]

I think I watched it six times before I got out of puberty.

Why in the world did I want to be terrified? On top of the risk of being caught by my parents watching unauthorized TV, especially unheard-of late-night TV, I could hardly bring myself to actually *watch* these movies—but I could hardly look away. Every Sunday morning, after suffering through several sleepless hours, I made a firm resolution not to repeat my mistake the following week.

Of course, these were tame "B" movies made in the middle of the twentieth century; no graphic violence, no gore, none of the kinds of elements in the modern slash and scream movies. Slow-moving monsters that we never actually see hurting anyone; corny aliens that are obviously awkward men in rubber suits; vaguely supernatural forces that make slinking-chain noises in Victorian houses visited by teenaged refugees from the Mickey Mouse Club, out on a dare. These films worked on mild suspense, not shock and gross-out. They were probably not even actually scary, but my *fear of being scared* was a powerful enough attractant to whip me up every Saturday afternoon into what became a frenzy of horror by the witching hour. The previous week's Sunday morning resolutions were long gone.

I liked roller coasters until I was about 38 years old and they began to hurt. I've been heavily involved in rock climbing and alpine mountaineering for three decades at this point, and I've been in some scary situations. I don't really like them, those scary moments in the mountains. I like the athleticism and adventure of climbing—I don't like being afraid. That's not at all why I climb. Climbing is fun. Being scared is not.

Film, Fear, Pleasure

Most people would not describe fear as a pleasant emotion. The experience of terror, of being threatened, doomed, or on the brink of feeling some terrible agony, is quite naturally a negative feeling. The purpose of fear is to serve as a warning. People do not send chocolates or flowers as a warning. A tiger does not purr before he attacks you, nor does your heart beat more slowly right before he eats you. So why is there a massive industry dedicated to the production of fear for pleasure? Scary movies, skydiving and bungee-jumping, haunted houses on Halloween, and horror novels combine to make a multibillion dollar economic powerhouse. Why?

Fear for pleasure may have murky roots historically, but we do know that with the rise of the Gothic novel in the late eighteenth and early nineteenth centuries, Western culture became fascinated with the sensation of terror. This coincides with both the Terror of the French Revolution and the rise of newsprint and what we now call "mass media." In other words, everyone knew about the great French Terror and its central object of fascination: *le guillotine*. And let's face it—news of suffering is as fascinating as it is repellent. Gothicism in literature and art in some ways was closely related to the Romanticism movement of the same period. Both were fascinated by powerful emotion, the wildness of nature, the strangeness of the supernatural, and the power of the sublime, which could transport you out of your own present consciousness. These Gothic novels—lurid tales about nuns being raped by cardinals in convents, young girls being carried off to moldering castles followed by enforced marriages to moldering old men after their fortunes, and of course tales of vampires as well as mortals who live a good life by day and another life by night—were forbidden reading in polite society.

They were thus wildly popular.

The very first films had a startling, sometimes even terrifying effect on their audiences. Short clips showing trains arriving in stations, waves crashing toward the viewer, and criminals aiming their blasting guns right at the camera caused screaming and defensive ducking among some. Pictures that *moved* were brand new, realistic, and potentially terrifying. Some early narrative movies began to exploit the power of film to control the emotions of the viewers—and particularly the emotion of fear. The first film version of Mary Shelley's novel *Frankenstein* was not the famous flattop version made by Universal in 1931; it was filmed in Thomas Edison's studio in New Jersey in 1910.[2] In fact, the first two decades of the new century—the century of film—saw the production of a number of silent horror masterpieces, notably the creepy *Nosferatu* (1922), an unauthorized rip-off of Bram Stoker's novel *Dracula,* and the surrealistically artsy German film *The Cabinet of Dr. Caligari* (1920). Both of these still play well today, though most modern viewers unfamiliar with very old film conventions find the pacing and the simple camera work a bit of an acquired taste. Nonetheless they are drenched in menace. By the middle of the third decade horror was a well-established genre with its own set of techniques and its own stars, led by the great Lon Chaney Sr.—the creator of the bloodcurdling being known as the *Phantom of the Opera* (1925). There was no need for a soundtrack; the audience would be screaming quite well enough on its own.

Techniques of suspense developed further in the golden age of big studio horror films (1930–1940) as moody, atmospheric masterpieces such as *Dracula* and *Frankenstein* (both 1931) ushered in the era of the classic "monster movies." Single villainous creatures provided the threat and terror, and at the end of the film the creatures were destroyed (although they were often resurrected for many a sequel). Evil was clearly defined and always defeatable by good. Evil was always a monstrous aberration from the natural. The forms of the dangers changed as times changed—art is always responsive to the larger cultural context. As has been widely observed, many suspense and horror films of the 1950s featured a menagerie of atomic mutants that were little more than concrete forms given to the fears of nuclear radiation. Powerful psychological horror themes became widespread in the 1960s and 1970s, building on the foundation laid by Alfred Hitchcock's *Psycho* (1960). William Friedkin's horrific supernatural thriller *The Exorcist* (1973) was the 1970s counterpart to *Psycho*; like a rabid, delinquent child of Hitchcock's film, this movie smashed taboos and shattered attendance records, all the while causing extreme emotional distress among many audience members (the stories about people fainting, vomiting, and generally freaking out are not entirely apocryphal). It seemed the more people heard about how utterly horrifying *The Exorcist* was, the more people were drawn to it. At the same time, the seventies also became a period of "nature wants to kill you" films—movies about every conceivable species or natural force going berserk. These were the stepchildren of a Hitchcock film, *The Birds* (1963). The granddaddy of them all is of course Steven Spielberg's 1975 blockbuster *Jaws*. Moby Dick with attitude, as I like to put it. We were *all* going to need a bigger boat.

These two fear-inducing movies (Friedkin's and Spielberg's) were in many ways the very first "blockbusters" and brought to the forefront of the business of Hollywood the idea that *terror makes big profits* if well-produced—and they also opened the door to the wave of increasingly explicit, graphic, gory, and taboo-breaking films of the 1980s and 1990s. As we close the first decade of the twenty-first century, we are now deluged with movies that have become so graphic and gruesome that they are often referred to as "torture porn" or "gore-nography." Every conceivable way to violate the human body on the screen has been explored and presented in visceral minutia. I do not watch these movies. What possible value could they have? What would be the point? But I am interested in both why they are made and why they are as popular as they are. And I have to say I wonder what in the world these movies might be doing to a generation of people—especially young people—who watch them. The body is as sacred, and as vulnerable, as the soul and the mind. I tell my literature students that to a certain extent "you are what you read." I believe this holds true for film as well.

This is a far too brief and generalized history of horror films, but it will suffice to show that frightening movies have always been a major segment of Hollywood fare. Fear sells tickets. Perhaps the greatest irony about scary movies is that one of our greatest and most universal human fears is a fear of the dark (which is really a fear of the unknown). So, really—"horror" plus "film" is a natural, you see.

Movie theaters display their wares in the dark.

What You Are So Afraid Of

The grounding premise of this book is that fallen humans suppress certain basic truths about God and his universe. This takes many forms: we suppress an inbuilt sense of his existence, we suppress whatever evidence for his existence may come our way, we suppress the witness of conscience by supplying alternative explanations for its annoying presence, and we suppress knowledge of our own natures, telling ourselves that we are either inherently good, or that some people are good and some are bad, or that morality is an illusion. The final willful act of suppression is that we suppress the fact of suppression itself. We tell ourselves that all we want is the truth, when that is the last thing we actually accept. But truth cannot be suppressed entirely, perfectly, or permanently, and it "bubbles back up," resurfacing as reconstituted core elements of cultural production. I want to again clarify that we cannot make a one-to-one mapping here—culture is not just a directly reconfigured diagram of truth. It is not a Lego building that has been partly dismantled and then rebuilt. Culture is far more complex than this, and I am not at all sure its mystery can fully be unraveled. Rather, I am saying that the recognition of truth elements in cultural artifacts helps us do two things: we can better interpret and understand our culture, and we can see that even rebellious human culture demonstrates to us that we are exactly as God says we are.

The strange conjunction of fear for pleasure is rarely considered, at least in a theological framework. Fear is basic to human psychological nature. While I see no point in denying that fear has a number of purposes, including self-preservation, I don't think the usual explanations about the origins of fear can quite explain why we also find certain kinds of pleasure in an emotion that is not, in fact, pleasant.

Fear is perhaps the most difficult feeling to suppress; "it will out," just like truth. Many suspenseful film scenes are built on our knowledge of this fact, as when we are empathetically frightened for a character hiding in a closet while a dangerous killer searches the room. Letting the fear express itself, as either a whimper or a scream, will bring about the feared end—the killer will hear and strike. Silence—suppression—is safety. But self-control while fearful is no easy task. In 1959 a rather low-grade film whipped up quite a marketing frenzy based upon this knowledge. *The Tingler* has a silly plot involving a scientific discovery that fear is actually embodied in a parasitic organism that attaches to the spine; when your spine tingles, the only way to get rid of the parasite is to scream. If you hold in the scream, you will die of fear. The marketing gimmick involved installing vibrating buzzers in random theater seats without audience knowledge. Near the end of the film, this "tingler" creature escapes into a movie theater. Then it looks like the film "breaks" in the projector, and we see the shadow of the "tingler" crawling across the lens—and then the screen (the real one) goes black. The "tingler" has escaped from the movie. The audience is now in total darkness. A voice from the soundtrack cries out that the "tingler" is in *this* theater, and you'd better scream to save your life—and that's when the seat-buzzers go off. Movie world and real world meet unexpectedly and everyone dumps their Cokes and greasy popcorn buckets on their dates. The high-decibel response to the gimmick, as you might imagine, had a galvanizing effect on the next audience waiting in line outside, tickets in hand.

There are really only two categorical objects of fear: fear of the natural world and fear of the supernatural world. There is indeed much to fear in the natural world, and these objects of fear make their way into many movies, such as *The Birds* and *Jaws*. There is also fear of the unknown, the "super" natural—the things "above" the natural, material world—and of course many horror films are built upon this fear. The supernatural is terrifying because the extent of its power cannot be predicted. Almost all fears can be reduced to a fear of the unknown, including the fear of *not* knowing what is going to happen next. Uncertainty is, quite literally, dreadful. This is what drives the greatest moments of suspense and terror in movies. It is not the knowing—it is the not knowing. The two categorical objects of fear meet in the one great universal fear—the one fear that is widely observable in the *natural* world, but holds open the door to the *supernatural* one. That universal fear is death.

We have an inborn ability to experience the warnings of fear when in the presence of natural dangers. For people like me who climb mountains and cliffs as a sport, part of the challenge is learning to control the extremely powerful natural fear response to danger. What is more interesting, however, is the response that apparently all humans have in the face of a supernatural force, real or imagined.[3] Even people who are strict materialists and do not believe in anything beyond the natural, observable material world can easily be frightened by a movie with an effectively presented supernatural element. You know it is a movie; you know it is fiction; you know these things aren't real. Yet your heart pounds and you jump during the scary moments. Why? There isn't always a buzzer under the seat.

I don't think it is just because of a suspenseful plot. I think all of us share a vague recognition, or at least a suspicion, that there *may* be more to the world than meets the eye. One of Hamlet's most famous lines in Shakespeare's play addresses this three-way confrontation between skepticism, uncertainty, and belief: "There are more things in heaven and earth, Horatio, than are dreamt of in your philosophy."[4] In fact, I believe there is *much* more. I also believe that part of the fallen human condition is that this knowledge is strongly suppressed, and in turn the suppression itself is suppressed. As a result of the conservation of truth principle, however, we enforce a double movement that overturns this very suppression: first, we make fiction, including movies, featuring supernatural elements; second, we often find these fictions terrifying, even though we believe they are fiction. It has long been said that art imitates life even as life imitates art. I would add to that. We do not believe our not believing.[5] *Our fiction imitates and undermines the fiction of our unbelief.*

It is indeed a strange truth about humanity that we tell ourselves stories that bring about the negative and uncomfortable emotion of fear. Yet—perhaps—not so strange. The actual psychological processes of deliberately induced fear are worth considering. Anytime we watch a movie, we manage quite an amazing feat. On the one hand, we know that what we are experiencing is fiction; it is carefully constructed, produced, and presented as if it is naturally occurring in our conscious experience of the real world.[6] This is why effective movies "transport" us, like all great art, as Longinus taught two thousand years ago. When you're watching a really well-made film, you don't realize that this is what you're doing, at least not in the forefront of your consciousness. But at the same time you *do* realize what you're doing. In other words, your mind does double-duty; you in a certain sense become two persons—one grounded in reality, one in fantasy. This book deals with this phenomenon differently based upon different genres and specific movies, but perhaps the most interesting question we can ask is, what happens when we enter the filmic creation of fear, which terrifies us even when we know it is not real?

In order to answer this question, we need to consider one more kind of fear, as yet unmentioned. This is the fear of God. There are two kinds of fear regarding God: the reverential trust, awe, and fear of giving offense that characterizes believers and the fear of those who do not believe—their fear that they might be wrong. A variation of the second fear can be seen in the person who is sure there is a God of some kind but does not want to follow him and thus lives in fear of judgment, however vague that fear may be. I believe the present fallen state of man is such that our previously natural fear of God—awe, respect, submission, and fear of offending—has been blunted, suppressed, and reduced. It has changed its object, to be precise. Instead of fearing God, we fear any number of other things, whereas if we feared God rightly we would fear nothing else wrongly.

If there is a God, one whom we naturally (and rightly) should fear; and if we have suppressed this truth, as Romans 1 says we have; and if, as I am arguing in this book, powerful truths such as these cannot and do not remain suppressed, then perhaps we now have a way of understanding the business and art of fear for pleasure. If God (and fear of him) has been removed from the forefront of our conscious minds, yet we are "built to fear" something infinitely greater than ourselves, something awesome, terrifying, mysterious, and incomprehensible, then we find ourselves predisposed to replace fear of him with fear of *something*.[7]

The full-blown abject terror of an infinite God—unmediated by grace—would be overwhelming and impossible to bear. And try as we might, we cannot entirely vanquish our sense of God or our creeping fears regarding him. The fear is inescapable. It is also unbearable. The only thing we can do is develop techniques to cope with the fear, just like a mountain climber or a skydiver does. The fear has to be managed—it has to be *controlled*. Uncontrolled fear is crippling. I believe that one way this management can be undertaken (and it can be done very effectively) is through storytelling. Fiction is a management tool through which suppressed truths slowly reemerge in bits and pieces, chunks and tatters, despite our attempts to bury the way the world really is. Narrative in general, and the very powerful, reality-replacing narrative art of film, can present to us an entirely convincing object of fear that has nevertheless been controlled, tamed, and reduced to a manageable package. One moment we are petrified in the dark theater—the next we are walking to the coffee shop laughing with our friends. Not so with deity.

What does the Bible say about the fear of God? The concept of "the fear of the Lord" is widely misunderstood, even by many Christians. It is quite often mocked by those who do not believe and who think that believers feel like I did while watching late-night scary movies as a kid. But this understanding is not at all accurate. The fear of God is taught everywhere in Scripture, and it is a fairly simple idea that we find consistently in all parts of the Old and New Testaments. The psalmist teaches that "the fear of the LORD is the beginning of wisdom; all those who practice it have a good understanding . . ." (Ps. 111:10). Wisdom—not to be confused with intelligence or knowledge, though they are all interrelated—begins only with a rightly reverential awe and respect for God, as well as a fear of offending him. Fearing God always features this moral and ethical component: "by the fear of the LORD one turns away from evil" (Prov. 16:6). Fear of God, repentance, and slow but steady moral growth are intimately bound up together. "Behold, the fear of the LORD, that is wisdom, and to turn away from evil is understanding" (Job 28:28). Refusing to fear God is the clearest marker of a foolish person, according to Solomon: "The fear of the LORD is the beginning of knowledge; fools despise wisdom and instruction" (Prov. 1:7).

Paradoxically, the God who is worthy of fear promises those who trust in him that they do not need to be afraid of him in the normal, fallen sense. God's words of comfort to Abraham in Genesis 15:1 are typical: "Fear not, Abram, I am your shield. . . ." There is marvelous irony here. The one thing in the universe we really should fear— God—protects us from himself by enacting his grace for our benefit and his glory. Thus, if you fear him you have no need to be afraid. If you do not fear him you have every reason to be afraid. The most frightening verse in all of Scripture is Hebrews 10:31: "It is a fearful thing to fall into the hands of the living God." What God asks is more than reasonable and in fact becomes easier the more we trust in him. He asks that we respond only as we should, with awe, respect, and obedience in the face of his sublimity, his infinity, his power, and his holiness. If we do not do that, then we find ourselves living enslaved to various other fears, none of which is pleasant.

For a believer, fearing God is a *sublime, deep pleasure.* That is what the ultimate fear is—pleasurable. It is not supposed to be negative, uncomfortable, or debilitating, but rather edifying by showing us who and what we are in terms of an almighty and infinite being. The fear of God, ironically, is not fearful for a Christian. Because we are wired to gain pleasure from the fear of God, yet as a race we do not so fear him, we find ourselves in the rather perverse position of experiencing certain pleasures coming to us in the form of highly manufactured and densely controlled fears packaged as entertainment. I believe this is why "fear for pleasure" has become such a profitable sector of the film industry. We want to have something to fear, and yet we want to maintain control over that fear, to limit that fear within prescribed boundaries, which we can never do in the case of the "fear of the Lord." Fearing God cannot be bounded, yet we can trust his care and love for us, his promise that he will not harm us. The precise opposite is the case in horror films: the evil entity wants to harm us—but we can control it, because we know it isn't real.

Our problem is that in our grievously foolish and fallen nature we don't think God is real either.

Showered with Fear

The modern horror film begins with Alfred Hitchcock's black-and-white 1960 masterpiece of shock, *Psycho*. The movie is a brilliant example of audience manipulation, utilizing everything from promotional materials to editing techniques to terrify viewers.

I clearly recall the first time I saw the movie. (I had heard for years that it was horrifying beyond belief, and so I was already set up to be shocked). It came on television late one evening, so as usual I crept downstairs for my dose of nightly terror. This wasn't "Creature Feature," with some guy in a rubber suit jumping out of a lake and chewing up B-grade movie starlets. This was a 10 p.m. network screening of "Hitchcock's Masterpiece of Terror," as it was being billed. I was about fifteen and of course completely obsessed with seeing the movie and petrified at the same time. All I kept hearing about was a famous scene involving a shower. I had wrongly assumed the scene was famous because it was racy—wrong on two counts. I was fit to be tied while watching, because for the first half of the movie, absolutely nothing happened; it was a boring soap opera with no psychos in sight. This is of course masterfully designed by Hitchcock. Just as was supposed to happen, I was nearly lulled into sleep by the time "Marion" (Janet Leigh) repents of her theft and decides to take a symbolic shower at the Bates Motel—where there is always a vacancy. Suddenly I realized something was about to happen. I leaned forward. I saw a shadowy form approach the shower curtain. Suddenly the camera cut to a screaming woman's mouth, and an instant later a dark figure ran out of the bathroom. Janet was on the floor, and the camera was twisting in a close-up of her dead eye, then the bathtub drain. Nothing much had happened as far as I could tell. The famous scene lasted about four seconds and was not scary in the least. I turned the movie off, completely deflated. I had been expecting to be horrified, and I felt cheated of my well-deserved fear. I mean, I was the little kid who was terrified by the old dead lady's bug-eyes in *Black Sabbath*. *Psycho* should have been almost unbearable.

Several years later I saw the whole film without all the TV edits that had butchered it the first time. This time I was even more relaxed when the (in my initial judgment) vastly overrated shower scene came around. Like most people who see it (whole) for the first time, I was completely overwhelmed with terror, but could not look away. For the next hour of the movie I was on the edge of my seat, expecting more mayhem, but there are really only two more scary scenes. These are creepy, but can be almost comic. But that shower scene still gets under my skin. I hardly like to be in the room when I screen it for a lecture on the incredibly complex editing sequence it features—over seventy camera angles and fifty cuts in under three minutes. The tame four seconds I had seen several years before had reduced the movie to a tense soap opera—I had not seen *Psycho* at all.

The most interesting part of the film from a theological perspective is not the handful of scary scenes, it is the ending. After we have witnessed several gruesome murders, with several more in the background, we find out who is behind the crimes. At this point, the perpetrator is in custody, and the survivors gather in the police station. We then meet "Dr. Richmond," a psychiatrist played by Simon Oakland who presents a "pop-psychology," Freudian/Oedipal analysis of the killer's motives. We have never met the doctor before, and he has just a single scene with an extended monologue. The characters accept his explanation, and then we see the perpetrator again in a final chilling "self-talk" scene in a cell. The final frames contain a slightly subliminal superimposition of a decayed corpse's face. And the movie is over.

Any depth of thought about this ending should leave the viewer deeply unsatisfied. If we are to take the conclusion seriously, then the whole movie is just a gimmick wrapped around a single ground-breaking horrific scene of violence in about the most private and vulnerable situation any of us ever experience: naked in a shower. A walk-on cardboard character that explains the entire plot away in four minutes is what critics call a "cheat"—it is an easy way out of a plot problem. The Greeks had the *deus ex machina,* a god lowered down from above the stage by a mechanical device, to solve the problems and bring easy resolution; *Psycho* features a modern dress-up version of this device—the all-knowing psychiatrist. The precisely wrought tensions, carefully drawn characters, lovingly and painfully vision-oriented camerawork all go down the drain—like Marion's blood—because it is explained away by comic-book psychiatric reductionism. This doesn't mean the movie isn't good—in my view it is superlative and unequaled in its kind—but like all cultural production it is *desperately incomplete and thus unsatisfying.* When was the last time you went to a museum to look at one painting, and then left satisfied? Art functions by increasing desire for more art. As Solomon says, "the eye is not satisfied with seeing, nor the ear filled with hearing" (Eccles. 1:8). There are people who have never watched a single movie; who do you know who has seen *only* a single movie?

Why am I saying this? Not to critique a brilliant film in a negative way. To the contrary, I find the movie especially fascinating because of what it cannot and will not do: deal unapologetically with the existence of actual human evil. Most people do not know the back-story of the film: Hitchcock bought the rights to Robert Bloch's 1959 novel, which is based on the true story of Ed Gein. Gein committed unspeakable atrocities on his farm in Wisconsin in the late 1950s. His crimes were so heinous that the newspapers suppressed them. The killer in *Psycho* is a timid amateur compared to the reality on which he is based.[8]

It's just too painful to say that all people are sinful and can and do act with incalculable evil. It is much more comforting to separate out *some* people and say they are ill. This allows us to think we are not like them. But while outward acts will vary among individuals, our minds are much alike and entirely infected with sin: "The heart is deceitful above all things, and desperately sick; who can understand it?" (Jer. 17:9). *Psycho* is a perfect example of the suppression of truth and the origins of culture. We'd love to believe mankind is basically good. Yet we see evidence to the contrary, and we produce fictional narratives that show people acting with motives ranging from mildly selfish to horribly evil. But since Hollywood is in the business of selling tickets, not just making art (or teaching theology), the filmmakers have a problem: if you show mankind as evil, you are insulting your paying audience. So while the plot depends—as all plots do—upon conflict, upon the incursion of evil upon others, the evil must be sanitized, diagnosed, and dispensed with in modernistic, scientific fashion. So a movie that is powerfully driven by atmosphere (primarily visuals—the dialogue is quite wooden) turns to a brief verbal explanatory monologue that deflates the film's driving force, which is a painfully exacting representation of evil in the context of a normal, boring life. And since Hitchcock's other films take psychiatry very seriously (as in 1945's *Spellbound*), we can be confident we are to take Dr. Richmond's monologue seriously, even while it causes the film as a whole to collapse as a satisfying fiction. But would it be better to show evil as evil, and show it as being as evil as it is? After all, movies are safe because they are just fiction, right?

But *Psycho* opened the door to what has come to be known as the "slasher film" genre, and we now have a massive catalog of hack-'em-up movies, some cheaply produced, others with very high production values and major star power behind them. If these movies are indicative of what we're like, then half of us wear hockey masks on Halloween and go around dismembering teenagers for sport, and the rest of us just wish we had the guts to do so. So many of these movies are made, I can't keep track of the titles—they line entire walls in video stores. Increasingly inventive methods of cutting, stabbing, slicing, and pulverizing the human form are dreamed up every year, and the power to shock jaded audiences seems nearly depleted. A simple knife in a shower won't do; perhaps slow evisceration of pulsing organs, followed by cannibalism might get the audience's attention! It's a long way from "Cesare," the wild-eyed but stumbly-bumbly somnambulist in the silent *Cabinet of Dr. Caligari,* who only threatens with his eyes and does little more onscreen than carry a girl off into a quaintly nightmarish surrealist set.

Reducing human evil by any variety of motives is standard fare in narrative film, though not all movies take this tactic, and it surely isn't the only one that can be used to jolt viewers and start their adrenaline flowing.[9] Supernatural horror is particularly effective because it is not tied to the rule-bound natural world. The unknown is frightening because we do not like uncertainty. This is why people are afraid of things like darkness, being lost, major changes in life circumstances, and public speaking.

The Shining (1980), based on the novel of the same name by horror writer Stephen King, is one of the greatest examples of a film that features fear of the unknown. The film works because the terror is psychological, not just supernatural. Neither the characters nor the audience really know for sure what is real and what may be just in the minds of the characters. The hotel may be haunted by a large number of malevolent spirits, or certain members of the Torrance family may be hallucinating or crazy. Or perhaps both. Why don't they just check out of the hotel if it is so scary? That's the genius of the plot, and the power of the fear: they can't leave. Jack Torrance, a marginally successful writer working as an off-season resort caretaker is living with his wife and son in the Overlook Hotel in the Colorado Rockies for the entire winter. They will be alone in the hotel—really alone, as it is snowbound for months at a time. But something apparently is in the hotel with them. And it is *extremely* frightening, as anyone who has seen the film can attest.

So the setup is very effective: trapped in a small world they cannot escape and tormented by a frightening power that may or may not exist. There is no way out, no way to either defeat or even understand the danger. And while the movie spares us ever so slightly (some family members escape the horror), it still reserves another great moment of terror for the final shot, which pans slowly across a series of historical photographs from the hotel's past. As we come to the last photo, with vintage party music playing gleefully, we zoom in ever so slowly to see, in attendance at a gala ball many generations ago, one of the current characters wearing a devilish grin and staring straight out at us. How could this person from the present be in a picture from the past? This shot foregrounds the core idea of being haunted, which means having the sense that you are not alone: *there is something beyond time there with you, and this someone is supernatural and perhaps to be feared.*

Stanley Kubrick's final shot does two things. First, it serves as a brilliantly subtle metaphor for the idea of the "moving picture" as we see a series of framed still images on a table moving *slowly* past our vision, such that we can see and analyze them all carefully. This of course is precisely what does *not* happen with an actual "motion picture"—its actual photographic "stillness" (many thousands of tiny photos) is hidden by moving it past the eyes at twenty-four frames per second. Second, it completely disorients and destabilizes all of our previous interpretive possibilities about what may have been going on in the plot. The final shot seems to be saying that it is not the Overlook Hotel or even its guests that may be haunted. It is the movie, or rather, it is *movies* that are haunted. And we are no less haunted than the movies we make and watch. We are *in them*, even as they are in us. We stare into them, as into a reflective pond, and what we see is ourselves inside the movies, staring back out at ourselves.

Which one is the ghost?

Into the Depths

Robert Zemeckis's *What Lies Beneath* (2000) is a highly entertaining and truly chilling modern masterpiece, with excellent production values, a great story, and an outstanding cast. Zemeckis is a master of misdirection in this film—this one fooled me repeatedly and delivered some genuine shocks and real frights. It is very much concerned with this same idea of naturalism versus supernaturalism. It is not insignificant that we humans are so haunted by the idea of being haunted. The question is bound up with the central image of the film, which is the image of surface and depth: what in fact does lie beneath? Claire and Norman Spencer are the perfect couple: he's a high level academic doing medical research, and she's a talented though retired Julliard cellist who spends her time with her husband, her daughter (who's now left for college), and her lovely old waterfront home. But all is not as it seems, and Claire becomes convinced that her house is haunted.

Her sense of the haunting grows after several odd occurrences, many of which occur in the presence of water: steam, a bathtub, the lake. The question is, how clearly can you see through a watery surface to what lies beneath? It's a great visual metaphor, and Zemeckis uses it to startling and unpredictable effect. This film is loaded with visual plays on reflections in mirrors, water, and other surfaces, and even more disconcerting, the extreme limitation and distortion when we try to look *through* water to see what may be there.

The opening moves set the metaphor—the camera, accompanied by slightly creepy music, is moving painfully slowly through murky lake water. Visibility is low and dependent upon uneven moments of light that appears to be penetrating from the surface. We can hardly see at all, and this is very disturbing. We edge forward through seaweed and bits of mucky debris, and suddenly the plants part to reveal what appears—for a split second—to be a sickly, purple female face. As the music crescendos the camera rapidly pulls back, the water clears, and we see Michelle Pfeiffer's face as her eyes open and she bursts upward out of her claw-foot tub as if startled. We have no idea how these two underwater "locations" might be related or why. Perhaps Claire was daydreaming under the water. She pulls the plug and the movie begins. But the doubled image of surface and depth is the controlling idea for the film.

This film has some really chilling moments, I must admit, and I'm not easily frightened because I generally think I know all the tricks by now. Remember, I have years of clandestine "Creature Feature" viewing under my belt! I first watched this movie by myself in order to prepare a lecture on suspense techniques; I have to admit Zemeckis got me, and got me *good*. There were at least four moments where I did not "see it coming," and the final moments of the penultimate scene, which takes place underneath the surface of a body of water (where else with such a title?), still make me shudder, not just out of fear but out of a sense of poetic yet terrifying justice. So what did I do after getting rather embarrassingly spooked watching it in my campus study all alone? Why, I took it home of course, and sat my wife down to watch it. I strategically positioned myself so I could watch her watching the unexpected scare scenes. I'm not sure which was more fun: being scared myself on the first viewing or watching her being scared silly during the second. (Of course I wouldn't do such a thing very often to my dear wife, because she *hates* scary movies.)

One of the most effective scenes involves a character paralyzed by a drug and left to drown in a slowly filling bathtub. The camera's POV (point of view) shots—which have hardly ever been matched for sheer audience-identification in a suspense scene—capture the feeling so perfectly that I find myself holding my breath during the entire sequence. It is a loving homage to Hitchcock's shower scene, and perhaps more distressing. The result is not *Psycho's* rapid-fire violence but rather the slow sensation of drowning.

To my thinking, the finest single moment in the film occurs just before this scene and shows the paralyzing drug taking effect. It shuts down motor ability (so you cannot respond to your environment), but leaves the mind lucid (so you know exactly what is going on around you). The subtle but rich sixteen-second shot is one of the best visual metaphors ever filmed. The camera, just above floor level about twenty feet from the two actors, slowly zooms in toward the paralyzed character, who is lying on the floor; then the camera seems to magically go underneath the now see-through floor and shows us both protagonist and antagonist characters from "beneath." They look as if they are suspended on a transparent floor, viewed from the basement.[10] In other words, we see things from an entirely different perspective now. We see that we have been entirely deceived by appearances, that good guys are not good guys. We now see the things the previously deceived character also now sees. With viewer/character identification now firmly established with this shot, we proceed upstairs to be slowly drowned in the terrifyingly haunted tub.

The film's ending is classic supernaturalism—it features perfect poetic justice, where the punishment fits the crime. This concept is, of course, perfectly theologically accurate. Real justice is always perfect and poetic, beautiful in its balance while terrifying in its execution. *What Lies Beneath* serves unwittingly and ironically as a perfect example in both theme and technique for my argument that that which is suppressed always reemerges to the surface. And just like the suppressed form that rises up from the depths to bring poetic punishment to the film's villain, the returning form, while recognizable, is always most definitely changed into what it was not.

The Exorcist

I hesitate to even talk about this movie, which is considered by many people to be the most frightening and disturbing film ever made. I have written essays on the film, lectured on it, and used clips and (in a few instances) the whole film while teaching at a large public university years ago. But it is by no means a movie that I like to sit down and watch. I feel unnerved just thinking about it, quite honestly.

I am primarily interested in its psychological effects and "spiritual" content. It does contain some highly offensive material, of course, and is not for the faint of heart. But if a movie about the devil possessing a young girl were not offensive, then what in the world would be? Several scenes are shockingly vulgar, but lots of movies are vulgar, and in worse ways. What is interesting to note about the film is that it *is* disturbing—it makes viewers genuinely uncomfortable. It causes deep psychological distress and even real terror that lasts, for many viewers, long after the movie is over.[11] After seeing it when I was probably sixteen, I went home and fashioned a crude wooden cross and stuffed it under my pillow for several weeks. I didn't really believe in God or anything. (I was far too sophisticated for that, I remember thinking.) But the devil scared me to death. Even though I didn't believe in *him* either. But I figured, why take chances? Those unauthorized and long-suppressed nights with "Creature Feature" had come back—in another form and with the vengeance of very frightening poetic justice for *me*. I did not wish to find out what lies beneath.

Few Hollywood movies have had the courage to deal so frankly with supernatural evil—with unrelenting demonic evil. It is easy to make a scary movie about demons or cultic wackos; it takes little imagination to portray Christians as nut-jobs and cranks (many movies do—*Carrie* for example). It is easy to take these subjects and make light of them. But there may well be a reason that *The Exorcist* struck such a nerve with the movie going public: a fear that the film may at some level be accurate, and that there could in fact be a supernatural enemy of mankind that can and does intervene in human lives. Now, I do not think that the scenario in the film is exactly a biblically sound one. I disagree with elements of Catholic doctrine and see very little contiguity between the Roman rite of exorcism and how demonic activity is represented in Scripture. Nonetheless I believe that the reason the film is so powerful is because it taps into a very basic human fear about both God and Satan. Interestingly, William Friedkin, the director, is a believing Jew, and William Peter Blatty, the screenwriter who penned the original novel, is a Catholic. Both have spoken quite openly about their faiths and said that they do not view the premise behind the story as fictional in the least. Is it any wonder that it took two artists who believe seriously in God and Satan, as well as human and demonic evil, to produce what many consider the most terrifying film ever made—not to mention an extremely lucrative one?[12] Few films that take themselves seriously have the courage to present evil so uncompromisingly, so convincingly, and with such conviction that no admixture of good and evil is present in the villain. Even if you don't believe at any level in Judeo-Christian theism, the mere possibility that this story might accurately represent basic structural elements of reality—*sharply defined good and evil in absolutely personal form*—is enough to give anyone nightmares. Because it foregrounds the uncomfortable truth (the biblical truth) that real evil is never merely abstract: *it is someone.*

We can be thankful for one thing: the same thing can be said about goodness. And his name is Jesus Christ.

Hollywood Invents Romance

Of All the Gin Joints, in All the Towns, in All the World, She Walks into Mine

"There are only two cures for love—marriage and suicide."
intertitle from *Spite Marriage*, Buster Keaton (1929)

"I was born when you kissed me. I died when you left me. I
lived a few weeks while you loved me."
Humphrey Bogart in *In a Lonely Place* (1950)

"I pray one prayer, I repeat it till my tongue stiffens. Catherine
Earnshaw, may you not rest as long as I am living! You
said I killed you, haunt me, then! Be with me always,
take any form, drive me mad, only do not leave me in this
abyss, where I cannot find you! . . . I cannot live without
my life. I cannot live without my soul!"
Laurence Olivier and Ralph Fiennes as "Heathcliff"
in the 1939 and 1992 versions of *Wuthering Heights*

A powerful scene halfway through the 1992 film version of *Emily
Bronte's Wuthering Heights* (a classy and more literarily accurate
remake of the classic 1939 adaptation) acts as the central plot-hinge.
Catherine Earnshaw is loved by two men: her poor childhood friend
Heathcliff and her rich husband Edgar. Heathcliff is tortured that she

married another man. She belonged to him, heart and soul; when she dies his torture becomes unbearable. We see her in an open coffin in Edgar's mansion, her beautiful face covered by a thin, silky shroud. Behind the coffin French doors open to the gardens. The room is empty except for Edgar, who gently places a tiny locket and chain in her clasped hands and then kisses her ever so slightly through the veil, with a look of sadness on his face. He walks out of the room. The door is hardly closed when the hand of Heathcliff (Ralph Fiennes) smashes through the glass door in the background and rips the door open. As Ryuichi Sakamoto's haunting score overwhelms the viewer with pathos and pity, Heathcliff staggers over to the coffin and violently rips the shroud off the corpse (Juliette Binoche), lifts her roughly from the box, and clasps her in an embrace that would probably injure a living recipient. He opens her hands, sees the locket, and hurls it away. He is racked with sobs and uncontrollable spasms all over his body. His loss is unbearable. "I cannot live without my life. I cannot live without my soul!" he cries out.

This scene (and this movie) is a favorite for both me and my wife. Every time I watch it, I want to grab her and say the same thing. Fortunately for me, she is still very much alive! Sometimes even a movie can make us realize how easily we forget how much blessing we have. As always, the first thing humans suppress about God is his marvelous goodness. He gives so much.

I'm a male, but I do not for one minute hesitate to admit that I love romantic movies. I always cry during both the 1939 and 1992 versions of *Wuthering Heights*. (Hey, I tear up when I'm teaching the *novel*. Students just love that kind of stuff!) But I'm not *completely* ridiculous. For example, I fall asleep during the 1998 version, which is pretty bad. And my least favorite movies are manipulative or schmaltzy or mindless romantic movies. Romance—in real life or fiction—is as delicate as filigree gold. You don't hammer on it unless you want to ruin it. For example, I absolutely despise the 1970 film ranked number nine on the American Film Institute's top 100 Romantic Movies list: *Love Story*, starring Ali McGraw and Ryan O'Neal. I sincerely wish every print of this horror show would spontaneously burst into flames and melt. (I doubt this miraculous event would be the result of any believable passion in the movie itself.) The famous tagline of the film is "love means never having to say you're sorry." That's the dumbest thing I ever heard.[1] This tepid, treacley story is actually ranked above *It Happened One Night* (1934), *A Streetcar Named Desire* (1951), *Marty* (1955), *Sense and Sensibility* (1995), *Witness* (1985), *Moonstruck* (1987), *The African Queen* (1951), *My Fair Lady* (1964), and *King Kong* (1933). All right, he's a gigantic gorilla and she's a short blond, but it is very romantic! And *Love Story* beat *City Lights* by one place. Were the AFI voters all blind flower girls that year or something?

Yes, it's true: deciding whether you love or hate a particular romance movie is not unlike deciding if you like a person and might want to spend the rest of your life with him or her. It is subjective and varies wildly from person to person. And it's a good thing, too.

Love and Boredom in the Real World

The Classic American Date: go see a movie together. Our culture is so film-saturated that this invitation is the easiest and most natural one to make. Think of all the movies you've seen where a couple goes out on a date to see a movie—often a romance! The Big Screen has indeed formed most of what most people think about most everything there is. Would it be possible to find a single young man or woman today whose ideas about romance were not formed in large part from watching the depictions of romance such as the one in *Titanic*? I find it ironic that going on a movie date teaches you how to be in love, at least according to Hollywood's script. Art and life crash into one another once again.

Our views of what is beautiful, attractive, and desirable come largely from movies. They have taught us (rightly or wrongly) what romance is and how it works, how it starts, how it grows, and how it either ends or lasts for a lifetime. More than any other medium, the movies have decided for us what a "sex symbol"—an idealized man or woman—is, what romance should be like, how love really works, and what it takes to make us happy in the realm of romance. Human cultural systems do exactly that: they teach us how to live, at least according to the system we find ourselves in. The goal of this chapter is to look at what Hollywood tells us about romance and look at what God says. As usual, a guiding tenet of our working theory about cultural production is the conservation of truth principle: the idea that basic truths about God and his rule over the world are built into all of us as taught in Romans 1 and implied everywhere in Scripture. These truths and their logical extensions are suppressed by sinful humanity so that we do not have to believe in God, but these truths about the real state of things slowly reemerge piecemeal, metamorphosed into new shapes. While these new forms may seem to support unbiblical views of the world, they in fact always point back indirectly to God and what he tells us about ourselves and our current fallen state. This is true about all human cultural production, and films about human love affairs are no different. In fact they present a unique case for the purposes of this book, because Scripture has much to say about human love as well as divine love.

Did you ever stop to think about what a wonderful gift God gave us when he designed love between a man and a woman? And that is exactly how he created it: between one man and one woman at one time, because that is all there was in the beginning. One man, one woman, one life, one love—there were no other options. Who else was going to take Eve on a date? Which other guy would have caught Eve's eye? What fellow, after flirting with Eve at a dance, would be asked to step outside by Adam? Nor did God ever intend for there to be any other ones, even though he planned to make more people in his image. But he didn't make romantic love to be merely an end in itself, to be just a source of great pleasure, joy, and satisfaction between two humans. His ultimate intention was for this one-to-one dedication and exclusivity to function as a beautiful sign in his infinite universe that points to his love for us and ours for him. He chose this simple, beautiful image—a groom and his bride—as an eternal metaphor for his marriage to his people.[2] This image is found all over Scripture, implicitly and explicitly, from Genesis to the Prophets and from the Gospels to Revelation.

For this reason, a thoughtful theological analysis of how filmmaking—our most influential form of cultural production for the last one hundred years—has presented the idea of romantic love should be a fascinating and enlightening exercise.

Brief Encounter (1945) was one of the first films to explore in a frank (yet still subtle) way the dichotomy between marriage and love that so many people experience in real life. This post-WWII film, quite shocking for its day, is narrated by a typical British housewife who recounts in a very matter of fact and unsentimental way how she stumbled into a "violent" love affair with a stranger. The story is told in her head while she is relaxing at home with her husband, whom she loves; she imagines it as if she is confessing it to him. "Laura" (Celia Johnson) meets "Alec" (Trevor Howard), a doctor who, just like her, is married and has two children. Their initially innocent friendship quickly develops into a passion, and they arrange brief, furtive liaisons to counteract the "problem" they have in their marriages. This problem is never stated explicitly but everywhere implied. The problem, and the justification of their affair, is boredom.

Boredom. The universal fear and the unfortunately common reality in marriage. I always counsel young couples to marry someone who will challenge them in every area possible. If you're married, the real temptation that must be resisted is the person who is "more interesting" than the one to whom you've promised faithfulness. Boredom is the great fear and the great killer of marriages.

When Laura and Alec meet at the beginning of the film, Laura is standing at the station waiting for her train home. She has been on her weekly shopping trip and at the end of the day is thinking about the rather dull life that awaits her. Oh, she does love her husband, but he is predictable, tame, and always the same. Life is routine, and there is nothing exciting, nothing *new*. When a passing train kicks up some grit into Laura's eye, she is rescued by a helpful stranger, the doctor Alec. He removes the grit, is sweet and kind and gentlemanly in a perfectly innocent way (which makes him all the more charming), and then goes on his journey home to his family. Next week they meet again due to his work schedule coinciding with her shopping schedule. And it begins.

The eye-grit rescue serves two purposes: it shows Laura as "needy" and Alec as a "rescuer," and this forms a significant part of how their relationship functions. Laura is not unhappy with her husband—she's just not excited about their life together. I see this meeting scene as a subtle message to the audience; the story of the removal of a speck of grit from her eye is a distinct and none-too subtle parallel to Jesus' parable of the dust in the eye: "Why do you see the speck that is in your brother's eye, but do not notice the log that is in your own eye? Or how can you say to your brother, 'Let me take the speck out of your eye,' when there is the log in your own eye? You hypocrite, first take the log out of your own eye, and then you will see clearly to take the speck out of your brother's eye" (Matt. 7:3–5).

The Lord's story about the dangers of hypocritical judgmentalism on moral issues is one of the best-known passages in all of Scripture. It beggars the imagination to think that the plot device of the speck removal by Alec at the opening of the affair is not deliberate, underplayed as it may be. We are instructed, regarding the story to follow: do not judge, lest ye be judged. Don't judge their little speck. You probably have a considerable log in your own eye and can't see clearly.

It's a slick move: the affair is presented as understandable, even if not entirely justifiable. Laura and Alec are just victims of circumstance, of fate. They're not looking to cheat, it just happens. Have you ever noticed the passive verbal structure of the phrase "we fell in love"? We are instructed from the beginning of *Brief Encounter* not to judge the adulterous affair, which is presented as a sweet, even innocent thing that gives meaning to a lonely wife's existence. On the one hand, yes, we should not judge uncharitably those who have fallen into adultery. They and those around them are suffering. On the other hand, we should call it what it is: a selfish act that arises from self-love, hurts a lot of people, and always has long-term negative effects. This film is powerful because it is so ambiguous. You can easily read it either as an anti-adultery film or as a pro-adultery film. Or, alternatively, as a nonjudgmental or antijudgmental film—both of which are of course judgments of one kind or another. The strange power of art always lies in ambiguity. Interestingly, boredom can quickly be cured by ambiguity, for ambiguity *is interesting because it is uncertain.* This is why many couples struggle with keeping romance alive after they are married and "the mystery"—the ambiguity of the partner—"goes away." What is left to discover? Predictability is frightening. In other words, what is desired is excitement, which means newness. New things are never boring; what bores us is what we already know so well.

In a different vein, *The Purple Rose of Cairo* (1985) is a brilliant Woody Allen film that is about romance movies: about their sway over us, about the complex relationship between fantasy and reality, and about the hypnotic power of the Big Screen when it comes to love stories. You see (Allen's movie tells us), what everyone really wants in their love life is a movie star. What everyone really wants is *to live in a movie.* How exciting would it be to find yourself in your favorite romantic adventure film, next to the gorgeous heroine or dashing hero, running through narrow Parisian streets in the rain, or hiding out in Algiers or Casablanca. But Allen complicates and then reverses this desire: inside of his movie, where people watch lots of movies, what the characters in *those* movies want is *to live in the real world.* They are bored with their fictional, scripted lives. They want a real life! This ironic reversal—everyone wants to get to the other side of the camera lens (or screen as the case may be)—absolutely nails the existential and theological problem of human existence: we are bored. We prefer fantasy to reality. Or, if we live in the fantasy world as a movie character, we want *real life.* Either way, we want what we don't have. Herein lies the real problem of faithfulness, a problem every one of us (married or not) struggles with, according to what Jesus teaches in the Sermon on the Mount about the identical nature of adultery and lust that is never enacted but remains in the mind's eye.

"Cecilia" (Mia Farrow) goes to the movies alone. Her husband is an abusive, lazy jerk with no sense of romance. But that's ok with Cecilia. The fantasy world of movies has blurred away the miserable real-life world, where she is an inept waitress in a diner and stuck in a dead-end marriage—in fact, a dead-end life—during the Great Depression. Her love for romantic movies consumes her life. She daydreams at work and imagines herself inside the movies she watches— movies filled with good-looking wealthy gentleman adventurers who are incurably romantic and drink very dry martinis. She watches the same movie over and over and over. She falls in love with the hero and (quite seriously) tells her girlfriend, "I just met a wonderful new man. He's fictional, but you can't have everything." The problem is, we *do* want everything, and that includes what we see in the fantasy world that the movies present to us. Many movies present us with a world greatly preferable to the one we find ourselves in. Who wouldn't want to live in them?

Some romance movies could be categorized as "perfect love stories." In this kind of plot a couple goes through some difficulty, but they end up together and happy. They go "off into the sunset" so to speak, with the explicit suggestion that they will be together and happy forever—the classic "fairy tale." This kind of ending is both satisfying and romantic. We'd all like to find that perfect love and have a fulfilling, joyful relationship that does not end. And never gets dull.

This of course does not mean that there are no problems. In fact a plot is nothing more than the introduction of a problem followed by its resolution at some level. No problems equals no plot, which equals no movie. But in the "perfect love" scheme, the problems are overcome, and it is this overcoming that usually brings the love to its deep and powerful final state. Difficulties bring a couple together; this is why couples who have it too easy, especially in the early years, often do not weather later storms well. You'll never see a truly perfect "Perfect Romance" movie—one with no pain and struggles—that actually works well as a story. Plot is conflict, and character development is working through difficulty. Love that works through pain to a solution and ends happily is love that is believable, desirable, lasting, and real. This is a central lesson that can be learned from the cross.

Satisfaction, Sensibility, Cinderella, and a Sinking Ship

One of the finest film romances ever made actually had its first incarnation as a television movie in 1953. *Marty*, starring Rod Steiger in the title role of the TV original and Ernest Borgnine in the 1955 theatrical film version, is a moving tale about a lonely middle-aged butcher who just can't find a woman. He is somewhat overweight and not at all good looking, and he is socially awkward. He is thirty-four and still lives with his mother. He has no prospects and spends his time with his other lonely buddies. His mother desperately wants Marty to find a wife, but he says openly that whatever it is that women want, he hasn't got it. His problem is the very common human problem of loneliness. We were made for companionship—we were not made to be alone, whether that loneliness is removed by marriage (if we are called to that) or close friendship. And of course, a deep intimate relationship with God is the cure to all loneliness. Loneliness is really a kind of boredom, where the mind desires to fix its attention on something but cannot find anything suitably interesting. As a result the mind turns inward but finds that terribly unsatisfying and painful. The irony is that we need someone else besides ourselves to make ourselves complete.

Every night Marty hangs out with his buddies, and they always ask each other the same question: "So what do you feel like doing tonight?" They are a group of friends bored out of their minds because their friendship is only partly satisfying and built around doing fun things together—and "the guys" are all so identical that it is like Marty being alone with several reflections of himself. He finally meets a similarly lonely middle-aged lady, Clara, who has just been ditched by a blind date. She is as awkward and homely as Marty is. They instantly connect, but his mother becomes jealous, and his friends taunt him about his choice. He strongly considers dumping her. Marty finally chews out his friends who are taunting him for going on a date with a "dog," though they haven't had any dates at all in recent memory and Marty isn't exactly Marlon Brando. He makes an impassioned speech: "You don't like her. My mother don't like her. She's a dog. *And I'm a fat, ugly little man.* Well, all I know is I had a good time last night. I'm gonna have a good time tonight. If we have enough good times together, I'm gonna get down on my knees. *I'm gonna beg that girl to marry me.* If we make a party on New Year's, I got a date for that party. You don't like her? That's too bad." Nothing could be more romantic! Marty has hope now. He finally realizes that caring for another person is the most satisfying thing in life. And—this is the key—*he hopes* he can get her. He does not think too highly of himself, he is not above her. Nothing kills romance like pride.

What Hollywood generally tells us is that you have to have a movie romance with a movie star to be happy. Life has to be filled with excitement and unending adventure to be romantic. Normal life doesn't cut it. You won't be happy in 1955 unless you have Marilyn Monroe or Jayne Mansfield by your side, or James Dean or Elvis Presley. But what this little film taps into is the (deeply suppressed) truth that real romantic happiness is grounded not in excitement *per se* but in satisfaction. And satisfaction is always a choice. Marty *decides to be satisfied.* He decides not to think he deserves more, and this makes him happy—and thus satisfied. He doesn't care what others think about his satisfaction. That's the great thing about satisfaction: it is so satisfying. Understanding this simple principle alone could save untold troubled marriages. Constant longing for some kind of fantasy is eternally unsatisfying. Just think about God's love for his people: could he have made a perfect people for himself after the fall? Of course! But he chooses to be satisfied in his love for us, and *then* to redeem us even while we are his enemies, and ultimately to recreate us *as* those perfect people.[3] And our part in this is to be satisfied in him and his ways. Sure, I could imagine a "preferable" god who would let me do whatever I wanted, who would permit me to be selfish and get away with it, and who would be satisfied with my dissatisfaction with him. But how satisfying would that be for either of us?

Sense and Sensibility directed by Ang Lee is another romantic film worthy of serious consideration by thoughtful viewers. The fact that it is based on a "highbrow" British novel betrays how well it works as an entertaining movie. Emma Thompson's sensitive, witty, and rich screenplay version of Jane Austen's novel surely ranks as one of the best novel/film adaptations of all time. Austen's fine-spun wit regarding early nineteenth-century British class consciousness, culture, and romantic entanglements is subtle, and only the sharpest craftsmanship could translate it successfully to the screen.

The story is not merely entertaining but also highly instructive. "Elinor" (Thompson) and her sister "Marianne" (Kate Winslet) both desire and need husbands—they have lost their inheritance. Marianne is a classic romantic, wearing her heart on her sleeve, while Elinor is reserved and cautious. They represent "sense" (wildly emotional romanticism) and "sensibility" (detached, rational control) in life and love. The plot is fairly complex and a delight to watch as it unfolds. The climactic scene, when the "sensible" Elinor finds out that the man she loves but believes has married another woman is actually still single and loves only her, is one of the most moving moments I've ever seen in any film. A lifetime of measured self-control, thoughtful repression, and carefully polite social behavior crumbles like an overtaxed dam bursting before a raging floodwater; she shakes and weeps with simultaneous shock, relief, love, and bewilderment. This really is the way love is meant to be experienced: near-total collapse in the face of joy, a recognition of blessing so rich it cannot be comprehended. *It is in no way* "sensible." But then, what is the proper balance between being sensible and being passionate? Marianne, who is not sensible, ends up terribly hurt because of her unwise emotionalism, and she finally becomes "sensible." Are we then to think that feelings are somehow dangerous in and of themselves? Should we think then that calm rationality escapes the effects of the fallen nature of man? Should we be cool, calculated, and safe in our love for mankind, for a spouse, for God? Or should we love with abandon, heedless of consequence? How would *you* rather be loved?

We all long to know that we are loved in the deepest sense, and many of us never know what that feels like. Humans disappoint one another on a regular basis. Nevertheless most of us look for the greatest love of our lives to come from another person as sinful and selfish as we are. It seems clear that human romantic love—designed by God to be a wonderful experience—is often but a pale reflection of God's magnificent love for us. Emma Thompson's emotionally wrenching weeping scene is thus a powerful cultural image of what our reaction to God's love should be like, but rarely is.

On the other end of the scale of subtlety is the 1990 romantic comedy *Pretty Woman*. This popular and incredibly successful film is very entertaining but really never sat right with me. A retelling of the Pygmalion story as well as the Cinderella myth, the film is a tale about a wealthy businessman and his growing affection for a prostitute who becomes his high-priced escort. Of course they eventually fall in real love. Making a comedy about prostitution is not an easy thing to do, and while some of the scenes and situations are admittedly funny, you feel a little bit as if you were watching a lighthearted treatment of something that in reality is a bit too heavy. It is a little difficult to believe that a man would fall in love with a woman he had paid for, and who had been paid for by many other men previously. (Not to mention her falling for a man who buys women.) Yet Julia Roberts's "hooker with a heart of gold" character really captured peoples' hearts and launched her career as a major actress. Her simple and ironically "innocent" winsomeness is what makes the story work. Interestingly, many A-list actresses turned the role down because they did not want to play a whore. The film was originally planned as a dark look at high-priced prostitution in Los Angeles, but slowly evolved into a nonracy, mild screwball comedy played for laughs. I think the positive audience response to the film is far more interesting than the film itself. I don't wish to be judgmental in a negative or unfruitful way, but I have wondered about the social consequence of such an absurd fantasy plot when many women are sadly trapped in the reality of sex-for-hire. But I also wonder why the movie, which really does have a silly and distasteful premise, was so wildly popular.[4]

Perhaps the story we should think through is the hope-filled Cinderella fairy tale and the Pygmalion myth, combined with the "redeemed prostitute" story.[5] This story is not a new one: it is in the Bible.

God commands the Old Testament prophet Hosea to marry a prostitute: "When the LORD first spoke through Hosea, the LORD said to Hosea, 'Go, take to yourself a wife of whoredom and have children of whoredom, for the land commits great whoredom by forsaking the LORD'" (Hos. 1:2). Hosea's marriage to Gomer symbolizes Israel's unfaithfulness to the Lord, which took the form of idolatry. The Israelites constantly fell into worship of the local pagan deities, which made God the "faithful husband" to Israel's "unfaithful wife." God later commands Hosea to buy his wife from a slave market and continue to love her: "And the LORD said to me, 'Go again, love a woman who is loved by another man and is an adulteress, even as the LORD loves the children of Israel, though they turn to other gods . . .'" (3:1).[6] So Hosea buys her for fifteen shekels and nine bushels of barley. In addition to this being a picture of God's love for Israel, it also shows his love for his New Testament bride, the church—those repentant believers who have been redeemed by

God's grace alone from their sin. But God does not just save people, he changes them—slowly and incompletely here and instantly and totally in heaven.

This image is powerful and hopeful. It has percolated through human culture for many centuries. It has surfaced in many stories, paintings, novels, operas, plays, and movies, and I think it shows up even in this silly comedy. Of course, Hosea the righteous "prophet" is replaced with a "profiteering" corporate raider (played by Richard Gere), and Julia Roberts is no miserable street whore but a high-priced, glamorous, and essentially happy call girl. Nonetheless, the story arc strongly implies that she will be much happier with a rich man who actually loves her and does not need to "buy" her. And yet the classical role of the redeemer is always to "buy" the object of affection out of whatever form of slavery he or she has been enslaved by—that's what it means "to redeem." As always, irony percolates slowly to the surface when we look closely at the products of the culture factory.

On a very different and considerably more wholesome plane is *Ladyhawke* (1985), an enchanting movie starring Michelle Pfeiffer and Rutger Hauer that explores (in the format of a medieval fantasy-morality tale) what happens when two passionate lovers are unable to be together. This is the result of a curse placed upon them by a jealous third party; the unusual form of the curse is the clever conceit of the film. The story captures the agony of a love that cannot be made complete in any way. The resultant longing and grief is familiar to anyone who has loved but been separated from the object of affection. The deep desire shared by Navarre (Hauer) and Isabeau (Pfeiffer)—who are cursed in such a horrific way that they cannot ever be together—is exactly the kind of "Romeo and Juliet" syndrome that only causes a love to grow stronger. This is a classic plot device in love stories from minor movies like *Ladyhawke* to sweeping blockbusters. For example, an entirely different level of moviemaking is found in James Cameron's massive romantic epic *Titanic* (1997), but much the same kind of story is told. This is one of the highest earning films of all time; its gross revenues are approaching $2 billion. Moviegoers were separated from their cash in a way that "Jack Dawson" and "Rose DeWitt Bukater" never could be separated from each other.

This movie is easy to pick on, and I've certainly done my fair share of that in lectures. The often ridiculous dialogue between Jack (Leonardo DiCaprio) and Rose (Kate Winslet) can be quite cloying (he quite graphically teaches her how to spit with verve and accuracy), and the frenzied multiple viewings by teenage girls crushing on DiCaprio, which brought in hundreds of millions of dollars during the initial theatrical release, have been the subject of much derision. But on the whole the movie does in fact play very well. It is long, engaging, and visually beautiful, has a great soundtrack, and lays out a classic romantic plot trajectory. Love really does blossom in life when a couple meets and overcomes obstacles as a team, learning to laugh together even in the face of powerful opposition and painful circumstance. The spectacular backdrop of the film—the gorgeously recreated luxury liner—and the ensuing disaster combine with the plot to make a memorable "happy tragedy" that sweetly hinges upon the deep power of a life-long love. It is made all the more poignant because the central story is told in flashback by an old woman who still recalls the honeyed sensations of young love. This movie garnered such a strong emotional response perhaps not so much because of the young-love scenes of DiCaprio and Winslet, but because the image of a very aged woman still in love and glowing with the purity of her life-long dedication plucked such a chord of desire among all its viewers. Who wouldn't love to be loved powerfully—forever?

The Funny Thing about Love
Romantic comedy is among the most popular of all film genres. These lighthearted treatments of the ups and downs of relationships are easy to sell to the public. They end happily, whether the couple stays together or not. These are the classic "feel good" movies. Thus they are the classic date movies: in a handy little twist, the movie you watch on your date foregrounds romance (no guy takes a first date to a war movie—not if he wants a second date), shows you how to be romantic, opens up the whole subject of romance to conversation, and provides

the couple with the shared experience of laughter, which I believe is important in any healthy relationship.

You would be hard pressed to find someone who does not like this kind of movie when it is done well. Romantic comedy presents two things we all have interest and experience in: love and humor. Many actors have built their careers on the genre, and most "top movies of all time" lists feature many of these. Romantic comedies are also very good moneymakers. They can usually be made fairly inexpensively, and because they are popular, happy films that often showcase major stars, they sell a lot of tickets. In many ways movies open up helpful conversations about relationships, love, life struggles, and so forth for the friends and couples who watch them. You can learn a lot about a person by "talking movies" with them.

In one of the most talked-about movies of the 1980s, the delightful *Moonstruck* (1987), Cher proves that she is a fine comedic actress. She plays a strong-willed thirty-seven-year-old single woman from an Italian family in Brooklyn under intense pressure to remarry (her first husband was hit by a bus). She becomes unexcitedly engaged to a rather weak "mama's boy" who is several years older, but then finds herself falling passionately in love with another man—the worst possible one under the circumstances. The film turns on the truism that when you really do love someone, he can drive you crazy and really hurt you. Therefore you must avoid being with them, but you can't, because then you're even more miserable. The more you try to resist that "wrong on every count" person whom you find irresistible, the more you fall in love with him, and the more powerful the attraction becomes.

This is the classic setup for the subgenre of the "screwball romantic comedy," which is a variation of the romantic comedy. These plots have one constant across all the examples. The movie always starts off with the worst possible match, and that situation is reversed by the end of the movie. The humor in these films works by irony, as I pointed out in the chapter on comedy: the audience knows things will work out, because it recognizes the elements of the genre and it knows that the man and woman who hate each other at the start of the film will find each other tolerable by the middle and irresistible by the end. The couple trades acerbic verbal barbs through the whole movie. The classic literary counterparts are Shakespeare's comedies featuring dueling couples, such as *Much Ado about Nothing* and *The Taming of the Shrew*.

Are these stories unrealistic? Is there hope (much less wisdom) in a match between two people who start off despising one another? What makes a "good match"? Have you ever noticed that most real-life relationships actually reverse the story arc of a screwball romance? Instead of starting off with dislike and ending up madly in love, many couples actually start off madly in love and end up in mutual dislike— or intense dislike—of each other. In this case art and life do not imitate each other except in a mirror. The image is reversed.

But perhaps the story arc of these comedies is more realistic and more hopeful than it at first might seem. Love takes hard work, determined growth, painful adaptation, and above all else an increasingly accommodating spirit of forbearance. Screwball comedies always show a couple initially at odds but finally coming together as a result of overcoming some shared difficulties, usually some external challenge that they team up against. Perhaps it *is* possible to start as enemies and end up in love.

The classic model and the first great example in film history of the screwball romantic comedy is *It Happened One Night*. This marvelous film still plays better after seventy-five years than the vast majority of the more recent screwball comedies to which it gave birth. It is one of the very few films I would be willing to call a perfect movie. It is a personal favorite because it is one of the first movies my wife and I saw right after we got married—and we laughed hysterically through the whole thing. The lightning fast repartee between the major characters, rich socialite "Ellie Andrews" (Claudette Colbert) and poor, hard-drinking newshound "Peter Warne" (Clark Gable), is fabulous and sets the standard for all such "abrasive/attractive relationships." As the plot develops (she is on the run from a controlling millionaire father, and he needs a gossipy news scoop to save his job), the relationship changes from mutually parasitic to mild mutual toleration to sweetly powerful teamwork and tender care. But then it all falls apart due to a misunderstanding. Near the end, Ellie's father asks Peter if he loves her. Peter responds disdainfully, "Any guy that'd fall in love with your daughter ought to have his head examined!" Her father keeps pressing, does he love her or not? Peter retorts, "What she needs is a guy that'd take a sock at her once a day, whether it's coming to her or not. If you had half the brains you're supposed to have, you'd done it yourself, long ago!" They continue: "Do you love her?" "A normal human being couldn't live under the same roof with her without going nutty! She's my idea of nothing!" Peter shouts. The interrogation is now very heated, and the father shouts in his face, "I asked you a simple question! *Do you love her?*" Peter shouts right back, "YES! But don't hold that against me, I'm a little screwy myself!"

There is in fact something about romantic love that not only defies logic but is "a little screwy." It is especially screwy—that is, it is unpredictable and makes no "sense"—to start as enemies and then find yourselves united by real love. Furthermore if, outside of God's will and law, you give yourself over to a shallow form of romantic attraction, you will end up doing a lot of damage to yourself and others. However, inside of God's will and law, when giving yourself over to godly romantic love (like we see in the Song of Solomon), you not only end up satisfied but edified. Godly marriage is joyful. And yes: even enemies can be reconciled. But it seems to make no sense to those who reject its premises. As a result, most "romantic" relationships are troubled. And these kinds of relationships provide much fodder for film plots.

Not all love stories end happily—in real life or the movies. In fact, the majority of couples do not ride off into the sunset together. Many romance films build their plots around troubled or doomed relationships. These are among the most powerful romantic movies. A strong romantic attachment that ends in disaster—the "Romeo and Juliet" type of plot—is one major variation; another is the dysfunctional relationship, where one member (or both) is unfaithful, or abusive, or personally troubled so that the relationship is fraught with problems. You could call these "car wreck" romances, and they can be effective but also unpleasant to watch. This goes to the extreme in movies like *Who's Afraid of Virginia Woolf?* (1966), which is a little over two hours of Elizabeth Taylor and Richard Burton hating each others' guts and using all the resources of language to do so. It is an antiromance movie if there ever was one.

Leaving Las Vegas (1995) is a similar exercise in misery, telling the story of an alcoholic (Nicholas Cage) who decides to drink himself to death in Las Vegas and a prostitute (Elisabeth Shue) who becomes his friend. Their agreement is that she will not try to talk him out of drunkenness and he will not try to talk her out of prostitution. This is not the formula for a happy relationship. As depressing as the film (and their relationship) may be, it still shows forth the burning desire for love, acceptance, and security that is only ever found with God. I think the reason the movie rang so true with viewers was because it is a powerful picture of the life many people lead, even if it isn't publicly visible.[7] You don't need to be a drunk or a prostitute to feel miserably trapped in a meaningless existence. Even if you manage to provide yourself with a constant stream of pleasures—even an overload of alcohol and sex—you quickly become dissatisfied and disillusioned. Even if you find a lover, like the characters in this film do, the best thing you can find is a temporary, crippled joy that you live in fear of losing.

The Authority on Love

What does the Bible say about romance? Not so much, percentage-wise, and a great deal, substance-wise. Scripture is as dense as a text can get. God does not waste words. The basics of what the Bible says are clear: God designed marriage to be the natural outlet and location for romantic love and its physical manifestation in human sexuality. Outside of marriage, you will run into inevitable problems (there are enough problems with relationships *inside* marriage!). God has designed people for commitment and trust that lasts a lifetime. The failure of marriage, or any relationship, always has a human cause.

When God creates Eve for Adam, Adam's response is as romantic as anything any man has ever said: Eve is "bone of my bones, and flesh of my flesh," and I don't think this is merely a reference to her being fashioned from Adam's own flesh. She is as much a part of him as any other part. He is incomplete without her, and while she "derives" from him, she is not lesser than he is before God.

The myth that Hollywood has created about romance is that the key to love is a combination of super-idealized beauty, unending excitement in life, and an open-minded attitude toward physical intimacy. Corollary to that "positive" primary myth is a subtle but powerful "negative" submyth that we see running implicitly through many movies and explicitly in others. This is the myth that committed, faithful, lifetime marriage between "normal" nonidealized couples is unsatisfying, boring, and no fun compared to what you'll have when you follow the Hollywood script for romance. But here's my question: who do you think would actually be more likely to spend a happy, fulfilling lifetime together: Marty and Clara (the "dogs") or Jack and Rose (the fantasy movie stars)? People naturally struggle with the unsatisfying reality of life when they compare it to the fantasy world of movies; this is part of the reason movies are so popular. We want to think of ourselves as smarter, stronger, and better looking than we are, and this is supported by the phenomenon of viewer-character identification. Careful production—from camerawork to editing to sound design—draws us into the movie, and we begin to participate as if we are there. Our consciousness is co-opted at a certain level, and we leave the real world and enter the world of the film. Then, when the credits roll and the celluloid fantasy is back in the film can, you look at your life and feel slightly disappointed with "the real." Like Cecilia in *The Purple Rose of Cairo*, we prefer the pleasures that aren't real to the ones that are. The problem with myths of course is that while they are useful, they can only do so much. The deeply unhappy lives of many people in the industry that is Hollywood should tell us that the myth they've created is just that.

God himself chose marital romance—one man, one woman, one lifetime—as *the* metaphor for his love for us and our devotion to him. Yet in our cultural representations of love and marriage, the wonderful design of God is suppressed and neutralized. Nevertheless this suppression always ultimately collapses in on itself and points back to God and the beauty of his design. Romance movies contain, in scattered bits and pieces, fractured elements of the image of the true Divine Romance. As Heathcliff, probably the greatest romantic male in literary and film history, says, true romantic love is like the sharing of a soul: his loss of Cathy is an unbearable kind of death of himself. "I cannot live without my life. I cannot live without my soul!" Yet these romanticized images of super-idealized lovers have left us stranded in a state of boredom. Every woman wants her Heathcliff, and every man wants his Cathy. Boredom becomes the actual state of *homo romanticus*, and continual excitement the only cure. As a result, we willingly choose fantasy over reality. On the one hand we are simultaneously fascinated and horrified by candid pictures of gorgeous actresses without makeup; on the other hand we continue to believe the airbrushed movie-poster photos and carefully lit, digitally enhanced scenes from the movies we watch.

Choosing to be satisfied is the key; this is what Marty does. And this is what God does. He is satisfied with his bride. Do we deserve this? That is *precisely not the point*. As William Munny says in his famous line in *Unforgiven*—one of the most theologically weighty lines ever spoken in a movie—"*deserve's got nothin' to do with it.*"

God is a passionate lover of his bride. Real romance was always designed to be passionate, constant, consistent, unchanging, permanent—and a function of marriage. The reason viewers respond so strongly to Emma Thompson's weeping in *Sense and Sensibility* is because deep down we want someone to love us like that. We long to have our sensibility broken by sensuality—but a sensuality that is perfect, faithful and can be perfectly trusted. One that is in fact holy and singularly devoted.

But we tend to not fully trust the one true lover of our souls, and we try to replace him by suppressing the truth of his love and substituting a pale movie shadow version of the metaphor of romance for the very thing the metaphor points to. God has purchased us by spending himself; this is as romantic as you can get. The mark of a good husband is that he would give his life for his wife—not just by taking a bullet, but by literally surrendering all the little, irreplaceable moments of his life for her happiness. And what a man desires is a forever woman who is endlessly beautiful in her total dedication to his happiness. They may indeed start out even as enemies, as we do with God. And yes, those whom you love can drive you crazy and can hurt you. And while ambiguity is interesting and exciting, we need to learn that the excitement of continually discovering a person you love is much like the continually unfolding excitement of loving God and getting to know him better. Choosing to be satisfied always leads to satisfaction. There is always more to learn, and more to love. This is why real romantic love lasts a lifetime.

And that is what makes it romantic.

> I will seek him whom my soul loves.
> I sought him, but found him not. . . .
>
> Let him kiss me with the kisses of his mouth!
> For your love is better than wine. (Song 3:2; 1:2)

Film Noir

The Dark Side, or Solomon Goes to Hollywood

"You don't know how much I've missed all of you. And I
   promise you I'll never desert you again, because after
   'Salome' we'll make another picture, and another and
   another! You see, this is my life. It always will be. There's
   nothing else—just us . . . and the cameras . . . and those
   wonderful people out there in the dark. . . ."
               "Norma Desmond" in *Sunset Boulevard* (1950)

"How could I have known that murder can sometimes smell
   like honeysuckle?"
               "Walter Neff" in *Double Indemnity* (1944)

FILM noir may be the most fascinating area of movie history for Christians interested in thinking about theology and culture. The French term means "black film" or metaphorically "dark film," and in general refers to a certain kind of popular movie produced in the 1940s and 1950s in American studios. These films share a certain look and tone and have other similarities, but beyond that it can be difficult to define what is meant by the term. The most basic element that film noir seems to exemplify is a gritty, cynical view of human nature at its worst. Many (but not all) of these feature police procedural, detective, or mystery plots, and often revolve around adultery, murder, or

165

other edgy subjects normally considered "borderline taboo" during the middle of the twentieth century.

Great film noirs include *The Maltese Falcon* (1941), *The Big Sleep* (1946), *Murder, My Sweet* (1944), *High Sierra* (1941), *Gilda* (1946), *The Postman Always Rings Twice* (1946), *Laura* (1944), and many others. More noirs, known as "neo-noirs" were made in the 1960s and especially in the 1970s, most notably *Chinatown* (1974) and *Taxi Driver* (1976). There are also noir elements in many films of the 1980s and beyond, such as *Body Heat* (1981), *Blade Runner* (1982), *Reservoir Dogs* (1992), *Red Rock West* (1993), *The Matrix* (1999), and *Memento* (2000). (*Blade Runner*, *The Matrix*, and *Memento* are treated in depth in other chapters.) Significantly, Quentin Tarantino's wildly popular *Pulp Fiction* (1994) is an obvious takeoff on classic noir. Three of the greatest classic noirs, *Double Indemnity* (1944), *Sunset Boulevard* (1950), and the lesser known *Scarlet Street* (1945), will be the focus of detailed analysis in the present chapter.

Film noir movies—like horror films—are compelled by their very nature to deal with what I call "the Hollywood/evil paradox." Movies depend on narrative ("story"); narrative depends on plot (the relational structure of the events that occur in the film); plot depends on conflict; and conflict operationally presupposes two or more forces in active opposition to each other. There are many ways to formulate this binary structure, but the simplest is "good versus evil." Some early westerns use this structure explicitly: good guys wear white, bad guys wear black. In later films, the clarity of the distinction is often blurred. We are all familiar with the flawed hero or the villain with the good streak—the "grey character." One variation is the notion of "the Force" in the Star Wars series. The Force itself has no pure, essential nature for good or evil; it does have a dark side, however, which must be resisted. It has a kind of yin and yang balance. George Lucas's films are thus strongly dualistic on the exterior, though ultimately they actually function as a popularization of Eastern Monism. Individuals make choices about which side of the Force to follow, but these decisions can be reversed, and of course the Force is universal and binds everything together into a holistic universe. This is what provides the dramatic tension for Luke Skywalker (who always wears white): he has an opportunity to choose the dark side and rule alongside his father, whose choice to follow the dark side transformed him into Darth Vader (always in black). Similarly, at the end of the first trilogy, Luke is able to rescue his father from the dark side, because Vader chooses to save his son—he finally makes a good choice. Another example is Oskar Schindler, the main character from Stephen Spielberg's *Schindler's List*. Oskar is the hero, risking his neck and spending his entire fortune to save Jews. Yet this hero is no paragon of morality across the board; he is a heavy drinker, a liar, a manipulator, and a womanizing adulterer. In other words, *he is exactly the way humans are in real life*. All heroes have flaws. All saints are also sinners. Liam Neeson's portrayal of Schindler is endlessly fascinating because it is not, in the broadest sense of the word, deeply fictional. It tells the truth about humanity.

This is why film noir is so interesting and why the Hollywood/evil paradox is so intractable—it is a "problem" for movies that cannot be solved and cannot be avoided. Humans in general (and of course artists and filmmakers are included in this group) do not want to believe they are capable of real evil (especially great evil), that they are naturally selfish and consistently self-interested, that our default mode is one of shameful thought and behavior. The primary result of the fall is that we deceive ourselves about our own nature. "Many a man proclaims his own steadfast love, but a faithful man who can find?" (Prov. 20:6). Yet we are faced every moment with the visible reality of human failure, selfishness, and outright evil. We see it constantly in others, and (of course) we see it rather less often in ourselves. My own oft-made tongue-in-cheek definition, "sin is what other people do to *me*," always draws uncomfortable laughter from classrooms and audiences. It hits rather too close to home. Our natural fallen human tendency is to do everything possible to suppress the idea of evil *as evil*—particularly when it comes to our own sinfulness. Humans have devised many strategies to explain evil away, to manage it. I would say this is one of the most important core elements in the formation of every philosophical position—how we deal with the messy problem of human evil. An embarrassingly wide continuum of explanations has been crafted to handle this Herculean task. We can say "'evil' isn't really evil," or "evil is relative," or "evil is sickness, privation, social ill, or some form of lack"; we can even try to make various kinds of anthropological arguments about human nature. We can say "all men are part good, part evil," or "some are totally good, some totally evil," or "there is no valid category of good or evil regarding human nature," or any variation of these. We can admit that there has been evil in the past, but we have outgrown it or evolved morally into better beings. No one ever quite likes to say that all people are always totally depraved and sinfully evil and that we cannot change ourselves. This idea—above all else—must be suppressed, and the suppression must be suppressed. And it is. But it comes back.

The Hollywood/evil paradox is a function of this theological position. Those who produce narrative film are essentially storytellers who run a business. They must sell their product or else stop making it. The movie business is just that—a business. As humans, both the producers and the consumers of the film product have an overwhelming desire to believe they are good or that the "problem of evil" is *explicable*. Some form of badness or evil is necessary to constitute a plot. When was the last time you saw a movie where two people met, fell in love, got married, had a happy, faithful, fulfilled relationship, with all of their material and psychological needs met, then had a couple of great kids who never got into any trouble? You've never seen such a movie, and you never will. Someone has to be unhappy. Someone has to cheat, or kill someone, or break the law, or become a drunk, or run away from home, or get kidnapped by Serbian nationalists. No evil equals no plot equals no movie equals no money. Thus the paradox: while we convince ourselves we are good (or at least not depraved), *our most powerful art form is built upon the revelation that this is a lie.* Morally simplistic movies—with uncrossable borders between good guys and bad guys—are in fact more theologically suspect than films with flawed heroes and bad guys who love their children; moral ambiguity is the marker of the human condition. This is not to say that God is morally ambiguous. He is not. But the inescapable result of the fall of man is that man cannot discern his own nature accurately, cannot understand true justice, and does not really understand good *or* evil. God is not ambiguous. We are.

Film noir is especially fascinating in terms of the theory of the suppression of truth and the origins of culture. Every story about raw evil breaks through the powerful urge to suppress the truth about man's condition, and man is thus portrayed in many instances as he actually is. Film noir is man against himself.

Welcome to the Darkness

Film noir is famously difficult to define, and with good reason. It is more than just a look, more than just a mood or tone, and certainly more than a genre. Elements of noir can be found in many nonnoir films, and noir-ish qualities are recognizable as "something familiar" by almost all moviegoers: vertical shots looking down deep art deco stairwells in tenements with a two-man chase scene going down, down, down the square spirals; shadowy figures with strong backlighting; a door opening slowly in a dark room illuminated only by intermittent flashes of a neon sign, followed by a burst of gunfire (visually echoing the flashing sign), and finally by a hand slumping to the floor; and, of course, sultry women waiting in their love-nest lairs—a cocktail in one hand, a loaded gun under their pillow . . . and an inviting smile on their lips.

Despite these difficulties, some movies seem to have certain "codes" marking them as noir or noir-ish, though not all noirs have all the elements. For example, film scholars have argued vigorously for years whether Alfred Hitchcock's stylish *Vertigo* (1958) is film noir. Commonly found in true noir are dark themes dealing with the underbelly of human society and human motivations, bottom-rung criminal activity, the *femme fatale* character who inevitably brings about the destruction of a naïve male character, and laid-back but very tough and cynical ("hardboiled") male leads who are detectives, private investigators, killers, or sometimes just wrongly-accused everyday Joes. The setting can vary, but the common location is urban—sometimes New York but very often Los Angeles during the foggy, rainy season of late winter. Plots are often simple on the surface yet feature twists and double-crosses as they progress. (*The Big Sleep* is famously impossible to follow. Just about all we know at the end is that Bogey and Bacall get together.) Characters in noir are almost never what they at first appear to be. By the end of a noir movie, it appears that no one can be trusted, though many noirs feature a single "golden character" or person of untouchable virtue, often a nubile young woman. Additionally, these films were among the first to feature a "hero" who might be called an "anti-hero"—a likeable but deeply flawed character sometimes no better than the actual "bad guy" being pursued. Longtime film tradition, as well as various censorship regulations, had generally required the bad guy to be all bad and the hero to be all good—he might have an internal struggle with temptation, but in essence the hero had to be far better morally than the bad guy. Female characters especially were to be of sterling moral character.

As anyone who has watched a lot of movies made between the 1930s and the present knows, many movies after the 1960s stir up these moral categories considerably; this is due in large part to the influence of the "dark films" produced between 1940 and the late 1950s. Perhaps the greatest single trait, even overriding the strong visual elements most people use to identify noir, is the already mentioned quality of moral ambiguity. This is not to say that there is no right or wrong in noir; on the contrary, "right and wrong" is the engine that drives noir, as it does all film, and I would say, all narrative art. I like to think of the strong noir visual element of black-and-white cinematography, with its sharp edges and deep contrasts, as a kind of visual metaphor for the tone of these gritty films; certainly the cinematographers often made that connection. But it is this very dependence upon categories of black and white, right and wrong, as represented in a very human art form that blurs the clarity of the distinction. For it is first in film noir that audiences can begin to question the true nature of a "good guy" and, more significantly, to notice themselves rooting for a "bad guy."

Noir generally has a distinct "look" or "*mise-en-scene*"—the overall visual appearance of a film's "world." Classic noir from the 1940s and 1950s is black and white, and is marked by strongly contrasting areas of light and dark, brightness and shadow. Use of powerful lighting from a single source provides sharp edges, strong silhouettes, and a powerful sense of either motion or stillness depending on whether a character is moving or not: noir is loaded with scenes of motionless characters waiting, watching, spying, or lying in wait. Much of the rest of the time they are chasing or being chased. Sometimes the noir screen has barely visible, unlit figures on an all-black ground; newer more sensitive film stocks and better lenses during the 1940s allowed experimentation with daringly low light levels, giving just the slightest hint to the viewer of what was taking place and making you feel as if you were right there. This gritty realism provided a claustrophobic and tense feel that audiences loved. Classic noir shots include dark interiors of cheap hotel rooms with flashing neon signs blinking through venetian blinds; deep shots looking down from high-rise building cornices as rain falls past the camera into space and soaks nefarious activities taking place below; and nerve-wracking stalk-and-chase scenes in foggy alleys and wharf areas.[1] Noir features lots of standard "hard-boiled" props: curls of smoke from cigarettes, tumblers of liquor, loud revolvers, large fast cars, women in black pumps and stockings, men in fedoras and trench coats, and plenty of violence and snappy dialogue to string it all together. Apparently the only reason these characters don't die of lung cancer or liver failure is because they are generally shot before the excessive alcohol and tobacco kills them! By today's standards the violence is quite tame (no explosions of blood, no bullet holes, no mangled bodies), but in the heyday of noir it was extreme. The dialogue is slyly loaded with sexual double entendres, not unlike Blues lyrics of the same period. In other words, not many of the main characters in noir regularly attend a good Baptist church.

Another common signature in many classic noirs is the *femme fatale* figure, or "deadly woman." She is always ethereally beautiful, charming and persuasive, and seductive. The male lead finds her irresistible—and so do many male viewers. She often comes across initially as naïve, weak, needy, helpless, and perhaps even childlike. As the plot develops, the initially naïve male lead—by now hopelessly in love and deeply entangled—finds himself bested by her superior wit and cunning. She plans only his destruction; he is a means to an end for her; and, if he would just look closely enough, he would see that she has a red hourglass on her belly, so to speak—she mates and she kills. These *femme fatale* roles were considered among the juiciest available for Hollywood's leading ladies, and they were fiercely sought after. Many actresses made their names with just a single such role, while others crowned their long careers playing the kissing killer in high heels.

The "deadly woman" is an ancient archetypal figure, traceable through various cultural incarnations through film, literature, and visual art all the way back to the ultimate *femme fatale*: Eve. "So when the woman saw that the tree was good for food, and that it was a delight to the eyes, and that the tree was to be desired to make one wise, she took of its fruit and ate, and she also gave some to her husband who was with her, and he ate. Then the eyes of both were opened, and they knew that they were naked . . ." (Gen. 3:6–7). Of course, viewing Eve as a classic *femme fatale* is a fallen misreading of both Eve and the fall itself.[2] It reads the effects back into the cause, while denying that this is what is being done. The strong misogynistic tendency to blame the feminine half of humanity as the source of male pain and destruction has taken many forms, and in some cultures women are still considered less than fully human. We see shades of the *femme fatale* figure in Delilah, Salome, Bathsheba, Helen of Troy, Circe, Morgan le Fay in the medieval Arthurian cycles, and in a great many fables, poems, novels, paintings, and operas. She is the origin of the classic "vamp" figure, and sometimes comes as an actual vampire.[3] In film history there have been and continue to be many variations on the deadly woman character, but the figure really hits her heights (or rather, depths) in classic noir. Essentially, she plays the man for a fool as a prelude to his destruction. She always has a hidden purpose or goal, and it is not in the man's best interest. Of course, we find her throughout the book of Proverbs (except, that is, in chap. 31!):

> For the lips of a forbidden woman drip honey,
>   and her speech is smoother than oil,
> but in the end she is bitter as wormwood,
>   sharp as a two-edged sword.
> Her feet go down to death;
>   her steps follow the path to Sheol;
> she does not ponder the path of life;
>   her ways wander, and she does not know it. (Prov. 5:3–6)

> For at the window of my house
>   I have looked out through my lattice,
> and I have seen among the simple,
>   I have perceived among the youths,
>   a young man lacking sense,

passing along the street near her corner,
   taking the road to her house
in the twilight, in the evening,
   at the time of night and darkness. (Prov.7:6–9)

With much seductive speech she persuades him;
   with her smooth talk she compels him.
All at once he follows her,
   as an ox goes to the slaughter,
or as a stag is caught fast
   till an arrow pierces its liver;
as a bird rushes into a snare;
   he does not know that it will cost him his life. (Prov. 7:21–23)

These classic warnings of a father to his son are practically the basis for many noir plots.[4] Solomon would say "run from the *femme fatale* and go find Mary Hatch in Bedford Falls and have yourself a wonderful life!" In direct opposition to the classic happy modest housewife of post-war America, the smiling Betty Crocker image, these glamorous, exciting, sexy, and dangerous women are like an irresistible attraction to a deadly force.[5] Flirting with them is like playing Russian roulette without an empty chamber. Men are all like Odysseus; they want to hear the singing of the Sirens, though they know this will cause their boats to crash upon the rocks. Well before the rise of modern feminism in the 1960s and 1970s, these strong but negative female characters worked in American film storytelling like deliberate reversals of Shakespeare's strong female heroines—they are utterly unlike Viola, or Beatrice, or Portia, or Rosalind, who are all brilliant, attractive, and good.[6] The "fatal women" of noir are brilliant and terribly attractive to men—*but they are not good*. They may *look* like Juliet. But they are all Lady Macbeth.

Noir and American Culture

Film noir has its origins in the pulp fiction (not the 1994 movie!) of the 1930s and 1940s. These were fast paced fictional works, mostly novels and magazine serials, with tales of cops, detectives, spies, dangerous women, gory violence, and brazen sexuality. Dashiell Hammett, James M. Cain, and Raymond Chandler form the major triad of "pulp" writers who both provided material and influenced content and mood. Many pulp writers also wrote screenplays. The cheap, pulpy paper these books and magazines were printed on supplied the name of the genre, and the sketchy characters and nefarious activities transferred easily to the screen. Bad guys are easy to portray. It comes naturally.

It is important, and theologically interesting, to consider noir in its historical context. Noir begins right at the end of the 1930s and first years of the 1940s. Its heyday was from about 1944 to 1960. In other words, we're talking about World War II and its aftermath. During this period of recovery from the Great Depression, American middle-class consumerism was born. More people had more money and more free time than ever before in human history. There was a mass exodus from claustrophobic urban dwellings and drought-stricken Midwestern farmland to expansive, user-friendly, bright, safe suburban areas. For many Americans this was like leaving a black-and-white Kansas for a colorful Oz. Labor-saving home appliances made the homemaker's life easier; automobiles made commuter life and family vacations much easier; radio, television, and inexpensive movie theaters brought information and entertainment in a constant audial and visual stream to every man, woman, and child in the United States. Post-World War II America was in many ways the epitome of the golden American Dream. So why was the dark, gritty, cynical world of film noir so powerful and pervasive at the movies? If everyone was so happy, why were some very popular movies so dark?

Any study of culture always brings up the question, does culture drive worldview or does worldview drive culture? What comes first, the movie or the *zeitgeist*? In other words, did these films from the 1940s and 1950s provide a picture of the way people in general looked at life, or did they in fact create a mood of darkness and cynicism? Or both? Surely, there were plenty of happy, lighthearted films produced in the same period, but rarely in film history do we see such a dark and troubled mode or genre as film noir. It is well established that the way America viewed itself in the postwar years was troublesome. For example, racism was widespread, organized religion was beginning to stagger under its own weight, and the possibility of geographic expansionism for the United States was essentially over. Did some of this malaise find its way into the dark films of the period?

After World War II, America saw massive economic growth, broad stability, and the rise of middle-class American life with all its cash flow, conveniences, and bright futures. Why such very dark entertainments? For example, we can compare the classic "Ozzy and Harriet" view of the happy American housewife, wearing her apron and low heels all day long while making homemade food for her hardworking husband, with the classic noir *femme fatale*, who is nothing but a seductress with manipulation and destruction on her mind. The former does not pack a pistol, and the latter does not bake cookies. Yet each vision calls up the image of its opposite. There may be here a cultural attempt to contain and control our knowledge of humanity's darkness in the form of such deadly female characters. Perhaps the bright and cheery outside, the "real world" of conventional American womanhood, could be a façade for an interior of self-absorption and corruption—not just of females, but all Americans, of America itself. We manage this always-suppressed knowledge by turning it into entertainment, giving the devil/woman incarnation as evil screen temptress just enough room to titillate while keeping a safe distance from her. The male protagonists, of course, are not so wise.

Scarlet Street (1946) directed by Fritz Lang is typical of the genre in many ways and encapsulates much of what I have just said. It is highly entertaining but extremely dark and ends up being downright uncomfortable near the end. Indeed, there's really no such thing as a "feel-good noir." That would be like a roller coaster without the first big hill or an opera without a spectacular scene with all the characters singing together. Edward G. Robinson plays Chris Cross, a milquetoast bank cashier who is married to a shrewish nightmare of a wife. Chris always wanted to be a painter but now must be satisfied with painting in his apartment bathroom on Sundays, under constant threat from his wife that she is going throw out all his "junk." Proverbs 21:19 comes to mind: "It is better to live in a corner of the housetop than in a house shared with a quarrelsome wife." Chris wears a frilly apron while he does the dishes, and his wife heaves insults at him. Typical of a man unhappy at home, Chris becomes entangled with Kitty, a beautiful young "working woman," not even realizing that she is a prostitute.

Analysis

She mistakenly assumes he is a famous and wealthy painter and that she can milk him for loads of cash. She manages to set herself (and her boyfriend/pimp) up in a fancy love-nest that Chris also now uses as his Sunday studio; Kitty and her boyfriend begin selling Chris's paintings without his knowledge and finance their life with the cash. The cutting-edge modernist style of Chris's work catches the eye of a major critic who shows up looking for the artist—and Kitty claims credit as the painter. This scheme works for quite some time as the love-smitten Chris is too blind to see what's really going on. At the same time, Chris hatches a plot to escape from his nasty wife. When Chris shows up and asks Kitty to marry him, she turns cruel and mocking, tells him the truth about everything, and calls him an ugly fool. Chris brutally murders her with an ice pick in a zombie-like fit. Kitty's boyfriend is convicted of Chris's crime and gets the death penalty, and Chris slowly loses his mind due to both guilt and his imagining Kitty and her lover together in eternity. This is not Hallmark Hall of Fame material. The one word you will not find in the promotional materials is "heartwarming."

The final sequence is painful to watch, as we see the aftermath of the *femme fatale's* destructive power in Chris's ruined life and tormented conscience. After the execution of the pleading boyfriend, several reporters recognize Chris on a train. One shares with Chris his theory about crime and punishment: "No one escapes punishment. I figure we all have a little courtroom, right in here [he points to his heart]. Judge, jury, and executioner." Chris is feeling very uncomfortable at this point, but the reporter does not notice. "The problem just moves in here where it can never get out. Right here in solitary. So what? So you go right on punishing yourself. You can't get away with it. Never. . . . I'd rather have the judge give me the works than do it to myself." This rather hokey and overly didactic little speech from a minor character works in the film because we have all experienced it ourselves. Carrying a burden of guilt is miserable, and all of us have felt the ironic sense of relief when we finally get caught, even though we don't particularly like that either.

This discourse on inescapable punishment jumpstarts the painful work of the conscience in Chris, and he moves from mild guilt to despair, to attempting suicide, and to a final madness. In the last scene

176

he wanders the city aimlessly only to see a wealthy woman buying one of his paintings at a gallery. The framed work is titled "Self-Portrait"; it is a painting of Kitty, done by Chris in the studio/love-nest and later sold by Kitty to raise cash for wild living. The massive irony of the entire story is palpable in this single moment as Chris's stunned eyes stare at the haunting image he has made of his own *femme fatale*, his deadly woman—*whom he has murdered for being unfaithful to him while he was being unfaithful to his wife*. The buyer and the dealer, not knowing the actual painter is right there, agree on one thing: this painting was "Kitty's" greatest masterpiece. Chris is hypnotized by the dead Kitty's painted eyes. Her image—made by him—rules supreme, and he cannot escape its power. Her powerful female eyes—painted by Chris—now transfix Chris once again. She controls him even from the grave. And we are just as transfixed as Chris by the images before us. Rarely in film do we see such Ecclesiastes-style irony dripping so thickly from the very screen.

The noir approach does not always feature detectives, cops, and gangsters, or even tangled love romances. In *Mildred Pierce* (1945), a "domestic" noir, Joan Crawford plays a single mother who works herself to death and spoils her daughter, Veda, so badly that Veda becomes an ungrateful monster. In this case, the daughter of a female protagonist becomes the *femme fatale*, though in a highly unexpected way. Many classic noir elements are present, including a flashback story structure, a voice-over narrative by the now-ruined protagonist, perverse plot twists, and frank handling of taboo subjects. Mildred eventually walks in on a love tryst between her daughter and her own second husband, Monty, who says "Oh . . . we weren't expecting you Mildred . . . obviously."

The Postman Always Rings Twice (1946), based on a novel by James M. Cain, is, like *Mildred Pierce* and *Scarlet Street*, a domestic noir. This makes the story all the more chilling; we don't have gangsters and killers but ordinary folk who become entangled in a series of terrible decisions bringing about a fatalistic and destructive conclusion. Frank Chambers (John Garfield) stops in at a rural diner for a meal and meets and falls in love with Cora Smith (Lana Turner), the wife of the owner. Frank and Cora are bored with life and enter into a torrid affair, hatching a plan to murder the husband, Nick, who is considerably older than Cora. The plot spirals down into a maelstrom of disastrous consequences and bizarre twists. Turner's powerful embodiment of Cora is among her finest performances. Even this domestic noir serves up a typically juicy (and nasty) brew: lust, adultery, conspiracy, murder, lies, and cover-ups. And more death at the end, of course, with some pretty acerbic poetic justice: Cora is tried alone for the murder, manages to get off on probation, then dies in a car accident—for which Frank is put on trial for murder and executed. The metaphoric title suggests that justice always comes around, just like the postman who will ring for you again if you don't open the door for him the first time.

But it is Orson Welles's *Touch of Evil* (1958) that really plumbs the depths of human depravity without pulling punches. Again, it is simultaneously disturbing and entertaining. Noir this dark is like a *femme fatale* itself: it draws in the viewer's gaze irresistibly even as it has little more than unpleasantness in store for us. It is one of the most theologically accurate films ever made as far as man's nature is concerned—and Welles is surely no theologian. But he knows how people act and is unafraid to portray diabolical human activity for what it is, and this movie, written, directed, and starring Welles, is no small commentary on the subject. It is surely one of the darkest masterpieces of film ever made. I find several portions of this movie almost too difficult to sit through when I screen it for film students. The image of evil here is far more than just a touch. Welles's portrayal of police Captain Hank Quinlan is nothing short of revolting. He is a mountain of a man who hobbles from place to place, lying, manipulating, planting evidence, degrading and terrorizing others, and basically making himself one of the least sympathetic characters in noir history—or film history as a whole. He makes Darth Vader look like Ebenezer Scrooge on Christmas morning.

In one sequence, Quinlan has the wife of his nemesis (good-guy Mexican cop Miguel Vargas, played by a hilariously overly-tanned Charlton Heston) kidnapped. She is stashed away, forcibly addicted to heroin, and framed for murder. Quinlan lures a Mexican crime boss to her room and in a scene of surreal horror yet absolute clarity, strangles the man quite literally on top of Mrs. Vargas's writhing semiconscious body. There are few scenes that so powerfully evoke sinful human nature in all of Hollywood history. There is no blood, no sex, no nudity, no cursing. Just a terrifying series of images that, more than anything else, evoke the scene of Cain rising up against his brother Abel. It hits a little too close to home. When I screen this film for a class, students almost always call it the most unpleasant moment of the semester (this is before the final exam is given, of course). Justice eventually catches up to Quinlan; but as he admits (moments before his death) that he has in fact planted evidence on many cases, he insists that all of the "perpetrators" were guilty.

> "How many did you frame?"
> "Nobody that wasn't guilty.
> "Guilty.
> "*Guilty.*
> "Every last one of 'em. Guilty."

This kind of film art crosses the line of entertainment and enters into the world of philosophy. It is an anthropological statement—a statement about *man*. It is a theological statement. It is as rich as a Vermeer painting, an opera by Wagner, or a Greek tragedy by Aeschylus or Euripides. Hank Quinlan and Chris Cross would find themselves right at home with Oedipus or Medea. And while these lines about universal guilt come from the lips of the vilest character in *Touch of Evil*, most viewers will be disconcerted to recognize it as fundamentally true. As William Munny says with the sour gravel of guilt in his mouth in *Unforgiven*, "We all got it coming, kid."

The justice of the diegetic world of the film requires that Quinlan pay for his crimes, and so he does. But this does not really bring justice to a world where innocent men are framed by a monstrous man with power. There is little satisfaction as Quinlan gets what's coming to him, either for Vargas or the viewer. It leaves us perhaps exhilarated, yet lacking deep satisfaction. Why, then, do humans produce such screen unpleasantness? Why call it art, or culture, or what have you, and why pay money to see it unfold on the magical screen? Similarly, how can people bear to watch *Schindler's List* or *The Exorcist*? Both are brilliant films that deal with evil in the most disturbing fashion imaginable, yet neither are movies you pop in when you want to be entertained. Despite this, film noir, which foregrounds the nastiness of humanity, remained not only marketable, but popular and widely imitated even after its golden era.

Roman Polanski's *Chinatown*, like many neo-noirs of the 1970s and 1980s, is similarly dark and brooding—and extremely violent.[7] With the official censorship of the Hays Office essentially gone, movies became much more violent as well as sexually explicit. *Chinatown* is probably the greatest masterpiece of neo-noir, reviving the genre in the mid-seventies and receiving eleven Academy Award nominations. Produced in the early 1970s, it is set in 1930s Los Angeles, and thus draws the audience into the classic noir setting. In a fascinating reversal of a common noir element, Fay Dunaway's character "Evelyn Mulwray" is not only *not* a *femme fatale*, she is the least selfish person in the cast. Even more recent noir-ish films, such as the Coen brothers' crime thriller *Blood Simple* (1984), their gangster homage *Miller's Crossing* (1990), and the brilliant black comedy *Fargo*, all have genealogies traceable to the classic noir era. A great many viewers today do not like to watch "old black-and-white movies," assuming they are boring, corny, shallow, or too tame. But when they take the time to look at some of the old classics after becoming familiar with the contemporary films descended from them, they often sense the déjà-vu of meeting a close cousin for the first time. When Jerry Lundegaard's little plot to have his wife kidnapped so he can raise some cash goes terribly wrong in *Fargo*, he wakes up not in the typical Fargo whiteout, but in the dark, dark world of the dark film—film noir.

Billy Wilder and the Blackness of Darkness

Let's look now in some depth at two of the greatest noirs ever made. Both were directed by the insuperably brilliant Billy Wilder: *Double Indemnity* and *Sunset Boulevard*. The two movies have a very different feel. The first is a gritty, rather cheesy straightforward crime/con-game drama wrapped in a soap opera romance. The second is slick, highly polished, and completely "over the top": it is set in Hollywood, and offers a deeply cynical yet playful look at the depths of depravity implicated in the pursuit of fame, whether that fame has been long lost or is being pursued for the first time. Both movies feature the classic noir elements of a fatalistic worldview with a doomed hero narrating the story of his own demise after the fact via flashback.

Both male leads offer an acerbic, cynical, witty voice-over commentary on his own naiveté and foolishness and lack of perception and self-control. Both movies open with the male protagonist either dead or dying. Now that it's all over—yet before it has begun—he's gained a little wisdom and wants to share it with us, the audience. The tone of the classic noir voice-over is not at all unlike that of Solomon in the Old Testament book of Ecclesiastes: the world is a crazy place, and the only thing about it that is predictable is that not much makes sense. There is no justice, no fairness, and not much in the way of hope. You stumble through a world you cannot understand, and then you stumble into a grave. Solomon's tone can be described in a single word: cynical.

Double Indemnity stars Fred MacMurray, Barbara Stanwyck, and Edward G. Robinson in three unforgettable, tightly interwoven roles. Wilder directed the film with his typical wit and eye for character detail. The plot is quite simple: an insurance salesman flirts brazenly with a client's classy yet sleazy wife. They fall in love and hatch a perfect plan to heavily insure—then murder—her obnoxious husband. The murder goes off without a hitch. Walter Neff (MacMurray) does the deed as the camera pans off ever so slightly to the icy face of nearby Phyllis Dietrichson (Stanwyck), who just barely manages to conceal a smile as her husband struggles for his life just inches away. The new couple is able to make it look like a rare kind of train accident, which carries a double payment from the insurance policy Neff wrote. But just as the insurance executives, particularly Barton Keyes (Robinson), begin to suspect Phyllis and then Neff, the cocky, gullible insurance salesman slowly learns that Phyllis has done this sort of thing before. Neff realizes he is only a fly in the web of a classic *femme fatale*.

How the tale is told is the key noir factor here. In the opening sequence Neff stumbles into the high-rise building in Los Angeles where his insurance company is based. He sits at his desk well after hours and turns on his Dictaphone. The tale unfolds as a long flashback where Neff's present-day voice offers wry commentary on the events of the past weeks. At the end of the movie, the flashback ends, and Neff is discovered in his office by his supervisor and friend Keyes, who has overheard the last moments of the recorded confession and now knows that Neff is the guilty party he has been searching for.

The movie works so well because of its classic film noir voice-over narration. In many films (such as *Sunset Boulevard*) a noir protagonist tells the story to us as a dead or dying man; Neff, it turns out, has a serious gunshot wound, and we do not know until near the end of the film who fired the shot. Our understanding of Phyllis's true nature is revealed slowly by Neff's recounting of what led up to the shooting. The entire tone of the film is driven by his wry, cynical retelling of how he ends up where he does. The moral: you don't know anything until you're dead. (Again, this sounds much like Solomon—by the time you've figured out how it all works, it is too late.) Like a fly buzzing calmly into a black widow's web, Neff flirts his way into a married woman's life, only to find out that *she* was manipulating *him* from the first moment they met. He was the marionette and she the puppet master; she has outsmarted him, out-planned him, and outwitted him at every turn. She is so bad that she makes even Neff look good!

After all the lying, adultery, murder, scheming, and double-crosses, the climactic scene comes. Walter has decided to kill Phyllis, and Phyllis has decided to kill Walter. She is dressed in a nightgown, waiting comfortably in an overstuffed chair in her living room. The lights are off, and there are horizontal stripes of light and shadow on the walls from the venetian blinds and the streetlights. She has a gun under her seat. The black widow is in her lair, ready to draw in the naïve male and kill him once and for all. Walter enters, playing it very cool. He is no more the gullible salesman. In the midst of this very dark and disturbing confrontation—after wounding Walter with one shot, but then finding herself unable to complete the task—Phyllis makes a shocking exclamation. Walter asks her why she doesn't shoot him again, why no fatal bullet? He has now taken the gun from her limp and passive hands. "Don't tell me it's because you've been in love with me all this time?" Neff asks her, as a very low, creepy cello note is played on the soundtrack. "No. I never loved you, Walter. Not you, or anybody else. I'm rotten to the heart. I used you, just as you said. That's all you ever meant to me—until a minute ago, when I couldn't fire that second shot. I didn't think anything like that could ever happen to me." Walter now has the sobbing black widow in his embrace, and he looks into her eyes as tears of love stream down her cheeks. "Sorry, baby, I'm not buying." Her eyes go wide with understanding.

"Goodbye, baby," he says with a sardonic smile as he looks into her eyes, almost lovingly.

Of course, he shoots her.

Most viewers find this a deeply satisfying moment. I have had students (in an evangelical Christian college, no less) cheer quite loudly at this point. Phyllis is an utterly unsympathetic character. There is nothing to like about her. That people considered Stanwyck one of the great screen beauties of her time makes this characterization even harder to accept. She is the gorgeous destroyer, irresistible even when you know it will kill you. Your only hope is to kill her first. In some ways, she is not a *femme fatale* at all; she is sin personified. And the game is kill or be killed.

In the concluding scene, we see Walter bleeding (and probably dying) after his confession; if he survives, he knows it will only be to go to the gas chamber. The final moments of friendship between Barton Keyes and Walter Neff—where Keyes lights a final cigarette for the doomed man, reversing the pattern established throughout their earlier scenes together—are the only truly tender moments in the whole film. Everything else is hard-edged cynicism. But Neff's final words to his friend, despite being delivered in male-friendship mock-humor, are the greatest words a person can ever utter: "I love you too." The entire tone of the film is reversed in just four syllables. Only here is the veil of cynicism pulled back to show us something real and worth having. Neff tells Keyes he was able to fool him because he was "right across the desk" from him. Keyes responds gently, "Closer than that, Walter," whereupon Neff speaks his final four words, words laden with the weight of a redemption he will never find. As Keyes is deceivable because of his love for his friend Neff, so Neff is deceivable because of his love for Phyllis. And who is Phyllis deceived by? Only herself, and only up to her last moments. She admits she is rotten to the heart and never loved anyone until after she shot Walter. At least . . . that's what she *says*.

How many people ever admit to themselves, much less anyone else, that they are rotten to the heart? How are we to take Phyllis's lines? I think the tone of the film strongly controls how the audience responds to her. The movie teaches us how to watch the movie. In all the years of teaching this film I've never had a single student cry out for Neff to spare her now that she has had a change of heart. Because she could be telling the truth, *or* she could once again be manipulating! She may not even be able to tell the difference herself; years of selfish manipulation make it impossible to know your own heart accurately—if you ever could to begin with. If we follow the tone of the film and do the "cynical reading" (the Neff interpretation) of Phyllis's final words, then we have become just like her and Neff and all the other cynical characters who populate the world of noir. Of course, if we do the "romantic reading" of her speech, and don't shoot her, and run off with her and the insurance money, she'll probably just poison us next week.

How do you choose between cynicism (which is an accurate view of human beings) and love (which is dangerous, but commanded by God)? For if ever there were two opposing forces—two ways of looking at the world—they would be love and cynicism. The noir-ish world of Solomon in Ecclesiastes and the Solomonic world of noir: these intersections are the epicenter of moral ambiguity.

In many ways, the cynical edge of film noir reaches its most extreme form in Wilder's second great noir masterpiece, *Sunset Boulevard*. It is quite simply the best movie made about movies—ever. It is also the most cutting self-critique Hollywood insiders have ever mounted against themselves, and it also happens to be wildly entertaining. Some Hollywood types were so insulted that they walked out of the film's initial screenings, most famously Louis B. Mayer, founder of MGM, who publicly chewed out Wilder. Truth hurts—especially when your "fiction" shows just how blurred the line between fiction and reality can become for many of those who produce the Hollywood fictions the world watches so eagerly. There has always been a question about the relationship between art and reality. Thinkers have wrestled for centuries with whether art imitates life or life imitates art, whether cultural objects simply reflect the cultures in which they exist or whether they actively form those cultures. One thing is for sure: Wilder's portrait of Hollywood culture is not very flattering.

This is one of the darkest films ever produced in Hollywood, undoubtedly because Hollywood is the subject, and *Hollywood is people*. Self-portraits are always the strangest form of art. They always tell the truth even while they lie. The title of the film comes from the famous street winding through the northern Los Angeles hills and down to the Pacific Ocean. The road is curvy, hilly, and very heavily used—in other words, it is dangerous. But the dangerous character in *Sunset Boulevard* is not the boulevard itself; it is Norma Desmond. She's terrifying, and yet pitiful. I'll never forget the first time I drove down this famous street, on the way to the research library at UCLA thirty minutes from my home. I was mortally afraid of blowing a tire and pulling into a driveway, and finding myself talking about faces and words and movies to an aging movie queen while she mourns her monkey.

This story about the film industry and what it can do to the human soul is absolutely blistering, even six decades after its release. It deals with the arts of screenwriting, directing, and acting; shows the costs and temptations of becoming famous and rich; delineates the manipulation by others and self so endemic to the artistic and business world that is Hollywood; brutally snickers at Hollywood wackiness; and calculates the cost of selling the soul for an image. Fame is shown for what it really is: the temporary acclamation of people who eventually turn on you and then laugh at you, pity you—or both. The message is simple: Hollywood kills.

The film opens with police and newsmen arriving at a huge, rotting old mansion on Sunset Boulevard. A dead man is floating face down in the pool; we realize that this dead man is the narrator who will tell the story about how he ended up like this. He tells us who he is and how the story began: out-of-work scriptwriter Joe Gillis (William Holden) is evading car repossession men when he turns desperately into Norma Desmond's driveway, thinking it an abandoned house. She mistakes him for an undertaker who has been hired to run a funeral for her pet chimpanzee. She then learns he is a screenwriter and is furious that a writer of movie words is in her home. Being a movie buff, Gillis recognizes her: "I know your face. You're Norma Desmond. You used to be in silent pictures. You used to be big." Norma's expression is priceless. At first she is smugly thrilled with the recognition of her face by a handsome young man. But when the compliment turns into an unwitting insult, she retorts, "I *am* big. It's the *pictures* that got small."

Norma Desmond (Gloria Swanson) had been the greatest silent screen star of them all, but her career faded away as sound movies replaced silents; this in fact was not uncommon in the early sound era. Now, decades later, she lives in her decaying mansion, attended only by her devoted and slightly sinister butler Max. She has hundreds of photographs of herself spread about in every room of her house, and she watches movies every night in her own home theater. The only movies she watches are her own. As Norma and Joe watch, she tells him these old movies didn't need "words . . . we had faces." She has immersed her consciousness in the visual image of her "celluloid self," as Gillis puts it later.

Norma hires Joe to do a rewrite of her "comeback picture"—a sappy script of her own devising where she will play Salome (a girl half her age) in a biblical epic to be directed by Cecil B. DeMille, who appears as himself in the film. The business arrangement leads to a live-in situation and before long a one-way romantic crush. Gillis can't make a clean exit because he is broke and desperate, and soon he is perfectly willing to essentially prostitute himself, even though Norma is, to say the least, simultaneously pathetic and repulsive.

She is so self-absorbed that it is difficult to watch, and we waver between pity and disgust. When Gillis tells her early on that he did not know she was planning a comeback, she flies into a rage: "I hate that word! It's a return! A return to the millions of people who have never forgiven me for deserting the screen!" Norma is convinced that legions of fans still love her; she receives fan mail every day, doesn't she? Gillis learns quickly never to cross this spoiled little child. Her tantrums are unmanageable.

The tough, masculine Gillis is rapidly emasculated by this bizarre *femme fatale*. "I didn't argue with her. You don't yell at a sleepwalker—he may fall and break his neck. That's it—she was still sleepwalking along the giddy heights of a lost career—plain crazy when it came to that one subject: her celluloid self, the great Norma Desmond. How could she breathe in that house, so crowded with Norma Desmonds?" As William Holden's character speaks these lines in voice-over narration, the camera pans and tracks slowly through the house showing us how virtually every square inch of space is littered with photographs of the young star in her heyday. She has created a memory-museum-mausoleum dedicated to her image, and she lives inside of it as the sole inhabitant.

The crystal clear cultural reference is to the ancient Greco-Roman myth of Narcissus.[8] Narcissus falls in love with his own reflection in a pond and pines away for love of the unreachable creature before him. He is so smitten he does not realize this object of affection is his own reflection. He eventually collapses from exhaustion, falls into the reflective water, and drowns, thus illustrating the dangers of self-love. Modern-day psychiatry would diagnose Norma (and Narcissus) with "narcissistic personality disorder," which is what the Bible calls sinful self-absorption. Whatever you call it, it is always destructive. The happiest people in the world are those who think about others and do things for them. Those who think of themselves and care only for their own needs and desires are the unhappiest. There are no exceptions.

Norma Desmond has been able to take this to a technological extreme with her "celluloid self," which has been carefully produced, reproduced, preserved, and repeated over and over again in her sight. She doesn't need a pond in which to see herself. Her life is lived inside a gigantic multidimensional technological mirror called "film" that reflects her image back to her from every direction. She is, ironically, perhaps one of the most perfect pictures of human sinfulness ever captured on film—and the film images of herself that form the object of her affection also engender her destruction.

In the final sequence (so brilliantly played that it simultaneously evokes horror and pity, exactly like classical Greek tragedy) Norma tells Joe Gillis that *he* cannot possibly leave *her*—she is a movie star! "I'm the greatest star of them all," she hisses. "Goodbye, Norma," Joe responds as he walks out, aiming his steps toward the real world outside. Alone, she whispers to herself, "No one ever leaves a star. That makes one a star." He cannot be allowed to walk away. Her gaze is fixed so solidly on her own image of herself that she has almost no grasp on present reality at all. She does not know, and has to be told, that the fan letters she receives are fakes sent by Max to keep her heart from breaking. Paramount and DeMille do not want to shoot her Salome movie at all. She has completely misunderstood the situation, believing only what she wants to believe. No one even knows who she is anymore, except a few old guys at the studio. Nor does she know herself in any meaningful sense. The human "Norma Desmond" has evaporated and been replaced by a celluloid image of "Norma Desmond" moving at twenty-four frames per second. For her, *meaning is movies*. There is nothing else.

As Joe walks out of the house, she shoots and kills him, closing the narrative loop and bringing us back to the opening scene of a dead man in a pool telling the story of how he came to be dead and in the pool. Surely Wilder must have enjoyed the ironic gender reversal of his killers and victims in this, his second major noir. This time, when the cynical man "isn't buying," the *femme fatale* still holds the gun.

The dead Joe Gillis, bobbing in the water with policemen all around, tells us with bitter cynicism in his voice that now he finally has the pool he always wanted. The view of him from underwater shows his absolutely blank dead face staring down into the clear and endless depths. (Significantly, the scene was not shot with an underwater camera, but by lowering a large mirror into the pool and filming from the surface in order to see Gillis's reflection.) Now Gillis himself is Narcissus, condensing the storyline of the original myth, gazing *and* dead at the same time, floating peacefully in that great Los Angeles status symbol—the private pool. He wanted the kind of fame that Norma had and lost; both were prostitutes with different wares on sale. Writers of spoken words had cost her the fame of her face. Norma Desmond, after shooting Gillis the screenwriter, stands in shock, stares into space, and says, "The stars are ageless, aren't they?" It is harder to imagine a creepier scene. But more is yet to come. Wilder will shake us until the last drop of gall is wrung from our souls. He works like a modern-day Sophocles, Aeschylus, or Euripides piling horror on horror until we stagger to the final cathartic release.

As the police arrive, Norma is upstairs doing her makeup. She's finally cracking up. She thinks she is about to act in a scene in a DeMille movie that will never be. She hears that the cameras are ready, but does not understand that the cameras in question belong to newsreel men who will record her swan song as she is arrested and carried away. She powders her face and comes to the top of the staircase. Max the butler—who had been one of her several husbands as well as the movie director who had discovered her years before—reassumes the directorial role and tells her to come down the stairs, like a princess in a palace, for her final scene. He cries out "action," and that's all Norma needs to hear. She begins to descend as Gillis's voice-over narration comments grimly: "Life, which can be strangely merciful, had taken pity on Norma Desmond. The dream she had clung to so desperately had enfolded her." Norma makes her dramatic, wildly overacted descent, greedily devouring what she thinks is admiration from the eyes of the crowd that has actually gathered only to watch her arrest. For her, reality is fast plunging into the abyss. Pity and horror—again, a throwback to Greek tragedy—is all the audience can see in the faces gazing at her. And as Norma reaches the bottom of the staircase, Wilder unleashes the final horror, one truly Greek in its tragic force.

The aging silent era diva is convinced the cameras are filming her in a new starring role that will revive her career. In her mind, the fantasy of film has subsumed the pain of reality—she is again young, beautiful, and beloved by millions. And now *she* has a speaking role. Now *she* is Narcissus. The camera, the film inside of it, and the screen upon which her image is projected are together the gazing pond in which she has drowned like mad Ophelia in *Hamlet*. In her soul, film has entirely supplanted reality and her very being—and she croaks out her final mad speech: "You don't know how much I've missed all of you. And I promise you I'll never desert you again, because after *Salome* we'll make another picture, and another, and another. You see, this is my life. It always will be. *There's nothing else—just us and the cameras.*" And here, in the most bloodcurdling moment in cinematic history, Norma looks directly into the camera, into our eyes, breaking the "fourth wall" and addressing the theater audience directly by saying, "*and those wonderful people out there in the dark.*" The audience is now implicated fully in her narcissistic self-destruction—and it is a terrifying moment, as her imagined audience merges with Wilder's actual audience, and as *we see ourselves as Norma/Narcissus* in the gazing pond of the screen before us. Norma is no longer imagining her own celluloid immortality, she is living it. The image has replaced, with absolute finality, the reality. Joe Gillis tried to tell her "the audience left twenty years ago," but she no longer can hear, because she is her own audience. And she is, of course, a Silent Queen. Yet Norma's infamous closing line, as she glides comically yet menacingly toward the camera and goes out of focus, says it all: "All right Mr. DeMille, I'm ready for my close-up."

It is difficult to imagine a film more cynical, or more accurate, in its view of humanity and human cultural production. The characters, Norma especially, can be viewed as caricatures—gross exaggerations of what they would "really be." But then again, that is what fallen humans actually are: caricatures of what they were designed to be.

If "Hollywood kills" is the message of *Sunset Boulevard*, then we could say that Hollywood is the real *femme fatale*. She mates and she kills.

Cynics and Their Mirrors

Should Christians watch movies that portray human nature so starkly and so negatively? Perhaps we should. The truths about our own natures are suppressed in a great many works of narrative art, but not in film noir. I would go so far as to say that noir is as biblically accurate about human nature as Hollywood has ever gotten. While we may wish to believe we are good, somehow we do not find (and should not find) a steady dose of "people are basically good" films very appetizing. Hence the attraction of noir and similar movies.

But what about the heavy dose of cynicism that dominates the tone of noir? Is that a good thing to sit and soak in on a regular basis? I would say no. But I say this for the same reason that I would tell you not to restrict your reading of Scripture to the book of Ecclesiastes, even though it is my favorite part of the Old Testament. I once spent an entire year teaching through it—about fifty straight Sundays, an hour each week. I felt rushed. (I'm not sure the hearers felt like I did.) I believe, based on the content of chapter 12, that Solomon wrote the book in his old age after a lifetime of wise observation of human experience. His tone can be characterized in a single word: cynicism. There is apparently no justice, no fairness, no pattern, no hope in human life. To use the modern sense of his repeated refrain of "vanity, all is vanity," life is meaningless. The only possible response is cynicism—a detached, uncaring, disengaged, unbelieving view of the world. *There is nothing to believe in.* And according to Solomon, man finds himself in this aimless and random world and is filled with an overwhelming desire to understand it, *to interpret it*, to find meaning.

"And I applied my heart to seek and to search out by wisdom all that is done under heaven. It is an unhappy business that God has given to the children of man to be busy with. I have seen everything that is done under the sun, and behold, all is vanity and a striving after wind" (Eccles. 1:13–14). As I have said, this is Hollywood according to Solomon and vice versa: the noir world of Solomon in Ecclesiastes and the Solomonic world of noir. It is the epicenter of moral ambiguity, the actual nature of fallen human experience.

If you find yourself in a world you cannot make sense of, and you desperately desire some ultimate meaning or purpose, and you choose to reject belief in God, there is only one place you can end up: the role of the cynic, what David calls in Psalm 1:1 the "seat of scoffers." You don't believe in anything at all. Of course most of us aren't born this way. In fact the common pattern is for youthful idealism to give way to middle-aged resignation, and finally aged cynicism. Remember Louis B. Mayer, the head of MGM who walked out on *Sunset Boulevard*? The story goes that his dying words were "nothing matters."

But there is a problem with cynicism.

It is profoundly dissatisfying. *This is not because of what it is, but because of what it is not.* It is the opposite of love, which is nothing at all like cynicism:

> Love is patient and kind; love does not envy or boast; it is not arrogant or rude. It does not insist on its own way; it is not irritable or resentful; it does not rejoice at wrongdoing, but rejoices with the truth. Love bears all things, believes all things, hopes all things, endures all things.
>
> Love never ends. As for prophecies, they will pass away; as for tongues, they will cease; as for knowledge, it will pass away. For we know in part and we prophesy in part, but when the perfect comes, the partial will pass away. When I was a child, I spoke like a child, I thought like a child, I reasoned like a child. When I became a man, I gave up childish ways. For now we see in a mirror dimly, but then face to face. Now I know in part; then I shall know fully, even as I have been fully known.
>
> So now faith, hope, and love abide, these three; but the greatest of these is love. (1 Cor. 13:4–13)

Cynicism is the opposite of true biblical love. It is death to the spiritual life; it is as far from the spirit of Jesus Christ as you can get.

If he had looked at humanity with cynicism, what would have happened to us? There is one important difference that I have not yet mentioned between film noir and the book of Ecclesiastes. Film noir has no chapter 12. This is where Solomon brings God into the equation of the depressing, meaningless world of mere human observation. God's presence, and knowledge of his presence, *radically alters the meaning of everything—in fact it gives meaning where there was none*. "The end of the matter; all has been heard. Fear God and keep his commandments, for this is the whole duty of man. For God will bring every deed into judgment, with every secret thing, whether good or evil" (Eccles. 12:13–14).

Now, this is one mirror, dim as it may now be, that we can safely fall into.

The End of the Matter

Movies and Meaning, Memory and Man

MEMORY is a mirror.

It reflects the past forward to us. Memory is inextricably tied up with consciousness and with both knowledge and belief. You only know what you remember. The same can be said of belief. You can't believe anything you've forgotten.

Strangely enough, the earliest memory I can recall and place in the timeline of my life involves a motion picture. I distinctly recall a series of images—in crisp black and white—on our family television in an apartment in northern Virginia. I was perhaps four. On the screen *(all the world's a screen)* is a room in some kind of old house or castle. A large table is in the middle of the room, and a wild-eyed man is chasing a terrified woman around and around the table in a classic pursuit scene. It is not an amorous chase but a scary one. I have no further recollection of this scene (I don't even know what it is from), yet it is burned into my memory for some reason. It may be because it is the earliest example of a moving picture I ever saw as a self-conscious human being. I sometimes find myself wondering if I would recognize this scene if I were to see it again. Would I remember? *Would I believe my own memory?*

Photography, and motion picture photography especially, also functions like memories. Both capture and reflect. Memory is a kind of organic technology that allows us to travel elsewhere, specifically to the past. Or perhaps we should say the past travels to us. Either way we are not limited to the present. I want to think in this final chapter about how memory, film, and human consciousness can be seen through a theological worldview grounded in the ancient revelation of Scripture, for Scripture says much about memory.

The Bible teaches that man falls into grief *when he forgets God.* The Jews are admonished over and over to remember always the great works of God. The whole Old Testament is essentially a history of forgetting. (Christians of course also forget.) Jews were to teach their children the lesson of remembering above all else, and when they asked questions about why certain things were done and said and believed, they were taught to recall God's great work in history. In Exodus 12:24–27 Moses teaches the Israelites how to handle the natural curiosity of children who wonder about certain beliefs and practices, in this case Passover: "You shall observe this rite as a statute for you and for your sons forever. And when you come to the land that the LORD will give you, as he has promised, you shall keep this service. And when your children say to you, 'What do you mean by this service?' you shall say, 'It is the sacrifice of the LORD's Passover, for he passed over the houses of the people of Israel in Egypt, when he struck the Egyptians but spared our houses.' And the people bowed their heads and worshiped." People are naturally curious; they want to know what things mean and why things are believed and practiced. There is nothing wrong with this. The past must be brought to mind, brought to the present. This is the essential function of both history and doctrine in the Bible—to remind us of things that were done, and things that were said *in the past.* Memory of the past is as much a key to faith as is looking forward to the future.

Memory is crucial to theology (you have to remember a doctrine to believe it). It is central to faith (you can't trust someone you have forgotten about). This is why the Old Testament emphasizes the importance of Jewish remembrance of the Lord. Similarly the New Testament repeatedly enjoins Christians to learn (and by extension remember) the teachings and examples of Christ. You can't revere what you don't recall. *Don't forget.*

Suppression: Memories and Memory

I have built the argument of this book on a reading of Romans 1 that emphasizes the human suppression of the truth of God. It would be foolish to contend that every element of culture down to the finest degree is a result of this suppression, and I have endeavored to avoid that extreme. Nonetheless, I think a strong case can be made that many of the most prevalent, powerful, and regularly repeated currents in human cultural production have their roots at least to some extent in this suppression of truth. But now I wish to provide a clarification, a turn or nuance to the argument. In the largest sense, it isn't just content knowledge about God that is suppressed. Suppression involves much more than just content. *The knowledge we have of God according to Romans 1 is not simply a set of abstract concepts that can be differentiated from our being.* These truths about God and his world are built into us at the deepest possible level. They are bound intimately to us through a central part of our consciousness, through who and what we are. I am speaking here about memory.

Functionally, what is actually suppressed is *memory itself*, not just specific memories. We could say "memory" *is* "memories." Our in-built memory about God has informational content, of course, but what seems to have happened is that the very function of memory itself is suppressed. We didn't just forget "stuff" as a result of the fall: we *forgot remembering, period.* This is why mankind does not just forget the information about God that is built into us; our very nature as rememberers has changed radically. We are made for remembering—for memory of God—but our memory is broken. We become, in Paul's words from Romans 1, "fools." This does not mean we are not intelligent. It means we cannot connect the dots of the universe because we have forgotten the purpose of the universe. It is precisely memory about God, which is implanted by God, *that fallen humans cannot bear.* Hearing about him in the present life produces either rage, ridicule, or conversion (see Acts 2:37; 7:54). What may be known of God—some of it perceived by observation of nature, some of it revealed internally, some of it perhaps even grasped by faulty human reasoning—is cached in the human memory.[1] If it is retained there, we must deal with it. But if it is suppressed, "quarantined," we can ignore it, at least temporarily. In a sense then, memory is the organic and spiritual "technology" by which we *should* know God.

Because fallen man has made God his enemy, this knowledge, this memory of God, must be suppressed. Furthermore I think a case can be made that is it is not just knowledge of God but the *entire human function of memory* that is suppressed, even crippled. If we are to function as conscious beings, we must have memory. But the core of memory, its original and ultimate purpose, is the knowledge of God. When we hold this knowledge back, we also severely restrict the very purpose of memory. Think of memory as muscles in the throat: they are designed specifically to swallow food, prevent choking, and keep the airway open. If we decide to suppress their use for either food or air supply, the muscles themselves will slowly atrophy, weaken, and eventually die. Similarly, we tend not to use our memory to remember God, which is its main design purpose. As a consequence, we function far below our intellectual and spiritual capacity, because both capacities depend on memory. But as we begin to function as maturing, increasingly self-aware humans—forming our self-consciousness by building up our memory cache as we leave infancy and become children and then adults—we inevitably dredge up our suppressed memory of God.

This is why motion picture narratives that deal with memory are so fascinating to viewers, and why they are so important in a theological analysis of film art. Narrative film itself functions like a kind of memory. It is a record (albeit manufactured, manipulated, and constructed) of something other than the present. And, like a memory, it pushes itself into present consciousness and takes us somewhere else. The more effective the film, the more effective the "transport" to whatever place it is the movie is designed to take us. Pictures take us places, including the past and the world of imagination.

Photography is a kind of "memory technology." I have seen photos of relatives and ancestors whom I have never met; I have a visual link to my own origins. "Motion photography" is even stranger. It copies reality with incredible precision and is uncanny in its effects on us. I have copies of old Super 8 family movies from my childhood, now stored on video. It is an otherworldly experience to watch myself interact with my parents in their early thirties, or observe my grandfather teaching me to fish for trout in 1975, or see what I got for my birthday when I was nine. It is a form of time travel. I also have recent video of my own family; I can relive last Christmas, my daughter opening presents, my two sons laughing next to her, my wife glowing from giving. I watch these not on a projection screen but an LCD computer screen that would have been quite unimaginable back when I caught that poor wriggling fish with my granddad. Human memory has always been heavily augmented by technology. In fact, we might say that in some ways our technological memory (these days stored in digital bits) is now supplemented by our feeble organic memories, stored in biological neurons by a process that is intensely mysterious. We have to ask, how can the immaterial "past" be stored in a piece of the "material present"?

As you might have already realized, this chapter focuses not on a genre or style but on a thematic core shared by several films. This thematic core is, I believe, richly theological, though it does not generally receive attention as such. I believe this theme shows very powerfully that suppressed truth works its way back to the surface layers of our conscious minds and finds outward expression in our cultural production. The films I analyze in this chapter all deal, in various ways, with the relationship between the nature of memory and the nature of humanity: to be fully human means to be connected mentally with the past. I find these movies extraordinarily powerful in almost identical ways, despite the great differences in genre, style, texture, and story. One is a black-and-white classic from the early 1940s; another is an early-eighties, cutting edge sci-fi noir dense with philosophy as well as violence; the last is an artsy, edgy psychological drama that deliberately and constantly disorients the audience—it is essentially a revenge tale about memory. How can you seek revenge if you forget the original crime or the desire for justice? Just as forgiveness demands forgetting, revenge requires remembering. And it is memory—that strange neurological link to the past that makes us human—which links these films together.

Citizen Kane (1941) takes us into the life of an early twentieth-century capitalist and media/political power mogul. *Blade Runner* (1982) carries us into the dystopian future world of Los Angeles where the distinction between humans and advanced androids is erased. The nature of memory is a focus of the tale, and ironically the movie is in some ways an echo, a memory of an earlier sci-fi film also obsessed with memory and the nature of man and technology. *Memento* (2000) drops us down unceremoniously into the world of a man who is unable to form new memories, so every minute of his life is a disoriented present with no genealogy of moments leading up to it providing context, certainty, and meaning. These three films—all of which I can recall with great clarity, for they act powerfully on my memory—are the last we shall consider.

Memory and Mirrors

Orson Welles's masterpiece, *Citizen Kane*, is consistently named the greatest movie of all time by a wide variety of film critics and film scholars. Plenty of regular moviegoers hate it.

I will not advocate here for whether or not it is the greatest film ever made. I find those kinds of categorizations of art and cultural objects a little silly, personally. But *Citizen Kane* is certainly incredibly important in film history for any number of reasons. Whether you love the film or hate it, it is a vitally important cultural object, and as such it merits close study and theological analysis. My first memory of *Kane* was formed when I was fifteen. I watched it with my father on television, because he had said something about it being a very famous movie. I watched it expecting great things; I was painfully disappointed. No one even got shot. I turned to him afterward and muttered, "A whole movie about a sled? Are you kidding me?"

Of course I was far too young to understand the film or appreciate its narrative complexity. This narrative structure excites near idolatry in fans of the movie and maniacal hatred in its detractors. Regardless, it is the way the story is told that I want to consider here. It is essentially a movie about memory.

Citizen Kane has perhaps the most fascinating backstory of any film ever made. Perhaps half of the interest I have in the film is based on the incredible story around its production and reception. How many groundbreaking movies have you watched that were made by a twenty-four-year-old who had never been to Hollywood before? Had never acted in front of a camera, never directed, or had any experience in cinematography? This describes the star, cowriter, director, and cocinematographer Orson Welles—young as a fresh college graduate—who pulled off a feat that has been called "the greatest film ever made" by more critics than any other.

The story is very simple, really. It follows the rise and fall of an American businessman. Nothing could be more pedestrian, and I freely admit to *Citizen Kane* detractors that it is not the most interesting story I've ever heard. But it isn't the story that holds my attention—it is the telling. And this is not to be minimized. *Star Wars* is a pretty hokey story, but the telling is fabulous. Tell it poorly, and you have a Saturday morning TV kid's show (which is where Lucas's film almost ended up after its dreary early cuts were shown to some very unimpressed executives.)

Charles Foster Kane is born poor, raised for his first decade or so at a humble boarding house in Colorado. His mother almost miraculously inherits a fortune in the form of a gold mine from a defaulting boarder who dies in debt. Charles, in classic Dickensian fashion, is sent to live back East under the guidance of the bank that manages his future fortune. The head fortune manager, Thatcher, becomes everything Charlie Kane hates, and when he comes of age, he expresses disdain for everything he owns except a small newspaper, which he then manages personally in the best tradition of muckraking yellow journalism, aimed mostly at exposing the corruption of Thatcher and his cronies. Over time, Kane builds his massive media empire and fortune across many fronts, has a family, and makes quick inroads into politics, almost certain to end in the White House. But his own weaknesses cause his downfall, and not just once. He becomes a heartless manipulator of everyone around him and eventually comes to his inevitable and lonely end—an end that takes the form of a powerful memory embodied in a single word.

This melodramatic soap opera has lulled many a viewer to sleep. But I think an attentive viewing—not just of the story but of the story as a groundbreaking way of telling a narrative with film art—will reward the careful viewer with the recognition of a movie that rightly deserves its spectacular reputation. More importantly, it influenced generations of film students, directors, cinematographers, editors, and screenwriters. It has cast a long shadow indeed. Why the fascination?

Welles decides to tell the story in a highly unconventional manner. Initially the viewer finds this nonlinear narrative rather confusing. Instead of following the normal life arc of a fully developed character (birth, youth, rise to power, eventual decline), Welles scrambles the story like an egg. We get different eras at different times, out of order. We see Kane's death and then his middle age, followed by late middle age and then youth. Some sections of his life are told more than once. How does Welles do this without alienating the viewer? He uses what he calls a "prismatic narrative"—the tale is told in nonlinear fashion by several characters who knew Kane, and their stories begin after Kane has died. We hear from his second wife, his worst enemy, his best friend, his business manager, and his butler. Along the way we hear fragments of his story from other sources as well: newspapers, radio, and passing comments from observers. These multiple perspectives are presented in a linear fashion as far as the film goes, but in no sense is his life story told in the order that it occurred.

By the time we get to the end of the movie, we think we have a thorough knowledge of the life of Kane. The movie uses a frame narrative to develop the plot: a news reporter named "Thompson" (William Alland) is tasked with finding out the meaning of Kane's last word: "Rosebud." Whatever it was, Kane's memory of it was his last conscious moment. Thompson goes from one person to the next—all of Kane's friends, relatives, and even the diary of his enemy, Thatcher—and builds his mountain of evidence higher and higher on the meaning of the mysterious word. Everyone tells him something different. No one knows for sure what the final gasp meant. No one even knows what Kane's life was all about; everyone who knew him sees him only in how he affected them. Finally the reporter concludes his investigation and walks away from the case befuddled. A female reporter thinks she knows why he failed: "If you could've found out what Rosebud meant, I bet that would've explained everything." Thompson, who has been fidgeting around with a box of jigsaw puzzle pieces, responds to her slowly and with resignation, "No, I don't think so; no. Mr. Kane was a man who got everything he wanted and then lost it. Maybe Rosebud was something he couldn't get, or something he lost. Anyway, it wouldn't have explained anything. . . . I don't think any word can explain a man's life. No, I guess Rosebud is just a . . . piece in a jigsaw puzzle . . . a missing piece."

All the memories of all the people who knew Kane cannot together produce the meaning of his last word—or of his life. As powerful as memory is (and the film constantly references the great power of memory), it is not enough to give either truth or meaning to life. The whole narrative is a series of complex, lengthy flashbacks. We see film clips of Kane and hear a radio interview. We hear him denounced by some, praised by others. We see and hear him romance women, make political campaign speeches, threaten, cajole, tease, joke, and argue. We watch Kane as he remembers his mother. *All these moments are memories.* His friend Bernstein recalls a momentary glimpse of a beautiful girl he saw but never met—half a century before. "A fellow will remember a lot of things you wouldn't think he'd remember. You take me. One day, back in 1896, I was crossing over to Jersey on the ferry, and as we pulled out, there was another ferry pulling in, and on it there was a girl waiting to get off. A white dress she had on. She was carrying a white parasol. I only saw her for one second. She didn't see me at all, but I'll bet a month hasn't gone by since that I haven't thought of that girl."

The entire film is an homage to memory. Of course not all memories are pleasant, and not everyone views memory as a blessing. Kane's friend Jed Leland (Joseph Cotten) recalls "Charlie" in detail—and disgust. He says to Thompson, "I can remember everything. That's my curse, young man. It's the greatest curse that's ever been inflicted on the human race: memory." Now, what would prompt such a sentiment? Did Cotten chuckle at the irony of memorizing these lines from the script?

The most common metaphor for both art and memory is the reflective mirror, and Welles uses this age-old image to great effect in *Citizen Kane.* At the end of the film, after all the different versions of Kane's life have been told by those who knew him, and we think we begin to see who he really is by these "composite memories," the young director and his brilliant cinematographer, Gregg Toland, throw us a final visual curveball. Our first view of Kane in the film involves seeing a tiny, distorted reflection of his dead body on the inside curve of a broken toy snow globe. Our final view of Kane is also in a mirror—also one that distorts. Charlie has experienced what is for him the last straw: his second wife Susan has left him, and he has thrown a massive tantrum and wrecked her dollhouse-like bedroom. He walks out of the room and finds all the staff members and guests in his huge mansion staring at him. He is publicly humiliated and privately brokenhearted at the same time. In his hand he holds the snow globe, which has some mysterious meaning to him. Kane walks past the crowd gathered in the museum-like hallway. The camera then cuts to a slightly angled shot looking across a long hallway, and we see Kane as he walks, left to right, in between a row of full-length floor-to-ceiling wall mirrors. There are mirrors on both sides of the wall; what we see in the angled shot is the set of mirrors in front of us (i.e., the camera). Of course we do not directly see what is behind the camera, but we see the reflection of it: it is another wall of mirrors. We are now looking at reflections of reflections. The camera pans slightly right, faster than Charlie is walking. In other words, his figure leaves the left side of the frame, even as he is walking into it. Picture the frame: we see Charlie, walking from far left toward the center, but as the camera's view swings well to the right, he goes out of the frame, and all we see now is a slightly angled view of a long set of parallel mirrors.

Now everyone knows that strange things happen with parallel mirrors. It is about as close to a visual image of infinity as we can get. A mirror only reflects what is in front of it. If what is in front of it is another mirror, we see the infinite bending away of infinite mirrors.

The camera is now in a still position for a few seconds, and, as expected, Charlie walks into the frame, still going left to right. Almost immediately his reflection appears to our right (his left), and then of course we see an infinite number of reflected Charles Foster Kanes, bending off to the right. In other words, we see the "real" Charlie, and we see the many "nonreal" Charlies—the mere images, identical to the original but without substance.

Then a startling thing happens. The set-up is so subtle that most viewers do not quite catch it until they've seen the film several times. I noticed it for the first time when, after many viewings, I was teaching a three-hour class on cinematography and philosophy in Welles's film. On a big screen Charlie walked across left to right (I was also walking around the room blathering on about infinitely regressive reflections and Platonism or something), when suddenly and unexpectedly *another Kane appeared* on the left side *of the screen!* Where did *he* come from?

I had always thought that what I had seen was Kane—the real Kane—reentering the frame and walking across and creating lots of reflections. I assumed that this was Welles's and Toland's way of saying, with a classic visual metaphor, that there were many versions of Kane. And that is precisely how the "prismatic narrative" is told. Everyone has their perspective. Add it all up, and you get the truth. But when I noticed for the first time that the "Kane" in the center of the frame was actually *just another reflection* and not the real Kane at all—and that I had never noticed this despite multiple viewings—I realized the shot was far more complex than I had imagined.

When the camera pans right and leaves the slowly-walking Kane behind, all we see in the frame are the infinite parallel mirrors. Everyone is fascinated with this phenomenon. So our attention is fixed on looking into infinity. When the first Kane figure comes in from the left, we assume it is the real Kane—Kane (1)—soon to be followed by Kane (2), Kane (3), and so forth. But we confuse the reflection for the real, the image for the reality, and we do not know that this is what we have done. Everything is displaced one notch; the "real" keeps moving down one to the left. When the "real" Kane shows up (if we even notice that he's the real one), we may feel a certain satisfaction that "now we have *the real thing*." But we don't. Because there is no real Kane. He's a fictional character in a movie, and a movie is just another piece of art, another mirror held up to the world as Hamlet would say should he have visited a Cineplex. I had misplaced the difference between the real and the not real, while watching a moving picture. I was back in the 1890s, ducking a train that would never hit me, a wave that was not wet.

I was a supposed "expert" teaching the film to my college students and had completely missed and utterly misunderstood the final and most important scene in the whole movie.

The question is: if mirrors—a marvelously simple bit of technology—can so mislead, then what can we say about memory? And movies?

Odysseus, HAL, and Other Replicants

Ridley Scott's visionary masterpiece *Blade Runner* did not come out of nowhere. It was made possible by Stanley Kubrick's visionary masterpiece *2001: A Space Odyssey*, released nearly a quarter-century earlier in 1968. George Lucas and Stephen Spielberg called Kubrick's film their personal "big bang," and they then opened up the whole movement of the blockbuster fantasy/adventure films of the late seventies and early eighties. Scott is a direct heir of their work, as they are of Kubrick's, but Scott is much closer to Kubrick as an artistic visionary whose work is often ahead of its time. In this way Scott has a visionary genius similar to Welles's in *Citizen Kane* four decades earlier. Both *Blade Runner* and *Kane* elicited some strong negative reaction in early viewers, but were later recognized as masterpieces and even have strong cult followings.

The central tie between *Blade Runner* and *2001* is that both films deal with core questions about the nature of the human, and these questions have to do with the necessarily related ideas of technology and memory. As strange as *2001* is, its basic idea is not really complicated. I recall watching it on the widescreen Senator Theater in Washington, DC, with my father, where Kubrick hosted the world premier. I was overwhelmed by the experience, but recall liking the film because it was primarily emotional and not overtly philosophical. The film is deliberately modeled at a basic level on Homer's *Odyssey*, the ancient Greek epic about a long journey home. The film suggests certain things about man's journey, particularly regarding technology and memory, that carry the viewer along with the same powerful epic sweep of Homer's twelve thousand lines of dactylic hexameter poetry. The movie is utterly strange, however, which attracts some viewers and repels others—a trait common in Kubrick's movies. Homeric epic is also powerful precisely because of its strangeness, its otherworldliness. Yet ironically the *Odyssey* is built around the familiar idea of the *nostos*, the Greek idea of a return to your home or your origin. *Nostos* is in fact the origin of our word "nostalgia," a kind of longing for or eulogizing of the past, a desire to return to the good we once knew, to live in our memories. We want to know where we came from, because that will tell us what we are. So *Blade Runner*, the grandson of Homer, is also about going home, about finding out just who and what we might be.

As I see it, Kubrick's film, which presents itself as a kind of visual-poetic history of man and technology, is driven by the fact that both are founded upon *memory*. Technology is dependent upon memory, and memory is a kind of technology. Both are strongly tied to "efficiency"—doing things better than before. Let me give an example of this. The moment early in the film when the prehistoric ape-man, apparently inspired by a weird black monolith, "invents" the first technology—a bone that is used to kill an animal and procure meat—is dependent upon memory. The ape-man looks at the dry bone, tentatively picks it up, and slowly realizes that it can function as a strong extension of his own arm, allowing him to kill an animal. Kubrick intercuts the ape's swinging of the bone with "imagined images" of the bone striking down an animal. Later we see him eating an actual dead animal; the implication is that he remembered his imagined act of killing, remembered the first act of swinging the bone, and then applied that memory. The bone is technology, and memory is what makes it useable. No memory equals no meat—the bone would stay a useless bone.

Next we see a confrontation between ape-man tribes. The tribe that has figured out how to use a bone, and remembered this technology, is able to win a fight over a crucial waterhole. A technologically-backward ape-man—he has no bone and no memory of a bone—is killed by another ape-man who has brought his bone to the fight and remembers how to use it. This scene is Kubrick's evolutionist version of Cain and Abel, and this is what all human technology has always boiled down to: technology has one or both of two uses. You use it to make yourself more comfortable (meat, air conditioning, a Mercedes-Benz C-Class), or you use it to kill the other guy (a bone, a Glock, a thermonuclear warhead). In many cases the latter purpose serves the former. You can bring a bone to a waterhole-ownership debate.

After killing the enemy with the bone he remembered to bring and use, the more technologically evolved ape-man is seized with a sense of his own power and, in one of the greatest shots ever filmed, hurls the bone far into the air in exultation over his newfound power to make his life better and to kill. The camera tracks the bone upward, and as it begins to fall back to earth, we cut to a vaguely bone-shaped spacecraft orbiting the planet millions of years in the future. It is one of the most unforgettable moments in cinematic history.

But we never think about the implication. Bone to spaceship. That's quite a transition! How did it happen? It happened because of human thought, which developed over time and which is utterly dependent upon memory. There can be no technology without the technology of memory—the storage and retrieval of the past. One idea can lead to another, but only when we remember the sequential ideas does technology progress. In other words, according to the film, the mind evolves because it recalls. When these creatures did not have purposefully functioning memory, they remained the same. They were inefficient. And when more efficient creatures endowed with memory and technology showed up, the inefficient ones lost out. The usual interpretation of the mysterious black monolith is that it is a symbol of technology or intelligence. I think that if it stands for anything at all, *it is memory*. The monolith shows up over and over again in the film, and each time it is linked with the past, with memory.

Near the end of the film astronaut Dave Bowman is in a battle of wills with his HAL 9000 computer. The machine has become a murderous sociopath. HAL is convinced he can never make an error. What this means functionally is that his logic circuits do not fail, and these logic circuits are dependent upon—you guessed it—his computer memory. In fact, as Bowman works to dismantle HAL, he physically enters the giant computer's Logic Memory Center. Now, in an age of multigigabyte memory devices that fit in our palms, it strikes us as rather quaint that a computer would be so large that you could actually go inside of it, but this was how the future of artificial intelligence was viewed in 1968. Computers did in fact occupy entire rooms. Now they can actually be miniaturized and placed inside of us for medical purposes. But what we get in *2001* is a human being quite literally inside the mind of a human creation—and trying to kill it. This killing does not take place with a bone but by dismantling HAL's memory. As this slowly occurs and HAL regresses backwards into a childlike state, he is filled with fear. He understands that if his memory goes, his mind goes. He will die. A strange fear for a machine to have, we might say. Yet even as a young boy I understood intuitively that this dismantling of a memory was nothing less than a *dismantling of a self*. This scene, indeed this whole film, is often viewed as a fable about technology. I think rather that it is a fable about man, and memory which makes him man and makes his technology possible.

The really interesting question of course is what would man make when his technology reached its maximum level? Would he try to recreate a man in his own image? And how would that man respond to his creation and his creator?

Blade Runner comes across on the surface as a science fiction/ action/detective story, but it is probably one of the more philosophically sophisticated films of the last fifty years. This is because its philosophical argument and its aesthetic presentation are so finely woven together in a rich filigree that they really become one. *Blade Runner* deals with the question of what it means to be human. The plot is simple: Deckard (Harrison Ford) is a blade runner—his job is to retire humanoid robots that get out of line. How do they get out of line? Mostly, they don't want to "die." They are supposed to have limited "lives" and just do the work they were made to do. But some of the more advanced ones want to be like real humans, to be free, independent, *and to live*. The very advanced androids, the "Nexus Six" models, do not always even know that they are not human. These robots are in fact organic machines called replicants. They are almost entirely indistinguishable from human beings. Of course, the problem is that this works the other way, too.

The technological key that their designers use to make the nearly-human robots function at such a high level—a human level—is that they give them *memories*. They are given not just the ability to remember what just happened, which would be necessary for even rudimentary machines or organic consciousness; they are provided with memories of a past that they never actually experienced. The designer "Dr. Tyrell" (Joe Turkel), a sort of Dr. Frankenstein character, explains to Deckard why the false memory collection is inserted into the androids: "We began to recognize in them a strange obsession. After all, they are emotionally inexperienced, with only a few years in which to store up the experiences which you and I take for granted. If we gift them with a past, we create a cushion or a pillow for their emotions, and consequently, we can control them better." Deckard is horrified when he realizes what Tyrell is only indirectly telling him. "Memories! You're talking about memories!"

The reason Deckard is so stunned is that he has just given the "android or human?" test to one of Tyrell's employees, the beautiful Rachael (Sean Young). The test took far longer than it should have because it seemed inconclusive. Eventually Deckard realizes two things: Rachael is a replicant, *and* Rachael thinks she is human. After she leaves, Deckard turns to Tyrell. "She doesn't know." Tyrell replies, "She's beginning to suspect, I think." Deckard is appalled. "Suspect? *How can it not know what it is?*" Scott's film taps into the ancient core of Greek philosophy found in the phrase "know thyself." Self-knowledge is the most important knowing that there can be and is in fact the center of self-conscious being. Furthermore, self-consciousness is nothing less than the sum of our memories up to and including the present moment. You are your memories, and you are the thoughts and feelings about the present and future as grounded in your experience and memory of the past.

In order to maintain control over the virtually human replicants, they are built to live only four years. If they were to last longer, they would build a significant store of memories and perhaps develop emotions, desires, and a dangerous sense of an independent self. In other words, memories lead to selfhood. The self is the sum of what we know of our past. This grows into a desire for a future—and both our past and future are grounded in a self-conscious present. This is the human state. *We are our memories.*

Dr. Tyrell tells Deckard what his technological/corporate goal is: " 'More human *than human*' is our motto." This extreme similarity between robot and human is due to the memory implants. Ironically this is very much the case for us humans: we do not know what we are, and in a very real way our memories—many of which are made by watching movies—are not always our own. Our views of the world and of ourselves often come from the screen culture that surrounds us. I am not saying this is either necessarily good or bad; I'm simply pointing it out. Even *Blade Runner* itself is an echo, a kind of remembering of *2001*. Instead of Bowman inside of HAL, we have the Tyrell Corporation inside of, well, by the end of the movie, we're not entirely sure who.

The intensely emotional climax of the film confirms this point I'm making about memory and consciousness. "Roy Batty" (Rutger Hauer) is the leader of the renegade androids and the final target of Deckard's hunt. After a terrifying chase scene where the hunted becomes the hunter, Batty has Deckard trapped: he is hanging by two hands, then just one, on the cornice of a high-rise building. All Batty has to do is let Deckard die. Just as the blade runner loses his grip, Batty grabs his hand and saves his life. He deposits the rescued man on the rooftop. Deckard is incredulous at the turn of events. Batty smiles gently at him and says, "I've . . . *seen things* you people wouldn't believe. Attack ships on fire off the shoulder of Orion. I watched C-beams glitter in the dark near the Tannhauser gate. All those moments will be lost in time . . . like tears in rain . . . Time to die." With the smile lingering, Batty closes his eyes, leans forward, and ceases to be. Deckard does not understand most of this speech. These are someone else's memories. But he does understand what Roy Batty understands: when he dies, his memories die. Deckard now pities Batty—and himself. Death, when it comes, will be the erasure of the self and the washing away of memories, like tears in rain.

At least, that's what the movie suggests, with extraordinarily memorable poetry, visual and verbal.

We All Need Mirrors

Leonard Shelby has a problem. He is unable to form new memories. His present experience is just that, and no more: present experience. As a moment or two passes, he forgets where he is, what he's doing, and what everything means. He does have a storehouse of memories from his life before the accident that injured his brain and caused his anterograde amnesia. Those intact memories involve his love for his wife and her murder. Leonard now lives in a state of constant forgetfulness, but he remembers one thing: find and kill the murderer. His memory is cast in the form of tattoos covering his body, which he reads (often in a mirror) to remind himself of the meaning of his existence: revenge.

Chris Nolan's *Memento* may be the most memory-saturated film ever made. It is all about memory, and it makes nearly unbearable demands upon the viewer's memory. The demands are so great, in fact, that most viewers remain as disoriented as Leonard Shelby even after repeated viewings; simply trying to recall the movie as a whole can cause a headache.

Leonard's condition is by its very nature confusing even for him. Like the replicants in *Blade Runner,* he doesn't know quite what he is. The manager of the hotel where he lives asks him about this. Leonard pauses briefly, trying to remember what it is like to be him, and then answers, "It's like waking. Like you just woke up." His constant experience is that momentary disorientation when we leave the dream world for the real one, wondering where the border is between the two. Except for him the momentary confusion is constant. He never knows where he has been or what he has been doing. He is always asking himself "where am I?" and "what's going on?" He does not understand himself or the trajectory of his life.

He tries (repeatedly) to explain this to people: "If we talk for too long, I'll forget how we started. Next time I see you, I'm not gonna remember this conversation. I don't even know if I've met you before . . . I've told you this before, haven't I?" His life is a life of forgetfulness. His condition is in fact the human condition. Leonard is *pars pro toto* for man.

This is the life of man: a constantly disorienting present, a quickly fading past, and an uncertain future. We have an intense desire to fulfill a purpose, to complete a mission—though we may be mistaken about that purpose, just like everything else. We are like Leonard. He is just an extreme case. But his condition is our condition.

Leonard's real difficulty is the nature of memory, and if memory is what it means to be human, then his problem is that memory is faulty even as we are fallen. He says, "Memory can change the shape of a room; it can change the color of a car. And memories can be distorted. They're just an interpretation, they're not a record, and they're irrelevant if you have the facts." His memory "condition" has one sure effect—he knows memory cannot be mapped directly onto the real world with certainty. That is one thing he does remember. Leonard Shelby does figure out how to function, and his functionality is built on two things: his notes to himself (some paper, but the important ones are tattooed on his body) and his acknowledgment that he is probably not really connected with truth. We all lie to ourselves to be happy, according to Leonard. Following Friedrich Nietzsche's classic nineteenth-century formulation that truth is an illusion about which we have forgotten that this is what it is, Leonard lies to himself, knows it, and keeps going as if his lies were true. Eventually lies become truth. In other words, he suppresses the truth and suppresses this suppression.

At the end of the film, Nolan has his protagonist perform an act that provides a tense visual metaphor for his own life and for humanity's arc in the universe: he drives his Jaguar coupe at high speed through the city with his eyes closed. This lasts for a frighteningly long time, and during this "test" of reality, Leonard carries on a soliloquy in his mind: "I have to believe in a world outside my own mind. I have to believe that my actions still have meaning, even if I can't remember them. I have to believe that when my eyes are closed, the world's still there. Do I believe the world's still there? Is it still out there?" He opens his eyes at this point, much to the viewer's relief. "Yeah. We all need mirrors to remind ourselves who we are. I'm no different."

What is a mirror, but a screen? And a screen, a mirror?

This speech gathers and asks tough philosophical questions from Plato to Kant and from Augustine to postmodernism. These questions always boil down to "what is real, and how can I know?" This question itself is the real mirror of our souls, and it is absolutely central in film art, where the real is replaced by a fabrication with our willing consent. Film reminds us who we are, and thus we are no different from Leonard Shelby. Movies are mirrors. We just forget this. But they are mirrors.

We are humans, driven by hope for some kind of restitution in our disoriented state, by our hatred of death, and by our overwhelming, burning desire for justice, sense, clarity, peace.

We are driven to know who we are.

The Womb of Film

Almost all the movies ever filmed were made in Los Angeles (or at least by people from there), where I now live and teach. A great many films are set in Los Angeles; even ones that aren't set in LA are quite often filmed here. My first few years living here were pervaded by a weird sense of occasional déjà-vu. I would think, *I know I've seen this somewhere before.* The first time I saw Tim Burton's *Edward Scissorhands* (1990), I lived in Maryland. I did not understand it. A decade later I moved to the very town for which Burton's brain-dead suburban-hell parody stands. It took ten years and a transcontinental relocation for me to get the joke; I had to move there and become a part of it.

Los Angeles is a history-less city. It has no memory. Orson Welles's brilliant career collapsed after he made *Citizen Kane* at twenty-four. He was asked for the rest of his life what had he done since 1941. LA is the town of *what have you done lately?* The city has no memory. Not that it has no actual history. Rather it is unshackled by the typical East Coast sense of self in history. The older buildings here have either been knocked down to build massive megamalls or the highways going to them, or they have collapsed in earthquakes, or they have burned up in massive wildfires. Los Angeles exhibits massive urban sprawl as opposed to vertical crawl, as in Manhattan. This is an interesting metaphor to think through, actually. The first time I flew across the whole developed area, I could not believe how huge it was. People now move into the inhospitable desert ninety miles out, and they are still "living in LA." It continually creeps outward, like some ancient ravenous empire in the Fertile Crescent, Assyria maybe. It slowly devours or co-opts everything in its path. Hollywood is the brain, celluloid is the chariot, and the movie theater is the mouth that persuades—or devours. It is a land of extremes: extreme beauty and extreme ugliness. The shallowness of the culture can be extreme in its depth. Here is the epicenter of the cult of celebrity, surface culture, the culture of youth, beauty, and wealth, the culture of the image, and the moving image. Los Angeles has made America and the world and, in some ways, the human in the twenty-first century. As much as we might like to joke about LA, it has made us what we are.

What about the mirror that Leonard Shelby speaks of? We all need mirrors to remind ourselves who we are. I'm no different. Which is the mirror—the movie or the audience?

All the world's a screen. What, exactly, would be the point of going to watch a movie—in Los Angeles?

This is a city that has no memory except its celluloid image of itself.

It is, after all, Norma Desmond's hometown.

"Remember also your Creator in the days of your youth, before the evil days come. . . ."

Notes

Introduction: Movies, Truth, and the Origins of Culture

1. William Shakespeare, *As You Like It*, ed. G. Blakemore Evans (Boston: Houghton Mifflin, 1997), 2.7.139–66.

2. Ex. 3:14; see also John 8:58.

3. What I am calling the "conservation of truth principle" is a kind of philosophical version of the law of the conservation of matter as well as the first law of thermodynamics in physics. I am not suggesting a materialist version of the concept of truth (i.e., "only the material is real"), but rather a similarity between the way the material world is presently recognized to work and the way the universe works as a whole in a biblical worldview—that is, both the material and the nonmaterial under God's direction and design.

4. William Shakespeare, *The Merchant of Venice*, Act 1, scene 2.

Chapter 1: Thinking about Looking

1. The term *diakrino* occurs in several different forms in Matt. 16:3; 1 Cor. 11:29; 12:10; and Heb. 5:14. The Greek carries the meaning of separating, distinguishing, judging, discerning, or making a judicial estimation (i.e., weighing the facts and reaching a proper conclusion). Discernment is a gift from God (1 Cor. 12:10) but also a skill that must be developed with practice (Heb. 5:12–14) in comparing the world with the Word. Many passages in Scripture deal with discernment, which we will discuss in the context of specific films in later chapters. Here is a brief list of some of them: Prov. 14:15; 16:4, 25; 24:3, 30–34; 25:28; 28:26; Eccles. 2:13, 21; 10:1; 11:5; Mal. 3:18; 1 Cor. 2:14; 12:10;

14:10; 2 Cor. 4:18; 10:3–7a; 11:3–4, 14–15; Phil. 4:8; Col. 1:9–10; 2:1–8; 1 Thess. 5:19–22; Heb. 4:12; 5:14; James 1:21.

2. See James 1:21: "receive with meekness the *engrafted word*" (KJV). This phrase in the original Greek text is "rooted-in word." God's message to us needs to be repeatedly read, studied, meditated on, and obeyed. Discernment comes through no other process.

3. Consider Prov. 24:30–32: "I passed by the field of a sluggard, by the vineyard of a man lacking sense, and behold, it was all overgrown with thorns; the ground was covered with nettles, and its stone wall was broken down. Then I saw and considered it; I looked and received instruction." The next two verses illustrate what was learned: laziness and foolishness leads to poverty and destruction. My point is twofold: first, we can (and must) learn from negative examples, and second, while looking at *anything at all*, we must be asking ourselves, "What does this teach me?" *The experience itself must always be viewed as an opportunity* for discernment, obedience, and growth.

4. By "biblical-critical discernment" I mean the habit of looking at everything around us through the discerning lens of Scripture. God's Word is the final arbiter of the value of everything (Heb. 4:12). But this does not mean we should use Bible verses as proof texts to attack and judge everything we think is wrong. Rather, biblical-critical discernment is the thoughtful application of solid hermeneutic (interpretive) principles to establish the meaning of biblical texts, which are then used to decode, contextualize, analyze, and make right decisions about whatever we encounter—be it a theological or philosophical argument or a song's lyrics or a talk radio debate or a scene in a movie.

5. Such was the case with *Blade Runner*, which the studio altered to make more upbeat and thus profitable; the film as originally released—a very dark "film noir" story with a tacked-on happy ending—did not do well. After its alteration, it simply didn't work as originally intended. Director Ridley Scott later released a "director's cut" version, which was a very different film, but one that more closely represented his thoughts about what the story was really about—what it means to be "human."

6. Heb. 5:14 and other passages show that the mark of the discerning Christian is not total separation from the world (which is impossible before death) but rather correct discernment of good and evil while living in the world. We can't make right, obedient choices until we know what the right choices are.

Chapter 2: Welcome to the Real World

1. Paul is an excellent example of someone working hard to understand other worldviews in Acts 17. He discusses the nature of "the Unknown God" with the Athenian intellectuals, showing them that even their own pagan poets recognize that he must exist. Paul has clearly attained some level of familiarity with worldviews very different than his own, and he uses that knowledge to combat error

and proclaim the truth of the gospel. Similarly he fights the errors of Gnostic philosophy that were encroaching upon the believers in the Colossian church by explaining the error-filled content of that worldview (Colossians 2).

2. James Sire, *The Universe Next Door*, 3rd edition (Downer's Grove: IL: Intervarsity, 1997), 53.

3. Ibid., 85.

4. Nihilism is a "tar baby"—referring to the classic Uncle Remus tale about the impatient rabbit trying to fight an unresponsive mannequin made out of sticky tar. The more you try to argue and fight, the more entangled you get. Classic nihilism, at least as derived from Nietzschean thinking, is built upon the idea that language is arbitrary and cannot connect us in any meaningful way with reality. From the nihilistic point of view, then, any attempt to argue against nihilism is dependent upon language and therefore futile.

5. Ibid., 95.

6. This makes a great sticking point when discussing Christianity with those who think they can mount an effective argument from the standpoint of relativism. Everyone has some kind of standard, and yet if we actually come from random materiality, where did such a notion come from? It seems logically incoherent. If everything means nothing, then how do you justify your personal standards? There are plenty of things you don't want others to do to you, but why?

7. For a much fuller treatment, again see James Sire's *Universe Next Door*.

8. If this sounds like the cultic American religion known as "Christian Science," you are correct. This system, founded by Mary Baker Eddy in the nineteenth century, is a bizarre admixture of Christian terminology, Hegelian metaphysics, and Eastern pantheistic monism. It rejects matter as "mortal error" and claims that sin, sickness, and death are all illusions. Christ's miracles are explained as examples of his mind over mere "matter." It isn't Christian any more than it is scientific. It's Hinduism with a steeple.

9. I will discuss *Memento* in much greater detail in the final chapter.

Chapter 3: How to Interrogate a Movie

1. This is actually what the Greek root for our word "analysis" means: to break something up into its constituent parts for closer examination.

2. I believe this is the central issue in film art, in fact. Every genre in every period shows this common thread. Many of the most historically significant films have this theme as their central driving force, even if it is not openly stated. In fact, it may not be too much to say that film art is the best single indicator available in the world today to show us what man thinks about his own nature.

3. Not all films compress "story" into "plot" quite like this. For example, one of the greatest westerns of all time, *High Noon*, works incredibly effectively

at building suspense by constant visual reference to clocks that show passage of time in the film that matches the passage of time in the real world. The audience begins to identify with the characters who tensely await the arrival of the villains—at noon, of course!

4. Roger Ebert is well known for stating repeatedly that films are not philosophical arguments but emotional experiences. I believe he is right in seeing film as an emotive, affective event, but emotion is one of the most powerful ways to make an argument, according to Aristotle's discussion of rhetoric. Emotion does not necessarily short-circuit rational thought, but it can work powerfully to persuade without relying on logic or evidence. I find film to be philosophical *because* it can be so emotional.

Chapter 4: A Time to Laugh

1. A great film comedy example of this occurs near the end of *What about Bob?* (1991) starring Bill Murray and Richard Dreyfuss as an extremely neurotic patient and his psychiatrist, respectively. Murray is quite literally driving Dreyfuss crazy, and eventually "Dr. Leo Marvin" has a maniacal nervous breakdown. At this point, another physician comes by to treat Dr. Marvin, and he prescribes Prozac. "Bob" (Murray)—who everyone else knows is quite crazy—begins to advise the new doctor on psychopharmacology: Bob: "Excuse me, Phil [new doctor], but with these particular symptoms, is Prozac the right choice?" Lily (Dr. Marvin's sister): "You think Prozac is a mistake?" Bob: "Well, with this kind of manic episode, I would think Librium might be a more effective management tool." Phil nods in assent: "You could be right. I'll rewrite the prescription." The conversation is delivered in a deadpan clinical manner, as if Bob and Phil are medical colleagues considering a problematic diagnosis. The hilarity here is that the nutty patient has now changed roles with his psychiatrist. In fact, his long experience with mental illness and its treatment has brought him to the point where he can fool a physician, knows as much as a doctor, and can rightly prescribe a sedative instead of a selective serotonin reuptake inhibitor (SSRI). This little scene encapsulates the whole film, which forces us to ask who is sane and who is crazy—in terms of who is happy and fun and who is not.

2. In yet another horrible ironic twist, the existentialists, much like the ancient Roman Stoics, elevated to the highest virtue the right and the courage of suicide. The Stoic philosophers (whom Paul debated on Mars Hill in Acts) thought Paul was crazy because in their view of the world, escape from the body in death was the ultimate release from the misery of meaninglessness. And any "god" that would voluntarily re-enter his physical body after he had died would have to be insane to so degrade himself. This is why they laugh at Paul's conclusion to his sermon on the Areopagus, where he rightly brings the

core of the gospel to the forefront by insisting on the resurrection, which they "mocked" (Acts 17:31–32).

3. This famous shot is widely available on the Internet as a brief video clip.

4. This scene is widely available as a video clip on the Internet.

5. I discuss cynicism in detail in chapter 7.

Chapter 5: Exorcising the Psycho

1. The film is now in the public domain and can be watched in its entirety on the Internet. But don't waste time. Go right to "A Drop of Water." You'll be calling the plumber.

2. This film is in the public domain and widely available for viewing on the Internet.

3. Twice I have been in the presence of palpable (and in one case, visible) demonic activity. People who have been missionaries in places like New Guinea have told me stories that go far beyond my small experience.

4. *Hamlet*, 1.5.

5. "For what can be known about God is plain to them, because God has shown it to them. For his invisible attributes, namely, his eternal power and divine nature, have been clearly perceived, ever since the creation of the world, in the things that have been made. So they are without excuse. For although they knew God, they did not honor him as God or give thanks to him, but they became futile in their thinking, and their foolish hearts were darkened" (Rom. 1:19–21).

6. This is the mainstream Hollywood technique. The "naturalism" in nearly all narrative film has as its basic technique the erasure from the viewer's consciousness that it is a movie that is being watched. There are some avante-garde "artsy" movies that do not work this way; they push their "movieness" to the foreground as part of their style. These films can be really interesting and enjoyable, but they are a long way from supplanting the primary product that Hollywood makes for the consumer, which functions as a temporary replacement for reality.

7. I am obviously drawing a parallel with the previous chapter on comedy, where I argued that we are designed to laugh in joy.

8. In 2007 I was standing in line at a gas station near my home just north of Los Angeles, behind a man wearing a film crew T-shirt. You see a lot of these when you live twenty minutes from Hollywood. But this one caught my eye—the movie was about Ed Gein. I was too horrified to ask the man about it. The movie was released later that year and is a typical gore/slasher movie; it was widely panned by critics. It is not anywhere to be found on my list of movies to see someday.

9. *Schindler's List* is widely recognized as uncompromising in its portrayal of human evil.

10. I've used this film in class a number of times. Surprisingly, over half the viewers don't notice this "slide underneath the suddenly transparent floor" shot until it is pointed out to them afterward. It is extraordinarily subtle in execution and therefore very effective.

11. It has been well-documented by film historians that the film makes use of numerous subliminal and partially-subliminal effects, both visual and sonic. For example, there are numerous screen flashes, just a few frames and nearly invisible to most viewers, that intercut frightening images into the movie. Some of these occur during the exorcism scene (these are more visible), but some are found in other sequences. For example, during father Karras's dream there are several such cut-ins, and there are some moments when Chris MacNeil is walking through her house and demonic images flash for a few frames on kitchen appliances or on Regan's door. Karras's mother's face shows up in a billowing curtain at a crucial moment. The sonic subliminals are probably more disturbing in their effects; according to sound engineers working on the film (along with Friedkin's own admissions), dubbed into the soundtrack just inside hearing range are sounds of a vicious dogfight, the squealing of pigs in a slaughtering line, and angry bees buzzing furiously inside a jar. We have a natural physiological reaction of agitation and fear when we hear these kinds of sounds, even below our conscious levels of cognition. The film won the "Best Sound" Oscar in 1974.

I have lectured on the use of subliminal visuals in *The Exorcist* a number of times, showing freeze-frame shots to incredulous viewers who could not believe what they had missed at full speed. Most of these "subs" can now be found in brief Internet video clips.

12. The film was produced for twelve million dollars and earned well over four hundred million (eight hundred million in inflation-adjusted dollars)—an extraordinarily large cost-to-profit ratio.

Chapter 6: Hollywood Invents Romance

1. This sentence is not mine—it is a quote from *What's up Doc?* (1972), directed by Peter Bogdanovich and starring Ryan O'Neal and Barbra Streisand. The film is a loving homage to the great screwball comedies of the 1930s and is one of the funniest romantic comedies ever. Two years earlier, O'Neal had starred with McGraw in *Love Story*, which was a huge hit, and everyone was going around repeating the tagline. At the very end of *What's Up Doc?* the wacky Streisand character, openly mocking McGraw's sappiness, bats her eyelashes like a vamp at O'Neal and says, "Love means never having to say you're sorry." O'Neal, playfully mocking his character from the earlier film, pauses and says thoughtfully, "That's the dumbest thing I've ever heard." It is one of

the most hilarious character revisions ever, and a brilliant comment on Hollywood's presentation of the Romantic Ideal. Harvard University (where *Love Story* is set) has a tradition that the movie is screened for incoming freshmen, who yell out mocking commentary during the showing.

2. The best-known and perhaps clearest passage is Eph. 5:22–33: "Wives, submit to your own husbands, as to the Lord. For the husband is the head of the wife even as Christ is the head of the church, his body, and is himself its Savior. Now as the church submits to Christ, so also wives should submit in everything to their husbands. Husbands, love your wives, as Christ loved the church and gave himself up for her, that he might sanctify her, having cleansed her by the washing of water with the word, so that he might present the church to himself in splendor, without spot or wrinkle or any such thing, that she might be holy and without blemish. In the same way husbands should love their wives as their own bodies. He who loves his wife loves himself. For no one ever hated his own flesh, but nourishes and cherishes it, just as Christ does the church, because we are members of his body. 'Therefore a man shall leave his father and mother and hold fast to his wife, and the two shall become one flesh.' This mystery is profound, and I am saying that it refers to Christ and the church. However, let each one of you love his wife as himself, and let the wife see that she respects her husband."

3. Rom. 5:8: "God shows his love for us in that while we were still sinners, Christ died for us." See also Eph. 2:12–13: "Remember that you were at that time separated from Christ, alienated from the commonwealth of Israel and strangers to the covenants of promise, having no hope and without God in the world. But now in Christ Jesus you who once were far off have been brought near by the blood of Christ."

4. The film, budgeted at fourteen million dollars has grossed nearly half a billion dollars, a thirty-five-fold profit.

5. Pygmalion is the classical Greek story of a sculptor who falls in love with his beautiful statue that then comes to life, retold also in 1964's wonderful musical *My Fair Lady*.

6. The strong implication is that she has incurred debts she could not pay and was sold to settle them. She is thus a double liability and utterly unlovable.

7. Nicholas Cage won an Academy Award for best actor, Shue was nominated for best actress, and the film was nominated for best adapted screenplay and best director (Mike Figgis).

Chapter 7: Film Noir

1. John Alton (1901–1996) was perhaps the major cinematographer of film noir. His book *Painting with Light* (Berkeley, CA: University of California Press, 1949) lays out many of the basic principles of the cinematographer's craft of using light to create and control mood.

2. There is nothing whatever in Scripture to justify viewing Eve as a *femme fatale*. In fact, I would argue that the *femme fatale* figure is actually a creation of the sinful male imagination due to misogynistic attitudes *resulting* from the fall. Eve's offering of the fruit to Adam in Genesis 3 has no marks of deception or manipulation, and in 1 Tim. 2:14 Paul makes it clear that while Eve was deceived by Satan, Adam was not deceived by Eve or anyone else. He made a willful, knowing decision to disobey God's sole command, and in doing so, brought the fall and its curse to all humans after him. The fall is in Adam, not Eve. Furthermore, in Gen. 3:12, when the Lord asks Adam if he ate the fruit, he admits he did—but then blames the woman, and by extension, God, who made her! This moment is the origin of the *femme fatale* figure: Adam's tendency to blame a female for his destruction is passed along to all men. This is the engine that drives many examples of film noir, as well as numerous other examples of cultural production.

3. The ultimate form of the *femme fatale* is the succubus in classical demonology, a demon that assumes a material human female form in order to seduce and damn a naive male human. The male counterpart is the incubus.

4. One of my favorite noirs presents a total reversal of the *femme fatale* plot structure: *The Hitch-Hiker* (1953) is loosely based on a true story and follows two men on a fishing trip who pick up a male hitchhiker who turns out to be a demented murderer who tortures them psychologically. It is very creepy. It was directed by Ida Lupino—a woman.

5. Part of what is happening with these movies—the opposition of a dangerous and sexualized woman over against a safe homemaker—is a bizarre division of femininity that has at least some of its roots in the fact that the "Proverbs 31 woman" and the "Song of Solomon woman" have been unduly separated by readers. The woman of Proverbs 31—the ideal wife—is the *public* woman of virtue; the wife/lover of the Song of Solomon is the *private* woman of virtue. They are *both* virtuous women, as opposed to the nonvirtuous women of Proverbs 5–7.

6. These wonderful ladies are from Shakespeare's *Twelfth Night* (ca. 1601), *Much Ado About Nothing* (ca. 1600), *The Merchant of Venice* (ca. 1598), and *As You Like It* (ca. 1599), respectively.

7. Film noir went out of fashion suddenly in the early 1960s. But by the early 1970s it experienced a resurgence. These new films were far more violent and gory, and they were in color. Many basic noir elements remained but were taken to the extreme. The taboo subjects were no longer taboo, as exemplified by *Chinatown*.

8. The most important classical source of the myth is the Roman poet Ovid, *Metamorphoses*, trans. David Raeburn (New York: Penguin Books, 2004), bk. 3: 402–36.

Chapter 8: The End of the Matter

1. Rom. 1:18–23: "For the wrath of God is revealed from heaven against all ungodliness and unrighteousness of men, who by their unrighteousness suppress the truth. For what can be known about God is plain to them, because God has shown it to them. For his invisible attributes, namely, his eternal power and divine nature, have been clearly perceived, ever since the creation of the world, in the things that have been made. So they are without excuse. For although they knew God, they did not honor him as God or give thanks to him, but they became futile in their thinking, and their foolish hearts were darkened. Claiming to be wise, they became fools, and exchanged the glory of the immortal God for images resembling mortal man and birds and animals and creeping things."